SONG
BY
SONG

The Lives and Work of 14
Great Lyric Writers

by
Caryl Brahms and Ned Sherrin

ROSS ANDERSON PUBLICATIONS

Published in 1984 by
Ross Anderson Publications
22 Higher Dunscar
Egerton
Bolton
BL7 9TE

British Library Cataloguing in Publication Data

Brahms, Caryl
    Song by song.
    1. Composers – Biography   2. Musical revue,
    comedy, etc. – Writing and publishing
    I. Title   II. Sherrin, Ned
    782.81'092'2   ML390

    ISBN 0–86360–013–1
    ISBN 0–86360–014–X Pbk

Photoset in Bembo by
Northern Phototypesetting Co., Bolton
and printed in Great Britain by
Billings of Worcester

In memory of Burt Shevelove

Treasure chest of knowledge, wit, craft and friendship, and distinguished lyric writer.

ACKNOWLEDGEMENTS

A bibliography (as well as a selective list of principal shows and songs) appears at the end of this book, but it is important to acknowledge some particularly important sources. Alan Jay Lerner has published one of the most elegant and considered books on the musical theatre in his *On the Street Where I Live*; to approach his life and work without constant reference to it would have been impossible and to attempt to improve on his prose impertinent. Howard Dietz's memoirs *Dancing in the Dark* are also witty, comprehensive and, above all, charming. Ira Gershwin's approach in his *Lyrics on Several Occasions* is more idiosyncratic, but so rich in detail and so wise about the expertise of lyric writing that it has proved invaluable.

Collaborators too have picked up their pens to helpful purpose: Vernon Duke, in his autobiography, *Passport to Paris*, described his experience of working with several of the lyric writers; Du Bose Heyward, Joshua Logan, Hoagy Carmichael, Richard Rodgers and Hal Prince have all left perceptive accounts of their working relationships. Oscar Hammerstein II, in forewords to the songbooks of Jerome Kern, Rodgers and Hart and Rodgers and Hammerstein as well as to Vincent Sheean's *The Amazing Oscar Hammerstein*, provides enthusiastic appreciation as well as accurate information; so does Moss Hart in his foreword to *The Cole Porter Songbook*. Noël Coward has, of course, documented most minutes of his life in his own lively style in his autobiographies, and in his diaries on which we have drawn. Ronald Harwood has kindly contributed a personal account of working on a musical with Johnny Mercer; and Roger Woddis a brief parody of Oscar Hammerstein's verse.

Then there is the invaluable series of lectures, *Lyrics and Lyricists*, organised by the late Maurice Levine at the YMHA on 92nd Street in New York. The writers represented here who gave their testimony on those occasions include Dorothy Fields, Howard Dietz, E. Y. Harburg,

Johnny Mercer, Alan Jay Lerner, Sheldon Harnick and Stephen Sondheim. In some cases these lectures are a principal source of autobiographical detail and Mr Levine generously made his tapes available to us.

Gerald Bordman's *The American Musical Theatre* is unparalleled in its comprehensive sweep and has been particularly valuable in checking some early shows and songs and dates; Robert Kimball's books need no further recommendation; we have referred on several occasions to Max Wilk's *They're Playing Our Song* which includes many fascinating interviews.

We are grateful to Chappell, Carlin, Campbell Connelly, ATV, EMI, TRO Essex and Columbia Pictures Publications for permission to quote many lyrics in this book (a more detailed acknowledgement is given elsewhere). We have also included short extracts from E. Y. Harburg's two sparkling collections of verse, *Rhymes for the Irreverent* and *At this Point in Rhyme* published respectively by Grossman and Crown, and a self-parody of one of his most famous lyrics published in the New York Times.

We have also made use of the perceptive vignettes of Michael Arlen on Cole Porter, S. N. Behrman on life among the Gershwins, Herbert Farjeon on Noël Coward and of sharp appraisals of various shows by Clive Barnes, Robert Benchley and St. John Ervine.

We are also indebted to John Dankworth and Cleo Laine who inaugurated our involvement in the biographical song compilations which are the basis of this book. We first devised a Gershwin programme for them in 1970. Then, in 1975, David Kernan asked for a Sondheim collection for himself and Millicent Martin and Julia McKenzie which again started in much the same form at the Dankworth Theatre at Wavendon before going on to London, New York and most other places. The BBC mounted a *Song by Song by Ira Gershwin* show in 1977 and since then Yorkshire TV (and PBS TV in New York) has broadcast another thirteen. We are grateful to Yorkshire TV, to Vernon Lawrence, the director, Irving Davies, the choreographer, Peter Knight, musical director and Deke Arlon, associate producer, for all their help. Neil Shand was the invaluable script associate on those shows and we have preserved some of his sharper asides in our text.

The selective list of principal shows and hits has been assembled by Rex Bunnett, a peerless pundit and dedicated buff to whom we are also indebted for his co-operation when we were researching *Song by Song*.

At various stages, the manuscript has been typed by Dorothy Siggars and Julia Bankover. To both we are grateful.

Our thanks also to the Hulton Picture Library and to ASCAP for permission to use most of the photographs reproduced in this book.

C.B. and N.S.

CONTENTS

Caryl Brahms (foreground), Ned Sherrin (at back) and other members of the YTV *Song by Song* team. (*Doug McKenzie, Photographic Services Ltd.*).

FOREWORD
The Great Lyric Writer

His parents are Jews born in Russia, or just possibly Poland. Crowded together in a boat with many other immigrants, some of them also the parents of song writers, they sail for the New World. Before or after, but not in any case of which we know during, the voyage his mother gives birth to her son, the writer.

Crowded in one room on the Lower East Side of Manhattan his parents eke out a living and strive to educate their offspring so that he may enjoy the advantages which they are being denied. They fail to master the new language. One parent, father or mother, but usually father, emerges as a character; if they fail in this duty a grandfather does the job. Sometimes The Character drinks, sometimes he gambles, sometimes he womanises, sometimes he speculates. As the son grows older The Character becomes something of an embarrassment. The Lyric Writer has a a limited choice of higher education. Depending on the circumstances of his parents, he goes to City College at night and works during the day. His alternative is to enrol at Columbia. Whichever course he chooses he submits light verse to Franklin P. Adams' column, 'The Conning Tower'. He writes his first lyrics for Broadway revues or frothy book shows until the early thirties when, chased out by the Depression, he goes to Hollywood to work for films intended to lift it. Here he is paid large sums of money but misses the respect he enjoyed on Broadway. In the mid-forties he returns to Broadway and contributes a new seriousness to the musical play, a new respect for the plot and character and songs which reveal character or advance plot. He becomes acquainted with the word *integrated* as it applies to songs and sometimes as it applies to people. He has his greatest success. He writes several integrated musicals after his come-back, but with each effort his work grows a little less integrated and less challenging. He becomes bland. He begins to be revived and to become one of a chorus, asking why there are not more shows like there used to be. There are.

I

IRVING BERLIN

'There's No Business Like Show Business'

It is 1892. The family Baline, all ten of them, including little Israel, aged four, are sailing past the Statue of Liberty. They are tired, they are poor, they are undeniably huddled. They are only too ready to give themselves to their new country – their Promised Land. Their journeying had started in Siberia, in Temun, if that was how they spelt it; they were never to be quite sure. They were, however, sure of the fire which had destroyed their village and sure of the Cossacks who had kindled it. If they had lost their home by setting fire to it themselves and not through the Cossacks, it would have been sufficient . . . if they had starved in Latvia and not gone on to starve in Lithuania, it would have been sufficient . . . if they had frozen in Lithuania and not gone on to the icy Baltic coast, it would have been sufficient . . . if Baline the father had lost his job as a cantor because he lost his voice and not because of the pogrom, it would have been sufficient . . . if they had stood day in and day out beside the unfriendly sea and no ship had taken them to the Promised Land, it would have been sufficient; but a ship did take them.

And here they are starving on Ellis Island, waiting for the cousin of Baline the father to collect them, and meanwhile being checked and listed and ticketed and docketed and saying one to another, 'God Bless America!' 30 years later little Israel would write a song with that title. Twenty years after that he would pluck up the courage to publish it. If it had not sold a single copy, it would have been sufficient; but it sold a million. Hallelujah!

Four years after the arrival of the Family Baline in the Promised Land – no honey, some milk but 'always bread and butter and hot tea' – Baline the father died. He never quite made it as a cantor in the New World; an occasional slayer of meat in the kosher manner, yes; a teacher of Hebrew, yes; a choirmaster, yes; but not a cantor like he had been in Temun. However, working at all these jobs and all at the same time, Baline the father managed to move his family up from their first three

windowless rooms on Monroe Street to three slightly better rooms on Cherry Street. And by the time he died he had already put Israel, now eight, to school and given him a taste for the music of the synagogue. Indeed, the Hebrew chants appealed to Israel more than the American lessons. He was picking up the language easily enough among the Polish, Italian, Irish, German, Chinese kids of the Lower East Side.

On his father's death, little Issy could not wait to join his bigger brothers as a wage earner. He left school and went into newspapers – selling them. Proudly, he joined the queue of baby Balines who nightly emptied their two or three cents' worth into their mother's outspread apron. No threat, no temptation would part the child from his meagre earnings – not even being knocked by a ship's crane into the East River where, coming up for the third time, he was rescued by a kindly sailor. One fist still clenched the five coins it had amassed and held on to them until it opened them at home into mother Baline's expectant apron and faithfully deposited every one of the five cents alongside those of his brothers.

However, the temptations of the Bowery were too alluring to the ambitious, hard-working son of the late, unfulfilled cantor. It was not the glimpses of plentiful pink flesh flaunted from cathouse windows which beckoned him; nor the smell of beer, stale on the hot, evening air. It was the songs of singing waiters, wafting through saloon bar doors, as they went about their white-aproned work. As the evenings grew later and the white aprons grew more stained, little Israel tried to get in on the act; but he too had his early show business setbacks. Of course, his mother disapproved – him the son of a cantor who had sung regularly in the synagogue, at least in Temun. Of course, the saloons rejected him. He had to sing out on the sidewalks, holding out his cap and hoping for the best. His mother's apron accepted such contents as it collected; but he left home in the end, promising his mother that he would come back bringing her a new rocking chair. Almost unpaid, he crept into the chorus of Edward E. Rice's touring production, *The Show Girl*, and, by the time the play reached Broadway, Israel had been left stranded in Binghampton. He hitched his way back to New York; but, once there, he was not immediately allowed to exercise his cheerful chirrup.

At first he supported himself by the lowly task of guiding Blind Sol, a Hearts-and-Flowers-minus-the-violin-vocalist, round the back streets of the Bowery. However, his artist's ambition would not let it rest there. A glittering, if temporary, career as a song-plugger opened before him. Not plugging songs to the customers who had come to the famous Remick's store, shopping for sheet music; not subsidised by Harry von Tilzer to sing his popular melodies from the stage of a music hall; but paid – five dollars a week at that – by the said Mr von Tilzer to stand up in the balcony and join in the second chorus of a new number as though he had just picked it up, sounding for all the world like an ordinary member of the public, which was not hard considering little Israel's limited vocal capacity. What technique could not supply, conviction accomplished. Had he got to sing in the balcony at Tony Pastor's Music Hall and not had his own spotlight beamed upon him it would have been sufficient; but standing in its flattering glow there seemed to Issy to be no limit to what he could achieve. Soon he was back in the Bowery saloons, not begging the odd cent, but as an artist singing the whole night through. He sang to foreign royalty on slumming tours – the future George V of England no less. He composed parodies. Occasionally, he put together his own tunes. He hardly had time to realise that he had become sixteen. He was working regularly at the off-white 'Nigger' Mike Salter's Pelham Café in Chinatown with Chinatown Gertie's brothel on top and blood from the occasional Tong murder mixing with the beer on the floor.

'Slinging out hash and serving beers' was his own description of his job, years later. He amassed enough money to buy his mother a bright new mahogany rocking chair as promised. He learned to pound the black keys and the black keys only on the old upright piano at 'Nigger' Mike's. For his first song he did not even need the black keys. He was only called upon to write the words. A rival saloon, Callaghan's, had launched an Italian song, 'My Muriuccia Take a Steamboat'. 'Nigger' Mike needed a number to counter it. His resident piano player, Nick Nicholson, supplied a tune (using both black and white notes); Israel added the words in this co-operative effort to drum up trade, 'Marie from Sunny Italy'. It was an instant, if local, hit, from the moment Israel sang it with an occasional aide-mémoire scribbled on his celluloid shirt cuffs. If it had pleased the proprietor and not been published, it would have been sufficient. If it had been published under the name of I. Baline and not, owing to a printer's error, that of I. Berlin, it would have been sufficient. But looking at the published song sheet, under the imprint of Joseph W. Stern, the brand new Mr Berlin felt a brand new importance – even though he could not decipher the confusing jumble of black notes that appeared beneath his brand new name. All the lyric netted him was 37 cents for Momma's apron.

It was appropriate that he should move to a brand new job in a superior bar – Kelly's in Union Square. 'The Best of Friends Must Part', 'Queenie, My Own' and 'She Was a Dear Little Girl' were tried out on the customers, a threefold delivery midwifed by the pianist at Kelly's. A vaudeville act asked him for an Italian dialect number – ten dollars was at stake. Away in London an Italian waiter, Dorando, lost the 1908 Olympic marathon race because enthusiastic supporters helped him across the finishing line. However, he caught the imagination of the world and the brand new Mr Berlin wrote a song about him from the point of view of a barber from New York's Little Italy who had backed him to win and lost his little Italian shirt.

Unfortunately, by the time Berlin had finished his masterpiece the fickle vaudevillian who commissioned it had restructured his act and re-allocated his ten dollars. Unabashed, Israel, now twenty, summoned up his courage and took the song to 113 West 39th Street to a publisher, Ted Snyder.

Asked his name by Henry Waterson, Mr Snyder's general manager, the brand new Berlin was ready with a brand new given name, which he had given himself that very morning. 'Irving', he had decided, suited exactly his new status; and it was Irving Berlin whom Mr Snyder and Mr Waterson congratulated, patted on the head, did business with and paid $25. Issy Berlin had gone in with a lyric, and, further, made up a tune on the spot when asked if there was one. Irving Berlin emerged with a contract. Doubtless his mother was the first person to see it and, doubtless, her all-devouring apron collected the advance.

It was the first of many. 'I Wish You Was My Gal, Molly', 'I Didn't Go Home at All' and 'Do Your Duty, Doctor' were all worth $25 in Mr Snyder's ears. He even bought 'Christmas Time Seems Years and Years Away'. The phrase, 'I'm Dreaming of a White Christmas', did not occur to Irving for another 30 years. 'Sadie Salome, Go Home' was an operatic parody which prompted Mr Snyder to offer more than a one-off contract. $25 a week, every week, as staff lyricist, and royalties on top. Alexander Woollcott, Berlin's first biographer, makes this stage a landmark. 'He had turned a corner and found himself in Tin Pan Alley.' He also found himself on Broadway or, to be exact, *Up and Down Broadway,* a show in which he and Mr Snyder sang their own songs, 'Sweet Italian Love' and 'Oh That Beautiful Rag', from their two pianos. By now, 'Dorando' had notched up $4,000, too much for even Momma's capacious apron. Irving moved her and his brothers into a bigger apartment and started minding his royalties for himself.

Financial stability did nothing to diminish the energy with which he pursued ideas for songs. He borrowed from the classics, Berlining 'The Spring Song' as 'That Mesmerising Mendelssohn Tune', (Mesmer, the Mesmeriser, was pretty topical in 1909); he borrowed from his friends' conversation – George Whiting had only to invite him to the theatre because his wife had gone to the country for Berlin to reply with 'Hooray, Hooray!' and to speculate that she probably 'thought it best, you need a rest', adding, 'that's why she's gone away!' A night spent together at the piano with Mr Snyder produced a tune and they had a song. The indiscretion ended Whiting's marriage; but little Irving had a hit. He borrowed, above all, from the new wave of Negro musicians and performers who were spreading the new music and new dance crazes from Sunday night sessions at Jimmy Marshall's hotel on West

53rd Street and Louis Martin's Café de Paris. Among the regulars at Marshall's were vaudeville performers like Ada Overton Walker, Abbie Mitchell and Bert Williams, who had already starred in the *Ziegfeld Follies;* songwriters like Alex Rogers and Will Marion Cook, famous for 'Bon Bon Buddy, the Chocolate Drop'; musicians like Will Dixon, the 'Dancing Conductor', Jim Europe, who organised a Negro orchestra, The Clef Club, and 'Buddy' Gilmore, the trick tap-drummer. At Martin's Place, Maurice, the notorious elegant Negro import from Paris, remembered nowadays only through the posters of Toulouse Lautrec, introduced the 'Danse des Apaches' and the concept of the gigolo. He was glamorised by his billing as 'the high priest of the decadent dance', and by rumours that not only had he broken a white woman's neck in a tango hold, but that he was either a genuine Parisian Apache or the illegitimate son of a French aristocrat. In fact, he was a native New Yorker coming back to triumph just up the road from his home town slum.

> All New York flocked to see him, waiting breathlessly for the climactic moment when his pretty blonde partner leaped astride his hips and, clinging to his waist with her bent knees, swung outwards and away from his body like a floating sash. (*Incredible New York,* Lloyd Morris)

We can safely assume that all New York did not include the Momma Baline. However, in these and other night spots – Bustanoby's, Murray's Roman Gardens, Maxim's at the Café Madrid, Reisenweber's, which boasted three dancing floors, and Rector's 'Souper Tabarin' on Broadway – the new-fangled 'cabaret society' spread the word, or rather the rhythm. A mixed bag of Fifth Avenue dowagers and brash young people, Broadway stars and showgirls, prostitutes and cake-eaters, tycoons of the 'Tenderloin' and the Madames whose brothels they protected, gambling big-shots, politicians from Tammany and playboys from Wall Street, risked joining in or wondering at the dances which the new music inspired – 'Toddling the Todolo', 'The Texas Tommy', 'The Bunny Hug', 'The Grizzly Bear', 'The Turkey Trot', the one step or the tango.

It was no spectacle for Momma Baline, the cantor's widow, even when the dances had been koshered by those nice clean-cut Castles, Vernon and Irene; but Irving was poised to provide the National Anthem of the new music. So great did his success at popularising ragtime become that a wicked inaccurate rumour persisted from 1911 that he kept a little black boy locked up in a room turning out hits which had the authentic Negro sound. It all started with 'Alexander's Ragtime Band'. Irving had a brand new piano now. It was specially constructed by the Wesser Company to enable the man who could only thump out a tune on the black keys in F sharp, to change key by adjusting a lever under the keyboard. In retrospect Berlin admits that 'Ragtime was written years before I thought of the phrase . . . what I did was to crystallise it.' His first shot was called 'Alexander and his Clarinet'. He tried it out on his début at the Friars Club. It was another sign of his rising status that he was formally welcomed to this exclusive show business haunt by George M. Cohan, whose speech was less than subtle. 'Irving Berlin', he opened, 'is a Jewboy who named himself after an English actor and a German city . . .'. The ragtime song did not go well that night but Irving was convinced that he had something. He remembered an unused instrumental piece he had in the trunk. He had placed it in a Folies Bergère revue without a lyric. That failed. Again he had faith; he toyed with the old lyric, and the new tune. Nearly they fitted. The new words promoted Alexander from clarinettist to leader of the entire band. That way it scanned. Finally, the new song found its way to the iron lungs of Emma Carus, who trumpeted it out during a vaudeville engagement in Chicago. 'Come on an' hear!' The house rose to her as they did to Jolson when he introduced it in Dockstader's Minstrels. 'Come on an' hear!' Berlin himself performed it at Hammerstein's Victoria Music Hall. 'Come on an' hear!' Before long the entire nation came on and heard and sang and danced to it. Everybody was 'doing it'. Wherever you looked you could see a ragtime couple over there. You could also watch them throw their shoulders in the air. Irving had two hits without even thinking about 'Yiddisha Nightingale', 'Yiddle on Your Fiddle', 'Play Some Ragtime', 'Goodbye, Becky Cohen', and 'Dat's-a My Girl', let alone 'I Want to be Down Home in . . . D–I–X–I Don't Know How to Spell It'. Almost it might have been Temun.

Any worries Momma may have had about the fast company young Irving was keeping were swept away one day when he picked her up in a cab and drove her from the East Side up into the clean air and greenery of the Bronx and installed her in a fine house with a fancy maid and a kosher cook. If he had provided her with a fancy maid it would have been nothing like sufficient . . . however, as it was, she looked around and it looked good and all she needed to complete the picture was a nice Jewish girl for her good hard-working Jewish boy. True, there was a nice girl on the scene; but she was not a Jewess. Her name was Dorothy Goetz and she had had a stand-up fight with a rival singer for the commercial advantage of being the first to sing one of Irving Berlin's songs ('Yiddle on Your Fiddle'). She lost the battle; but she won the war. She got Irving. She was his first love.

Tragically, she was to die within months of their marriage, of a typhoid contracted on their honeymoon in Cuba. She was twenty, he was 24, and inconsolable. His new brother-in-law, Ray E. Goetz, an impresario, dragooned him into going on a visit to the Europe from which he had sailed as a child twenty years earlier. But the black mood persisted until Goetz prescribed a more direct therapy. He advised Berlin to let his emotion work for him – not against him. 'You're a man who writes from your emotions,' he pointed out, 'use them.' 'When I Lost You', the result of that prescription, broke Berlin's block and became his first deeply felt ballad. By now he was a partner in the music publishing firm of Waterson, Berlin and Snyder. The board's unanimous decision to publish the song resulted in a sale of a million copies. The next year he bounced back to write comedy songs – 'When the Midnight Choo-Choo Leaves for Alabam' – and to make a triumphant appearance at the London Hippodrome, billed as 'The King of Ragtime'. When he got out of his very first London cab the doorman at the hotel was whistling 'Alexander's Ragtime Band'. He gave his English public that. He gave them a specially composed 'International Rag'. They begged for more and got 'Yiddle on Your Fiddle'. And the London *Daily Express,* in that style which it has not forsaken down the decades and through two wars, wrote, 'Go where you will, you cannot escape from the mazes of music he has spun. In every London restaurant, park and theatre you hear his strains. Paris dances to them. Berlin sips golden beer to his melodies. Vienna has forsaken the waltz, Madrid flung away her castanets and Venice forgotten her barcarolles. Ragtime has swept like a whirlwind over the earth and set civilisation humming.'

Back in New York songs burst from him as often as shows burst upon Broadway in those prolific days. 'In My Harem', 'Rum Tum Tiddle', 'If You Don't Want My Peaches You Better Stop Shaking My Tree' and 'Cohen Owes Me Ninety-Seven Dollars' – the latter written, no doubt, from another deeply felt personal experience.

In 1914 he wrote his first Broadway book-show under the patrician management of Charles Dillingham. For the moment he gave up the idea of treating his public to a ragtime opera but not of using the notion as a frequent publicity gambit; it was to be 'not a musical comedy but a real opera on a tragic theme'. He applied his imagination instead to a vehicle for Vernon and Irene Castle. She was above matters of plot and appeared in the programme simply as Mrs Vernon Castle. For a man who was uniquely to cross the bridge from Tin Pan Alley songs to show songs this was a modest beginning; but at least there was a dance theme which bound the show together. 'Syncopated Walk' became a hit. 'Play a Simple Melody' survived, after 40 years of neglect. 'Settle Down in a One-Horse Town' and 'Lock Me in Your Harem and Throw away the Key' did not.

Writing show songs was an automatic way to get them plugged; but the ex-singing waiter, ex-second-chorus-balcony-exploiter was no slouch when plugging his non-show songs. His approach was simple;

first he would write the song. Once he had judged it excellent he would go to the telephone. If it was a sentimental song he would call Al Jolson. 'I've written a great song for you, Al . . .', invariably the sales pitch would begin. One of Jolson's favourite Berlin songs was inspired by a practical joke which no one discovered to be a practical joke until years later. Open-hearted Mr Berlin and sentimental Mr Jolson were much moved by a tear-jerking bequest which appeared in the unlikely pages of a bankers' magazine. A Chicago lawyer, Charles Lounberry, rejecting material matters, was reported to have left, 'to children exclusively, but only for the lifetime of their childhood, all and every, the dandelions of the field and the daisies thereof'. In spite of lumps in his throat and moistened eyes, Berlin expanded the sentimental imagery in his lyric 'When I Leave the World Behind', disposing of night-time to the dreamers, songbirds to the blind and reserving the moon above for those in love. In fact, a Miss Fritzi Scheff had the privilege of unveiling the song to the waiting world; but Jolson sang it whenever possible and Berlin cried all the way to the bank. That the original bequest eventually turned out to be a hoax did not dilute the sweet salt of the tears.

For a time the round of writing shows to plug his songs and plugging songs that were not in shows continued. *Stop! Look! Listen!* served to introduce 'The Girl on the Magazine Cover', 'I Love a Piano' and 'When I Get Back to the USA' but *The Century Girl* – a curious combination of waltz-time and ragtime, personified by the unlikely spectacle of Victor Herbert and Irving Berlin working alongside – produced nothing beyond Herbert's suggestion that Berlin might profit by taking piano lessons. Berlin gave it two days before abandoning it forever; 'I realised I could have written two songs and made myself some money in that time.' Real profit. On the song-plugging front, the firm of Waterson, Berlin and Snyder tried out a brand new sales line – advertising. They plastered Philadelphia with posters promising a brand new Irving Berlin hit, 'Smile and Show Your Dimple!'. The conservative Philadelphians resisted and Berlin put the song away in his trunk until he took the tune out years later for 'Easter Parade'.

Meanwhile, in Europe, a war had been going on. Berlin, serving at Fort Yaphank on Long Island, was still able to contribute to the *Cohan Revue of 1918* and to lie back and listen to John McCormack's recording of his 'Dream On, Little Soldier Boy' while telling the press, 'I don't believe the boys in France want sad, tearful songs . . .' Then, with Armistice Day six months away, he launched his secret weapon. *Yip, Yip, Yaphank,* an all-soldier revue, played for four weeks at the Century Theatre. On the last night the composer, producer, star, led the entire company marching out of the front of the theatre and into troop transports to his tune 'We're on Our Way to France', which was precisely where they were going to entertain their colleagues behind the front line. The score included 'Mandy', which Ziegfeld staged again in a flamboyantly civilian context the next year. But his biggest hit was 'Oh, How I Hate to Get Up in the Morning'. In a sentence of sublime show business idiocy another of his biographers has commented on *Yip, Yip, Yaphank's* arrival in France: '. . . two months later, the war that had been going so badly was over and won.' Did the Kaiser ever forgive Irving Berlin?

At least Ziegfeld welcomed him back with open arms, and *The Ziegfeld Follies of 1919* is widely held to be the best of the series. 'Ziegfeld Outziegfelds Ziegfeld', one headline summed it up. In response to a last-minute appeal from Ziegfeld, Berlin contributed the ultimate song-to-introduce-the-girls, 'A Pretty Girl is Like a Melody'. The appeal was another of those 'I've-got-some-costumes-I-need-a-number' managerial requirements. 'Mandy' had contrived to linger (' . . . here's a ring for your finger, isn't it a hum-dinger . . .') and the other new songs included 'You'd Be Surprised'. Every matinée, every evening, Eddie Cantor sang it, and they were. 'The Guy Who Guards the Harem' completed the main Berlin portfolio together with a topical Prohibition number, 'You Cannot Make Your Shimmy Shake on Tea'. 'It simply can't be done,' he announced. 'You'll find your shakin' ain't takin'.'

As a song writer Irving continued to be a devoted son turning his filial affection into crisp green-backs. 'The Hand that Rocked My Cradle Rules My Heart' and 'Was There Ever a Pal Like You' were both directed at mothers the world over. Fathers the world over could tap their toes to 'I Left the Door Open and My Daddy Walked Out'. Though the war had brought sorrow it also brought some opportunities for women. Berlin chose to celebrate the victory in 'Everything is Rosy Now for Rosie' and 'Since Katy the Waitress Became an Aviatress'. Cuba to him was no longer an echo of his first wife's death, but a subject for another song about getting out of the range of the Volstead Act and Prohibition – 'I'll See You in C.U.B.A.'.

By 1920 he was becoming The Grand Old Young Man, hardworking, contentious, litigious, protective of his copyrights and of the way in which his songs were arranged. He was observed breaking recordings of his tunes which he did not like across his knees and sending stern letters from his lawyers to the culprits by the first post. He still talked portentously to newspapermen about the syncopated opera he was never to write and the effect that American syncopation would one day have on opera the world over. He predicted that one day New York would be getting 'operas from Vienna filled to the brim with our own native jazz'. He split from Waterson, Berlin and Snyder and became Irving Berlin Inc. He found himself on a panel of eminent musicians – one of whom at least could not read music – judging a patriotic song contest. John Philip Sousa and John McCormack were Berlin's fellow judges. They gave the lowest prize of $50 to George Gershwin's anonymous entry. Berlin and Gershwin had met earlier when the nearly Grand Old Young Man had told the very young, young man that he had too much talent to waste as an arranger for the house of Waterson, Berlin and Snyder. 'Yes,' Gershwin had agreed with the sublime certainty of genius as yet unrecognised.

It was at this time that Berlin lost his mother and buried her beside his father in a Brooklyn cemetery. His working life was full. The first *Music Box Revue* gave birth to 'Say it with Music', 'Everybody Step' and 'They Call it Dancing' ('A man can squeeze all the she's with his hands and his knees'): in the second, a year later, the titles of the songs virtually describe their staging. 'Lady of the Evening', on moonlit rooftops, 'My Diamond Horseshoe of Girls', 'Crinoline Days' and 'Porcelain Maid'. *Music Box Revues* aimed to be as glittering as a Ziegfield show but funnier and more imaginative, in a much more intimate setting. Alexander Woollcott defined the production style: '. . . they emerge from tree-trunks and bird cages, spring up out of trap doors and lightly swing down from high trapezes. When this is not possible they walk groggily down interminable staircases of black velvet, managing the perilous descent as nonchalantly as possible in the circumstances of having to carry with them gowns of silver sequins weighing about a ton each.' All this on a stage which felt full in 1977 with four performers and two pianos for *Side by Side by Sondheim*. The third *Music Box Revue* sprayed orange-scented perfume on the audience while the tenor and Grace Moore sang of 'An Orange Grove in California' and, by the time of the fourth *Music Box Revue* in 1924, Berlin was still tirelessly writing and supervising everything and also found time to address the *New York Times* on the subject of his jazz opera: 'I hope that some day I may write an operatic score in jazz.'

Enough of dreams of opera, it was time for romance: and in Ellin Mackay, the only daughter of a rich, Catholic, anti-semitic and disapproving father, Clarence Mackay, head of the American Post and Telegraph Company, Berlin found it. Grace Moore once described the ballads she was given in the *Music Box Revues* as singing telegrams, so convinced was she that 'Remember' and 'Always' were direct messages from Irving to Ellin, passed without her father's knowledge. Berlin's official courtship had started badly. Clarence – known to the press as the 'Cable King' – took Ellin abroad to get her away from Berlin, not, as some romantic newspaperman imagined, to get a dispensation from the Pope so that she could marry him. Berlin's big numbers that year were 'All Alone' and 'What'll I Do?', and less romantic pressmen took the point. When Mackay got back, a statement from the stern father confirmed a defeat for Berlin which was trumpeted round the world by the fascinated society columnists. Rival songwriters cashed in with a song, 'When a Kid Who Came from the East Side Found a Sweet Society Rose', and Berlin, who was trying to write *The Cocoanuts,* was so besieged that he must have found it hard to distinguish between his real life predicament and the Marx Brothers farce on which he was working. Mackay and he feuded in statements, in letters and face to face. Mackay threatened to disinherit his daughter the day she married Berlin. Berlin said he would settle two million dollars on her if he did. Mackay boasted his pedigree. Berlin said his went back to Exodus. Exodus was his cue to get out. Finally, the lovers resorted to elopement. Married, they faced the press. Ellin assured reporters that they were supremely happy. They chose to go to Atlantic City where the bride repeated to the press that they were supremely happy. Father still refused to speak to Ellin; but when the pair returned to New York she said once more that they were supremely happy. 24 hours later they were back in Atlantic City where Ellin arranged a party for 60 close friends. Immediately after the party they made yet another journey to New York. They holed-up there and when they could no longer be reached for comment, which would perhaps have been predictable, they fled to London and the guard who barred the door to their suite at the Carlton Hotel gave his own statement to the press. 'They are supremely happy,' he said. Berlin presented Ellin with all the royalties from 'Always'. Deeply felt experience was doing its profitable work again.

The constant attention of the press, the bucketings about the world and an abortive attempt to collaborate on a Drury Lane revue provided a frustrating period for Berlin. Back in New York, society offered no balm. On the occasion of the wedding, the *Social Register* had noted the marriage of 'Miss Ellin Mackay, daughter of Clarence Mackay, and Mr Irving Berlin', adding, 'This is in accordance with the *Social Register's* custom of recording marriages when one of the parties is in Society.' On their return the new edition was no kinder to the cantor's son. It mentioned neither Irving nor Ellin. A reporter questioned the omission. The *Register's* rebuke was firm. 'Irving Berlin has no position in Society.' Society had an even sterner rebuke up its sleeve. Although the Berlin's little daughter Mary Ellin was a healthy happy child, their son, born in December 1928, was to die that Christmas morning and there were those in Society callous enough to point out that the Christmas Day tragedy was not an accident but 'God's punishment for marrying a Jew'.

Counting his blessings ('instead of sheep') as he entered 1929, Berlin could list a wife, a daughter, a fortune and his three most recent hits, 'The Song is Ended', 'Shaking the Blues Away' (the big success of his first Ziegfeld score for six years) and 'Blue Skies', which was interpolated into Rodgers and Hart's *Betsy* behind their backs and to their chagrin. It was, they held, a plot between the star, Belle Baker, and the manager, Ziegfeld, who added spotlight to injury by beaming one on Berlin as he acknowledged the cannonade of encores for his song on their first night.

On the debit side was the undeniable fact that the hits were isolated. Berlin's society wife did not encourage him to work as hard as had his Momma with her apron. She decreed that no one was to call him Issy who had not known him in his Bowery days, or was not a member of his close family. Nothing less than Irving was required from the rest of the world. Then came the crash which took with it most of Wall Street. First of all it took Clarence Mackay. One newspaper called his loss 'the greatest reversal of fortune of any rich American'. It did not leave his son-in-law unscathed. 'I was scared,' was Berlin's comment on the crash. 'I had had all the money I wanted for the rest of my life. Then all of a sudden I didn't. I had taken it easy and gone soft, and wasn't too certain I could get going again.' His uncertainty showed in everything he did. He was building a $200,000 house on East 92nd Street with one hand, and with the other stuffing songs into the trunk as soon as he wrote them lest they did not meet his standards. Indeed, he was no longer sure what his standards were. 'Putting on the Ritz' for Harry Richman and 'Let Me Sing and I'm Happy' for Jolson had crept out to do very nicely thank you; but for every song that got away a dozen were held back lest people laugh at them. With the new lack of self-confidence a new smoothness was growing, born of the new self-criticism. Music and lyrics were becoming more worldly and more refined. He and Cole Porter were friends through their wives. His popular appeal was still there; but for the moment he doubted it. One of his pluggers did not. He rifled the trunk and kidnapped a number, spiriting it to Rudy Vallee for his radio show with the tear-jerking information that Irving felt that he was 'all washed up'. 'Say It Isn't So.'

It was Mr Vallee's turn to weep. 'Say it isn't so,' he warbled to his wife, who was on the point of divorcing him. The marriage held. So did the song; and Irving's courage, never far below the surface, returned. Diving into the trunk himself he surfaced with 'How Deep is the Ocean'. Thus encouraged, Berlin felt able to attack a whole Broadway score again. In fact, not one but two. For Moss Hart's* *Face the Music* he had a hit with 'Soft Lights and Sweet Music' and, hard on the end of

---

* Moss Hart, sixteen years younger than Berlin, had made his Broadway début with his comedy *Once in a Lifetime*, pulled into shape by the established playwright and wit, George S. Kauffman. *Face the Music* was his second venture into musical theatre – the first, *Jonica*, was a failure. He was to go on to write the book for *Lady in the Dark* and to be associated with a number of Broadway hits as writer or director. Perhaps his greatest triumph was his direction of *My Fair Lady*.

Prohibition, another with the unlikely premise, 'Let's Have Another Cup of Coffee'. His second show with Moss Hart, again a revue, *As Thousands Cheer*, built around newspaper headlines, was even more magnetic – with 'Heat Wave', for Ethel Waters, and 'I Wanna Go Back to Michigan'. After further recourse to the trunk, 'Smile and Show Your Dimple' reappeared, decked out in an Easter bonnet with Easter roses on it as the tune for an Easter Parade. Berlin's explanation for the new success of the old flop was simple. 'A song is like a marriage. It takes a perfect blending of two mates, the music and the words, to make a perfect match. In the case of 'Easter Parade', it took a divorce and a second marriage to bring about the happiest of unions.'

All these hits reassured Irving and also cemented the newly mended rift with his father-in-law. Rumour had it that the dutiful son-in-law signed a cheque for a million dollars to ease Mackay's financial embarrassment. Other rumours said it was more. Ellin had made the first overtures, giving evidence in court on her father's behalf in a law suit, so saving him $100,000. When he married Anna Case, an opera singer from the Met, previously a blacksmith's daughter, the whole family was 'supremely happy'. Miss Case – Anna Mackay – died in 1984 at the age of 95, the same as her step-son-in-law, who was finally an orphan.

In spite of his frequent fears about what radio would do to the future sales of his music, Berlin embraced the medium in the thirties – this time as a performer. 'You have to hug him to hear him,' the comedian, Joe Frisco, had said of his voice; at least with radio they could put him nearer the microphone. Continuing to turn his back on the stage, he moved on through the mechanical media to Hollywood and movies. It was go-West-middle-aged-man time for the composers and lyricists of Broadway – Rodgers, Hart, Hammerstein, the Gershwins, Porter, Kern, Harburg, Arlen, Schwartz, Duke, Lane and Fields. Berlin, his confidence fully restored, was not prepared to accept anything less than the best terms on his arrival. Arthur Freed has described his attitude to a deal: 'It took longer to write one of his contracts than a whole script. But after it was done, he'd forget about the contract and give you anything you wanted.' He gave them *Top Hat*, with 'Top Hat, White Tie and Tails', 'Cheek to Cheek', 'Isn't This a Lovely Day to be Caught in the Rain?' and 'The Piccolino'. Research consisted of a boat trip to Italy with Moss Hart, eleven hours in Naples and the old upright piano transferred just in time to catch the next boat back to New York. He gave them *Follow the Fleet* – again for Fred Astaire and Ginger Rogers – 'I'm Putting All My Eggs in One Basket', 'Let's Face the Music and Dance', 'Let Yourself Go' and 'We Saw the Sea'.

In 1937 he gave them *On the Avenue* with 'I've Got My Love to Keep Me Warm' and 'This Year's Kisses'. Next year it was *Carefree* – full of music and love and romance, and 'Change Partners and Dance'. By 1938 he was an elder statesman and it was no longer essential that he should write new songs. Easier to take one of his old titles and throw some sort of story, a handful of stars and dozens of his other earlier hits at it. *Alexander's Ragtime Band* crammed in 28 Berlin titles; *Blue Skies* only slightly fewer.

Just as for ordinary mortals, so for Irving Berlin, the decade which was the thirties lasted only nine years. Once again he had a secret weapon with which to greet the new patriotism. There in his trunk lay 'God Bless America'. In 1918 he had tried it on his amanuensis, Harry Ruby, who flinched at the idea of yet another patriotic number. Always sensitive to a flinching guinea pig, Berlin had silently stowed it away. Now he went straight to his foolproof filing system in response to Kate Smith's request for 'a song like the "Star Spangled Banner"'. In 1918 Berlin would have been behind the times with 'God Bless America'; twenty years on it put him ahead of them and, since he gave all his royalties to the Girl Scouts of America, it put them in the black. Sentimental patriotism accomplished, he turned his hand, with even greater success, to his definitive musical essay on seasonal homesickness, 'I'm Dreaming of a White Christmas'. Written for *Holiday Inn* with Bing Crosby and Fred Astaire, it left him with Ascension Day the only high day in the calendar uncelebrated by an Irving Berlin song. The verse of 'White Christmas' which placed the singer firmly amid the palm trees of Beverly Hills was speedily dropped from the published song copy, when its composer sensed that it might seem to exclude audiences hungry for its wonderfully universal homesick sentiment.

Nor was he content to minister to the homesick only through the movies. *This is the Army* was the forties equivalent of *Yip, Yip, Yaphank*. Berlin with his upright piano went back to Fort Yaphank to absorb the atmosphere of the new army. He was determined to be thorough. His last return to Broadway, the soft political satire of *Louisiana Purchase*, had not been a great success, though it had yielded 'It's a Lovely Day Tomorrow' and 'Lord Done Fixed Up My Soul'. Apart from 'This is the Army, Mr Jones – no private rooms or telephones', the atmosphere of Fort Yaphank also suggested to him 'What the Well-Dressed Man in Harlem Will Wear', 'I'm Getting Tired So I Can Sleep' and 'I Left My Heart at the Stage Door Canteen'. Royalties went to an army charity and the show toured the theatres of war. For London he wrote a mercifully forgotten addition, 'My British Buddy'. The *New York Times* verdict on its effect, 'A new song is sweeping over London and its psychological punch is equal to another big chunk of lease-lend', is a blatant piece of chauvinistic over-statement.

There is a pattern for the comebacks of the great song writers in the forties. From the moment that Rodgers and Hammerstein broke the mould with *Oklahoma!*, it is as though all the other old warhorses, sensing their rivals racing to success, started pounding their pianos determined to produce their best work. And they did. Cole Porter, writing under pressure, romped home with *Kiss Me Kate*; 'Yip' Harburg found another rainbow in *Finian's*; and Irving Berlin was under starter's orders from the day Jerome Kern died from a heart attack suffered on a New York street, and the producers, Rodgers and Hammerstein, and the book writers, Herbert and Dorothy Fields, who had had the idea of doing a musical about Annie Oakley for Ethel Merman called *Annie Get Your Gun*, asked him to write the score.

There was some hesitation at the starting gate. Berlin, who was not sure if he could manage the hill-billy idiom, took the book away to his farm in the Catskills for the weekend. The bucolic atmosphere worked well. He came back with 'They Say It's Wonderful' and 'You Can't Get a Man With a Gun'. Having developed the habit of working down on the farm he went off for another weekend. This time he raised five fine songs, 'Anything You Can Do I Can Do Better', 'The Girl That I Marry', 'My Defences Are Down', 'Doin' What Comes Naturally' and 'I Got the Sun in the Morning'. It had always been his habit to thump away far into the night at the old upright piano, which he had long ago named his Buick. That weekend must have set some sort of record. In more urban surroundings he produced 'There's No Business Like Show Business', a song custom-built to keep the audience happy during a scene change. Once again he demonstrated his gift for transforming a simple thought into a universal song suitable for a special occasion. He had an instinct for anthems. His colleagues liked it; but not, apparently, enough. The next time he played the score to them he dropped it. Oscar Hammerstein asked where it was. Berlin had left it behind. Sensitive to first reactions as ever, he had interpreted their polite approval as rejection. A friend of Berlin's (one wonders if he remained a friend) once described *Annie Get Your Gun* as old-fashioned. 'Yes', Berlin said, 'A good old-fashioned smash!'

Or at least such a smash that he did not have to be driven to the Buick for another three years when, inevitably intrigued by Robert E. Sherwood's suggestion that they should work together on a musical about the Statue of Liberty, Berlin began thumping again. If *Miss Liberty* had been a hit, it would have been sufficient. Unfortunately, she was not. Set to an Irving Berlin tune, Emma Lazarus's words, 'Give Me Your Tired, Your Poor', were less potent than some of Izzy Baline's own patriotic pieces written during the intervening 57 years since first he passed the Statue of Liberty as a boy of four. But at least it was a long way from Temun. There was to be another hit, *Call Me Madam*, which called upon Merman again and presented her with a bouquet of songs, 'You're Just in Love', 'It's a Lovely Day Today', and 'The Hostess With the Mostes' On the Ball'. And there was a flop, *Mr President*, which, like

Miss Liberty, aimed perhaps too directly at the bullseye which Berlin's public expected him to select.

The Buick was sent to the Smithsonian Institute. Berlin no longer talked of writing a ragtime opera. The immigrant boy took up painting. He took up fishing. He continued to sue parodists, but his heart was not in it. 'I never had a hobby,' the driven, single-minded, anxious, wealthy, little man says. 'Song writing was my hobby.'

2

COLE PORTER

'Riding High'

Night and day he was the one, only him beneath the moon and under the sun; only him, that is to say, in his order of priorities. For Cole Porter, a socially talented, professionally gifted writer and composer of songs, financially secure even before he wrote them, was an only child – a dangerous thing to be if you were well-heeled in the twenties and thirties, indeed at any time – but then, like Henry James, Cole Porter could 'stand a good deal of gold'.

In the first place he came from a good deal of gold. It had been accumulated by his grandfather, J. O. Cole, a self-willed old autocrat who exercised his Midas touch from the moment he first fingered the real thing as a prospector in California in the 1850s. However, the method of this Midas was to exchange digging in the ground for digging in the pockets of his colleagues – he sold water to the thirsty and from the stock of his general store he sold generally and largely. He made a considerable profit; and soon he was able to return to the family home in Peru, Indiana, where he bought a brewery and expanded like an octopus in all directions. The old curmudgeon saved the softer side of his nature for his wife, Rachel, and his daughter Kate. Rachel he referred to as 'The Rose of Indiana', a cloying floral image not to be equalled in sentimentality until his grandson's first song-hit, 'Old Fashioned Garden'.

However, the inspiration for that song lay not in Cole Porter's soul, but rather in the purchase of a trunk of Ziegfeld's cast-off flower costumes by Raymond Hitchcock, the producer of *Hitchy-Koo of 1919*, who commissioned the fragrant fancy.

'Old Fashioned Garden Farm' had been the name of Porter's mother's old home in Peru, Indiana. Kate, the apple of her father's eye, made her son the apple of hers. In early childhood she added the middle name, Albert, so that his initials should spell a whole word, C.A.P. She did it simply because a gypsy told her to. She enveloped young Master Cole in care and concern, distancing him from his ineffectual father and protecting him from his formidable grandfather. The father, Samuel Fennick Porter, can be dismissed in a few sentences. He was used to dismissal in life. A druggist who married money, his sole positive contribution to his son's progress seems to have been to introduce young Master Cole to poetry and in particular to the convoluted rhymes of Browning which found an echo in the prosody of his songs in later years. However, unable to stand up to his father-in-law, Sam Porter tended to vent his frustration on Cole whenever the boy failed to grasp Browning's denser passages. Very early he lost the boy's affection to a mother who would not be satisfied with less than all of it. He did not die until 1927 after a seemingly interminable nervous breakdown. He had long since ceased to have any influence on his son. Young Master Cole's early photographs, and his mother commissioned plenty, suggest a shy and mostly solemn little marmoset peering out of velvet and lace and ruffles. Fitting out the slightly larger marmoset with the sailor suits and large straw sailor hats of the period did nothing to dispel the cossetted air. Piano lessons, lessons on the violin and French lessons, from the one genuine Frenchwoman in Peru, were all lavished on the embryo genius, man of the world and leader of society. On the way to the violin lessons young Master Cole found, all by himself, a dirty-book store which was to inspire a lifetime facility for the off-colour rhyming joke, in songs like 'But in the Morning, No!'.

When, at the age of ten, he started to write songs – his songs of innocence – they were greeted with nothing less than total euphoria by his mother. Early he learnt that his facility for music was a powerful weapon which he could exploit to gain love, and acclaim and admiration. For the next 60 years he sought all three as his life-time companions. He got less admiration from his grandfather who felt that he needed toughening and alternated tales of derring-do on the frontier with solemn drives across country to stare with a dour look at the workhouse: 'That's where you'll end up, my boy!'

At thirteen young Master Cole departed for Worcester Academy. The choice was his mother's. His grandfather wanted him to stay farming. His father was not asked. The manner of his going divided his mother and grandfather for two years. The object of their disagreement was delighted by his new surroundings. His arrival had been heralded by 'numerous trunks, pieces of stationery, paintings and an upright piano – a rather unusual assortment of possessions for the thirteen-year-old midwestern farmboy to bring to school in 1905, or, for that matter, any other year.' His instincts, as always, were to play the piano, to please and to become an East Coast gentleman. Mother had chosen the perfect headmaster to further this ambition. 'A gentleman never eats,' he instilled in the eager mind; 'he breakfasts, he lunches, he dines, but he

Cole Porter (*Hulton Picture Library*).

never eats!' Between Worcester and Yale the young gentleman popped over to Paris as a punctuation point. He had hardly visited Peru in the meanwhile. On the one occasion when he did return, his grandfather insisted on sending him down to the hayfield where young Master Cole contrived to faint within 30 minutes, came to himself in mother's arms and never returned to hay – save lyrically, some 30 years later, in the song 'Farming', where his lyric suggested that 'Dear Mae West is at her best' in it; and went on to conjure up a picture of what happens when the stripper, Margie Hart, 'starts churning her butter', and other bucolic *double-entendres*.

There was no question of keeping Cole down on the farm once he had seen Paree. Indeed Paris became the fascination of a lifetime.

However, his arrival at Yale was uncharacteristic. The half-finished young gentleman chose to conceal his self-consciousness by wearing gaudy pink and yellow shirts and ties. It needed all his ingratiating skill at the piano to endear him to his classmates, but so forceful was the manner in which he deployed it that he soon had them all – football hearties and scions of the social register, all the college society that counted with him – kneeling at his piano stool. He was prepared to play all night and all day. Riding and swimming were his only sports – no need to be one of a team there. What he did obsessively was to write and perform songs for the Glee Club and for any other amateur dramatic society which would take them, and all of them did.

Yale merged into Harvard when it became necessary to go on to the Law School in order to keep grandfather's funds flowing. In no time at all Porter got out of law and into music – though only his mother was told. Having got into music he had to get on to Broadway and he managed it with a semi-society, semi-professional production, *See America First*. Porter was ecstatic; but clear-eyed critics advised the public to 'see America last', and the show folded after fifteen performances. Porter was dismayed. He felt disgraced; his career was over. According to Clifton Webb (part of the professional contingent): 'I played a cowboy and an autumn flower. Others had roles not so believable.' The only song to make an impact was 'I've a Shooting-Box in Scotland'. Fred and Adele Astaire put it into their act. This was a swings and roundabouts time for Cole Porter. On the swings side came a windfall from grandfather J. O. Cole, who established a substantial trust fund for his grandson; against that, on the roundabouts, was his new-found depression. However, even this was turned to profit. His fertile imagination went to work and he let it be known that, shocked by his failure, he had done the only decent thing and gone off to join the Foreign Legion. To remember that he did not leave for France for a year and a half and that, when he got there, he did not enlist, would have ruined the symmetry of the story. A fantasy often appealed more to him than the unvarnished truth; and if fantasy was piled on fantasy the further away it took him from facts, the more at home he felt. However, he was variously reported as a legionnaire, an officer of the Zouaves, a member of the French Army, a corporal, a captain, an American aviator, and ADC to the head of a relief organisation behind the lines. Most of the time, it is safe to assume, he was behind a piano.

There he stayed when the war ended and the American forces went home. How to fill the days? Well, there was the study of counterpoint, composition, orchestration and harmony with Vincent d'Indy at his Schola Cantorum; but that did not last once master and pupil failed to agree. There were larger issues. Elsa Maxwell, the potential party-giver, must be met and made a friend; her attitude to Porter's music was less critical than d'Indy's. The friendship blossomed. There were parties to go to and people to meet. There were the last spots of midwestern gaucherie to polish off and the pace was fast enough to accelerate the sandpapering process.

Cast in the role of principal polisher was Mrs Linda Lee Thomas, a divorcee from Louisville, Kentucky, eight years older than Porter and fated to become his wife. She was a beauty, a leader of fashion and a woman of legendary, if sometimes wilful, taste. On one occasion she had her hands on the Hope Diamond for 24 hours and then sent it back, not because she feared its curse, but because she hated its 'dirty blue colour'. At seventeen she had married the sort of millionaire who could afford, on one occasion, to lose ten million dollars and shrug it off. He was also the first American known to have killed a man in a car accident. When he married Linda Lee he threw in a cottage in Newport, a mansion in Palm Beach, a New York town house, a yacht, a box at the opera, and a long list of jewellery. He was athletic, aggressive and a playboy. She was frail but strong; beautiful but determined. By the time they had been married seven years, she had closed her ears to countless stories of his liaisons with showgirls and continued to run her handful of homes with impeccable style and clockwork precision. One publicised infidelity finally broke the back of the marriage and she filed for divorce. Some years later Porter met the lady in question in London. 'Oh,' she said, 'I don't know whether I should meet you or not. You see I was your wife's ex-husband's mistress.' He had reason to thank her and did. Linda Lee Thomas emerged from her marriage with about a million dollars and settled in Paris where her beaux included Irving Berlin's future father-in-law, Clarence H. Mackay, the Duke d'Aosta and the Duke d'Alba. Friends who were not suitors included Shaw, Galsworthy, Winston Churchill and Bernard Berenson. The Porters were to make a marriage of perfect pitch and absolute taste. Two actors, one of consummate chic, the other ambitious to emulate her, both swanning their way through the Parisian *haut monde*, giggling a little, playing, privately, at Kentucky girl and Indiana farm-boy in a game they had invented in order to preserve their sense of proportion.

Young Master Cole had one genuine farm-boy's reservation. He could not yet afford to support Linda Lee in the manner to which her first husband had accustomed her. He went home to the farm to ask grandfather Cole to put his hand still deeper into his pocket. The old man refused; but Mother, as always, dug into her purse. The voyage home to Peru had yielded a bonus. It was on the ship that Porter played his songs for Raymond Hitchcock, the comedian who was launching his own revue, *Hitchy-Koo of 1919*. This was the opportunity for 'Old Fashioned Garden' to flower into a hit and, collecting his royalties, a couple of loans and his mother's subvention, Porter hurried back to Paris just in time to enter the twenties a married man.

The 'Coleporteurs', as they were known in Paris, began their delicate dance along the tightrope which they slung between work and play. They shared a determination to make his work succeed; but they concentrated at the same time on establishing the legend of an indolent, extravagant, charmed and charming playboy which never disappeared. Elsa Maxwell has recorded that while Porter was 'cutting capers all over Europe he was working hard and steadily, six hours a day, writing songs, experimenting with lyrics, polishing his technique and . . . building up a large inventory of songs.' Michael Arlen's famous paragraph etches precisely the public image which 'les Coleporteurs' were busily creating in Paris in the twenties:

> Every morning at half past seven, Cole Porter leaps lightly out of bed and, having said his prayers, arranges himself in a riding habit. Then, having written a song or two, he will appear at the stroke of half past twelve at the Ritz, where, leaning in a manly way on the bar, he will say: 'Champagne cocktail, please. Had a marvellous ride this morning!' That statement gives him strength and confidence on which to suffer this, our life, until ten minutes past three in the afternoon when he will fall into a childlike sleep.

Moss Hart, increasingly successful, arriving from America, sought him out in the Ritz Bar and delivered a dancer's Christmas present – a pair of solid gold garters. Porter promptly put them on instead of the gold pair which he was already wearing and which he presented to the barman.

The schedule also included a great deal of travelling. The caravan settled for a time in Antibes – lengthening the season there from spring into summer. When grandfather Cole died in 1922 they could afford to extend their kingdom to Venice – and a series of palazzos. The grander the palazzo, the bigger the parties. His verses were complaining that '. . .

these Americans are always entertaining'.

Their home base was 13 rue Monsieur in Paris, a few doors from the house Nancy Mitford was to make her home twenty years later. Linda could receive there with as much ceremony as she liked; and Cole could sally out to place a dozen or so of his songs – some in London revues which failed; some in New York in *Hitchy-Koo of 1922*, which also failed, never reaching Broadway. A score for an 'American' ballet for the Ballet Suédois, *Within the Quota*, moved Paris, but left America cold. Linda, excited by this more ambitious step, solicited libretti from Arnold Bennett, John Galsworthy and Bernard Shaw. None arrived through the letterbox at 13 rue Monsieur. John Murray Anderson, a leading revue producer, invited a score for *The Greenwich Village Follies* but sank the lyrics under a brash, gaudy production. Porter found himself back at Yale contributing three songs to yet another show. One lyric admitted that there was no concealing the fact that he was feeling bored. Bored with lack of progress.

1927, and it was time to go to work, even to be seen to be going to work. Some inner lack of confidence, some fear of rejection had pushed the pose of the bored playboy beyond a joke. Irving Berlin (the two Society wives, Linda Porter and Ellin Berlin, were the friends who brought the two dissimilar men together) urged Porter to get the feel of Broadway and of 42nd Street. Porter decided that a good lunch would be more pleasant and more purposeful; but he chose to have it with a good agent, Louis Schurr, who, he noticed, had an uncanny knack of finding the right jobs for his clients. Porter auditioned for Vinton Freedley and Alex Aarons, two producers who already possessed one composer, George Gershwin. They decided that they did not need another. However, E. Ray Goetz, brother of Berlin's first wife, next on Schurr's list, lacked a Rodgers and Hart. He decided to give Porter a chance to be both – the show was to be called *Paris*, it was to star Goetz's wife, Irene Bordoni, and it introduced Cole Porter in the most emphatic way with 'Let's Do It'.

Mr Schurr earned his lunch and this first introduction led to three shows with Goetz. *Fifty Million Frenchmen* and *The New Yorkers* were to follow. Neither was very substantial; but all were scattered with songs which solidified Porter's reputation. In one show the audience was taken on a tour of Paris, in another a tour of New York. In between composer and entourage took a tour of the world arriving in Venice by way of Hollywood, Hawaii, Japan, China, the Malay Straits, Nangpo Colony and Siam. Japanese railways fell short of expectations; and back in America Depression newspapers were brightened with the news that Cole Porter had hired a private train to get to Nagasaki. He also posted home a new song from practically every port, a gesture which attracted rather more favourable publicity. Like its composer, a Porter song was beginning to develop a knack of getting itself talked about. When 'Let's Do It' was shipped to London to decorate C. B. Cochran's revue, *Wake Up and Dream*, there was speculation on whether sexual innuendo would get it banned. However, the Lord Chamberlain congratulated the lyric writer on his exhaustive and scholarly animal research, especially the mating habits of grouse who 'do it' when they're out of season.

When 'What is This Thing Called Love?' was imported into New York, Walter Winchell, the notorious newspaper columnist, ran a campaign on 'Love's' behalf. More scandal attended another lyric. In 1926 Porter had written a song called 'The Scampi'; now he updated and upclassed it to 'The Oyster'. A leading critic, Gilbert Seldes, campaigned against the song on grounds of taste and secured its removal. It told of an innocuous day in the life of a social-climbing oyster, fed to a society matron and ultimately regurgitated into the ocean. The oyster had a taste of society, '. . . and society has had a taste of me'. The oyster may have been saved; but the song was not reprieved until the sixties.

When 'Love For Sale' was introduced in *The New Yorkers*, it too was condemned as 'in the worst possible taste'. The four white singers in a street setting peddling 'love that's only slightly soiled', were replaced by Elisabeth Welch in décor which suggested the Cotton Club.

Porter had already set the pattern for his work in the 1930s. And the thirties is his defining period. He had written thirties music in the twenties and he continued to write it in the forties and fifties. Also the music was timeless. It carried the shows. There might be extravagant clowning or powerful personalities on display, but no great effort was made to integrate either in what passed for a book. The pattern of his life meant working hard, still in as secret a fashion as possible, and playing hard, still in as public a fashion as possible. It meant dividing time between Europe and America; between Paris, London and New York – and increasingly California. Hollywood discovered Porter and he returned the compliment, relishing the climate, the extravagance and the hedonistic atmosphere. He enjoyed tweaking the tails of the apelike studio heads and he enjoyed even more making them cry with his most sentimental songs. 'Imagine making L. B. Mayer cry,' he laughed to a friend: 'What could possibly top that?' Porter had played him 'In the Still of the Night', a song destined for Nelson Eddy.

Tears and laughter. A Cole Porter show was now an event; eagerly expected by first-nighters, frequently dismissed by critics as not as good as the last Cole Porter show – the hallmark of an established reputation. The Porter first-night pattern was elegant, unique, unvarying. Mrs Porter's gift was always an especially designed cigarette-box usually run up by the Duke di Verdura and decorated with a jewelled motif relevant to the play. The evening would start with a small dinner party.

The guests arrived at the theatre laughing and gossiping just before the lights dimmed. Here they became part of a larger party, occupying perhaps the first three or four rows. Centrally seated, the host and composer, urbane and genial, would lead the enjoyment. No nailbiting at the back for Cole Porter; no nervous pacing the surrounding streets until the crack of applause summoned him back for the final curtain. Rising from his seat like any other satisfied first-nighter, he would continue to enjoy the festivities. 'Isn't it fun,' he would confirm. Some years later, he explained his iron-nerved attitude in an interview: 'The reason for my behaviour isn't that I'm confident of the play's success or that I'm totally without nerves. I'll put up my nerves against the best of them. But, for some reason, the moment the curtain rises on opening night, I say to myself, "There she goes," and I've bid goodbye to my baby . . . it belongs to the performers. And I become another $8.80 customer. That is why I take my friends along and make a night of it afterward.'

Gay Divorce was his next chance to make a night of it. Fred Astaire, appearing for the first time without his sister, was the star, 'Night and Day' the most famous and enduring song. There are several stories of its genesis and some of the confusion stems from Porter's penchant for fantasising. It was his contention that the music was inspired by a Mohammedan call to worship which he had heard in Morocco. One biographer holds that the verse was written on a beach in Newport; another, while conceding Newport, recalls Mrs Astor's words in the middle of a rain-swept luncheon party: 'That drip, drip, drip, is driving me mad,' she said, sending Porter racing to the piano to finish the verse he could not complete until he got the rhythmic inspiration. Biographers disagree about the song's success too. 'Cole was convinced that the song was doomed to a quick failure . . . the closing of the show after 248 performances killed any hopes he had for the song . . .' ill accords with 'So quickly did this number catch on that *Variety* reported it as one of the leaders in American record and sheet music sales for January of 1933, little more than a month after *Gay Divorce* had opened on Broadway . . .' Whatever its immediate impact, its longevity is not in doubt.

Nymph Errant brought 'les Coleporteurs' back to Europe. Based on James Laver's story of an indomitable English girl's successful quest to lose her virginity, it was a Cochran production which starred Gertrude Lawrence. The book was by Romney Brent, actor and writer, who worked on it with Porter while he took a cure at Carlsbad. Setting out from Paris, Brent was fascinated to watch his collaborator's thorough concern for his health and appearance. He travelled with a box full of cosmetics and medicines, and discussed the script with excitement while applying a variety of lotions to his face, taking a series of pills and carefully spraying his throat. His hypochondria was legendary and his medical research for 'The Physician' in *Nymph Errant* must have yielded him a treasure trove of symptoms: getting 'epiglottis' and 'bronchial tubes' in one stanza and then rhyming 'pharynx' with 'larynx'. *Nymph Errant*, a hit in London, was never filmed or taken to Broadway.

Cole Porter was now poised to write the show that would perfectly represent the musicals of the period between the wars. While *Show Boat* might presage change and a new serious dramatic backbone, that was not Porter's Theatre. Though Rodgers and Hart might be similarly entertaining with *A Connecticut Yankee* or *The Boys From Syracuse*, here again they were ambitious to extend the form or at least to try to admit more challenging subject matter. Shakespeare and Mark Twain were both Broadway risks. *Anything Goes* was the quintessence of the inconsequential Broadway musical about nothing at all, decked out with two handfuls of jokes, larger than life performances and an irresistible score. Porter's career from now on was a switchback bucketing between shows where his writing is less than his best, then soaring dramatically, to another royal flush of splendid songs, just when he is being written off and rejected; then out of triumph he would snatch despair again. And the despair was not only the despair of his admirers. He was constantly assailed by his own fears that he would never be able to be as good as he used to be. If Lorenz Hart wrote for his living, Cole Porter wrote for his life. But unlike Hart, he did not pour his insecurity into his lyrics. After all, it was not Porter's appearance, over which he took such care, which worried him; but his uncertainty about meeting his own high standards. His homosexuality was confident and discreet and its only possible manifestation in his lyrics lay in the brilliant, sibilant wit which so often distinguishes the homosexual. It is no coincidence that the three most glittering lyric writers in this book are Porter, Hart and Coward.

True to its form as the definitive thirties musical *Anything Goes* had a mongrel birth. Vinton Freedley, who had rejected Cole Porter in favour of the Gershwins back in 1927, split with his partner, Alex Aarons, after a Gershwin flop, *Pardon My English*, which lost them both a great deal of money. Freedley arrived in Europe determined to sign Porter for a new musical whose plot he only dimly perceived. It was to concern the wreck of a pleasure steamer – a cruise ship – and he wanted P. G. Wodehouse and Guy Bolton to write the book. Excited, Porter wrote several songs. Freedley was delighted. A more dilatory Wodehouse and Bolton turned in their script. Freedley was dismayed. He saw no way out of the shipwreck of his hopes until he heard the sad news of the actual shipwreck of just such a cruise ship off the coast of New Jersey. The USS *Morro Castle* went down with 134 lives lost and a wrecked pleasure steamer was no longer a possible premise for a frothy musical comedy. As Wodehouse and Bolton were by now otherwise engaged, Freedley was free to take his Porter score — 'I Get a Kick Out of You', 'Blow, Gabriel, Blow!', 'You're the Top' and 'Anything Goes' — to Howard Lindsay, who agreed to direct the show and spin out the songs with something that would serve as a story. All Lindsay asked for was a collaborator and sure enough a friend of Porter's literally got out her ouija board and came up with the name of Russel Crouse. On the first day of rehearsals, no script existed, but Lindsay was able to ad-lib a very presentable plot to the cast. Unfortunately, as the euphoria of their approval wore off, neither collaborator could remember the story line — the era was pre-tape recorder. They had to re-invent one by the time they reached Boston.

The 1934-5 season was bad for musicals on Broadway, but *Anything Goes* would have been special in any season. The first night was described as 'the greatest Gala since the Depression began', and one columnist confided to his readers that even the balcony was wearing chinchilla. The composer surpassed himself in aplomb by turning around airily in the interval and calling out 'Good, isn't it?' to a friend sitting in the usual three front rows full of friends. Ethel Merman, in her first Porter show — the first of many — became the ideal Porter singer.

Due for a holiday, the Porters took it with Moss Hart. Together with entourage they circled the world in the *Franconia* and, as they had decided to write a show en route, Porter also shipped 'a metronome, a typewriter, a small piano-organ, twenty-four black pencils, a quire of music paper, recordings of the songs of *Anything Goes*, a gramophone and three cases of Grand Chambertin '87'. The show that was born out of these raw materials was *Jubilee*, inspired by the forthcoming celebrations in London. Touble dogged the musical on the road, and on the occasion of the dress rehearsal in Boston, the leading lady, Mary Boland, alarmed by threatening letters, sought courage in the bottle and had to be withdrawn from the firing line. She played the first night; but when the show opened in New York she found her return from movies to the live theatre too demanding and had a few more nips which incapacitated her from time to time. 'Severe abdominal pains', it was called. She left the cast after four months. Porter, who had broken a lifetime's rule by investing in his own show, lost $18,000 and never forgave her. However, his world tour had yielded the tunes for 'Begin the Beguine' (born in Kalabahi Island, New Guinea) and 'The Kling-Kling Bird in the Divi Divi Tree' (born in Zanzibar), 'A Picture of Me Without You' and 'Why Shouldn't I?'. The harbour at Rio de Janeiro produced a gasp from Porter as he saw the dawn rise. 'It's delightful,' he said. His wife agreed: 'it's delicious.' Monty Woolley completed the sentiment, 'it's de-lovely.' The title phrase was there; but the song had to wait for *Red, Hot and Blue* before it got an airing. 'Just One of Those Things' came in during the Boston previews and Porter is said to have written it in eight hours – all but one word. He needed a three syllable adjective suggesting lightness to describe 'wings' and a passing architect at a party, hearing the request, promptly supplied 'gossamer', without a moment's hesitation.

The Porter lifestyle was now subjected to the strain of Hollywood. Its manner was very much 'his' and not 'hers'; and in the next three years their differences came to a crisis. Linda Porter was always supportive of her husband's work. She coddled both with single-minded devotion; but to her Hollywood was an amalgam of sun and vulgarity, warmth and vulgarity, actors and vulgarity and producers and vulgarity. She could find all those qualities in New York, Paris or the South of France without having to inhale the vulgarity. For a woman with an innate sense of style and chic and with an aristocratic, if impoverished, southern background, the place was intolerable. Moreover, it brought out the worst in her husband. He wrote some of his most maudlin songs for movie tycoons who were scared of his 'intellectual' reputation and were always relieved when he wrote down to them – with songs like 'Rosalie'.

Symptomatically, he relaxed his severe sartorial standards in Los Angeles, swapping his dark town suits for gaudy checks and stripes, in the bright colours which he had hardly donned since his first day at Yale. Furthermore, the louche atmosphere of Hollywood gnawed away at the discretion with which he had always conducted his promiscuous homosexual extra-marital affairs, and made them harder for his understanding wife to ignore. Musically, this period produced 'Don't Fence Me In' – inspired by a cowboy's poem and written for *Adios Argentina* (never produced). It was not unveiled until 1944 when it found its way into *Hollywood Canteen* and became one of Porter's biggest sellers. He had paid the cowboy $200. His pen flowed more generously for Broadway. For *Red, Hot and Blue* in 1936, he suppled 'De-Lovely', 'Ours', 'Ridin' High' and, for Merman, at the last moment, 'Down in the Depths on the Nineteenth Floor'.

Appropriately, in view of his new eminence, Porter disappointed a section of the press; but the show ran for 183 performances. It starred Jimmy Durante and Bob Hope as well as Merman. On the opening night Cole returned the gesture of Linda's first night cigarette-box by giving her a platinum case. Its lid, as the Park Bernet Catalogue was to describe it in 1967, was 'paved with a diamond sunburst set with numerous round and baguette diamonds on a divided field of faceted rubies and faceted sapphires and small diamond star motifs . . . from Verdura.' In spite of this charming gesture, their differences over Cole's fondness for Hollywood and its temptations were coming to a head. Perhaps the gift was an attempt to stave off the crisis. After spending the summer of 1937 in Europe together, they stopped speaking to each other. Linda stayed in Paris and Cole went to New York to prepare his new show *You Never Know*, based on a flop which not even Gertrude Lawrence and Leslie Howard had been able to save in 1925. The Porters, therefore, were in different continents for the central tragedy of Cole's life, his riding accident.

He was riding at Oyster Bay, Long Island, where he had gone to weekend at the Countess di Zoppola's house. Although he had not ridden for some time, he was determined to organise a party. 'It was a sudden caprice,' the Duke di Verdura has said, 'but Cole's caprices seemed sometimes to be made of steel.' Against the advice of the stables, he insisted on picking the most mettlesome horse. It reared at some bushes, and fell back on him. As he failed to kick the stirrups free, the frightened animal tried to get up and rolled back on one of his legs. It staggered and fell across him, crushing the other leg. Rushed to hospital, Cole Porter was unconscious for two days. Afterwards he remembered that he had spent the time waiting for the ambulance to arrive working on the lyrics of 'At Long Last Love'. If ever a hopeful fantasy was understandable, this was it. The two Porter women – wife and mother – met in family conclave over the transatlantic telephone and agreed that, if they allowed the amputation for which the doctors were calling, their patient would die of despair. Those years of Cole's spent tending his body, preserving his appearance, concealing his age, perfecting his presence could not be cut out in a single, unaesthetic slash. They were not to know that his legs would never heal or that he would be racked by pain for nearly 30 years. Until that time his courage and strength of will had only been called upon to overcome his rich beginnings. His battle had been against creature comforts; a struggle to be professional, when to be a sybarite was an easy and attractive destiny. An iron will had kept him on the right course, and perhaps as strong a sense of control is necessary to resist the blandishments of luxury as that required to conquer the assaults of pain. Porter was soon to prove that he could fight in both directions with similar courage, wit and resilience. His weeks in hospital, his months of convalescence, 30-odd operations over 30 years, his determination, not only to work again but, just as important, to play again, started as soon as he came to. To Elsa Maxwell he said, 'It just proves that fifty million Frenchmen can't be wrong. They eat horses instead of riding them.' His legs he christened Josephine and Geraldine. Josephine on the left was a comparatively placid girl. Geraldine was a 'psychopath'. The doctors wanted to do away with her; but he insisted he loved her and would not let her go. Linda, who was never to leave him again, felt that her judgment not to amputate had been vindicated.

It is hardly surprising that *You Never Know* was not a success; but he did finish the score and it included 'At Long Last Love' and 'From Alpha to Omega'; to J. J. Shubert, the omnipotent but not over-educated impresario who produced the show, the song was always known as 'From Alfalfa to Omega'. However, the show was a flop and in retrospect its composer thought the score was his worst. It was said along Broadway that Cole Porter was finished – so comprehensively that he promptly hit another winning streak. Lyrically, he remained in top form; musically, he was below par; but in *Leave It To Me* he was able to provide 'Get Out of Town' and 'Most Gentlemen Don't Like Love', adding that 'they just like to kick it around'.

Mary Martin made her début in *Leave It To Me*. She was preferred over a protégée of one of Linda Porter's friends, a girl with 'a thrilling voice'. 'Her voice *is* thrilling,' Porter agreed. 'What your friend neglected to mention is her protégée is a midget.' Miss Martin nearly wrecked her chance at her audition; she was dowdy and dull – until she started to sing. She never quite grasped the *double-entendres* in 'My Heart Belongs to Daddy'; however, as long as her clear enunciation ensured that the audience could hear the words, her upward look of innocence enabled them to guess the rest. *Wake Up and Dream* had been the last twenties musical to open on Broadway – on 30 December, 1929. *Dubarry Was a Lady* closed the score card for the thirties on 6 December, 1939. Once again, Porter's music was bolstered by Ethel Merman's voice – and the comedy was lifted immeasurably by the presence of Bert Lahr; but the success of the show lay more in broad, boisterous, bawdy humour than in the sleek sophistication that hitherto had been the Porter trademark. Although that same year he had written the lovely 'I Concentrate on You' for the movies, his biggest successes in *Dubarry Was a Lady* were cast in a different mould. 'Well, Did You Evah?', 'Give Him the Oo-La-La!', 'But in the Morning, No' and 'Friendship' suggest a conscious – albeit successful – attempt to please the groundlings.

When the show arrived in New York after a triumphant tour, it had a frozen reception at the 46th Street Theatre; and although Betty Grable, making her Broadway début, Merman and Lahr were well received, the score was not. Porter set off on a cruise immediately, correctly prophesying a long run, in spite of the press, and Linda, meanwhile, began to plan yet another home – this time in Williamstown, Massachusetts. She bought Buxton Hill, a fine old house standing on a slope in its own extensive grounds with a romantic view of the Berkshire Hills. In 1937 she had shipped to America the carefully assembled treasure trove that had filled 13 rue Monsieur – glass, china, furniture, pictures, books; now she set about installing them at Buxton Hill, both in the main house and in a guest-house in the grounds which she converted into a work-room for Cole. The last gesture changed his mind about the house after his initial objection to putting down roots yet again in another elaborate residence. While Linda was creating their new home, Cole was at work on his new show, a flimsier structure once again propped up by the formidable timbers of Ethel Merman. *Panama Hattie* was constructed along traditional lines by Herbert Fields and Buddy de Sylva. In a mixed press Merman was welcomed; but Porter's score got its now traditional reception. The most callous words came from John O'Hara: '. . . In the carping department belongs Mr Porter's music. Who'd have thought we'd live to see the day when Cole Porter – *Cole Porter!* – would write a score in which the two outstanding songs are called 'My Mother Would Love You' and 'Let's Be Buddies'? And written straight too; no kidding . . . Ah, well, he had a bad riding accident a year or two ago. This ought to teach him to stay in his Brewster-Ford and away from horses.'

It is ironic that *Pal Joey*, which opened two months later than *Panama Hattie*, and which was to take such an important place in the history of musicals, was based on O'Hara's short stories. It, too, had a divided press; but the division was provoked by its forward looking qualities while *Hattie's* offence lay in its conservatism. *Pal Joey* ran for 374 performances the first time around, *Panama Hattie* for over 500; but *Joey* has the place in history. The offending song, 'Let's Be Buddies', featured Merman and a moppet, Joan Carroll – the daughter, in the play, of Merman's intended. Miss Merman seeks to get through to the resisting child on wings of song, invariably her way of clinching an argument. The audience loved it; but it does show Porter following the popular-at-all-costs course originally charted in *Du Barry Was a Lady* with 'Friendship'.

The score of *Panama Hattie* also included yet another of Porter's now inevitable 'laundry-list' songs, 'I'm Throwing a Ball Tonight' – in going over her invitations, Merman was able to cram into one number Wendell Wilkie and F.D.R., Life, Look, Peek, Pic, Snap, Click and Harper's Bazaar, Monty Woolley, 'Cliff' Odets, both of whom 'tendered their regrets', Gov'nor Lehman, 'Commishner' Valentine, The Lunts, Grace Moore, Mae West and Father Divine, Gracie Allen, Fannie Brice, she asked Johnny Walker 'and Haig and Haig twice', once again 'No Dice!'. Alone in the classic Porter tradition stands, 'Make It Another Old-Fashioned, Please, . . . for one who's due to join the disillusioned crew . . .'.

Once again, as soon as *Hattie* had opened, Porter set off for Hollywood; but this time instead of bringing tears to the eyes of Louis B. Mayer, he was working for Columbia and Harry Cohn had him sing the score to his stenographers. It did not bring out the best in him and, though working with Fred Astaire again was a geat incentive, he considered *You'll Never Get Rich* one of his worst film scores. He was in better hands on Broadway with Herbert and Dorothy Fields as bookwriters for *Let's Face it* – based on *The Cradle Snatchers*, a 1925 farce. For the original show three gigolos were recruited by three wives who were convinced that their husbands were cheating on them. However, by 1941, the world of tango-teas and cake-eaters had been shattered and the three youths became three young servicemen, led by Danny Kaye. The ballads belong firmly in the new Porter-mawkish period:

> You are my favourite star
> A haven in heaven
> You are ev'rything I love . . .

But the bright premise of the show once again inspired point numbers in which the lyrics left their tunes a long way behind. In listing 'Fatality, morality, legality, finality, neutrality, reality or Southern hospitality', in 'Let's Not Talk About Love', thesaurus and rhyming dictionary must both have been working overtime. Then there was 'Farming', which satirised a current socialite fashion to till the soil of Bucks County, and which stretched a *double-entendre* far enough to suggest that 'Miss Elsa Maxwell, so folks tattle, Got well-goosed while de-horning her cattle'; while 'A Lady Needs a Rest' gave as the Lady's reason the fact that for a Latin boyfriend 'she keeps a private nest'. No wonder, now and then, a Lady needs a rest.

Porter wrote *Let's Face It* in his new work-room at Williamstown, which he christened 'No Trespassing'. By the time the show opened in Boston he had started to despair and fled the Colonial Theatre after the dress rehearsal muttering, 'I don't want them to witness my disgrace.' He seems to have sensed the changing climate of musicals and to have doubled his doubts about whether he could keep up with the new pace, and the new ideas. The new decade held all the portents for 'The American Musical as a conscious Art Form' – *Lady in the Dark*, *Pal Joey* and *Cabin in the Sky* were already on view and *Oklahoma!* and *Carmen Jones* were in the air. There were to be four Porter shows before his masterpiece, *Kiss Me Kate*, kept him up with the Carmen Joneses; two were hits and two flops, which is a very fair average for a passé invalid.

The hits – *Something for the Boys* and *Mexican Hayride* – had their high spots, but nothing so special that it would carry Porter easily over the crisis of confidence caused by the rejection of his work in *Seven Lively Arts* and *Around the World in Eighty Days*, two disasters inspired by two mammoth showmen, Billy Rose and Mike Todd (Todd, in his case, bowing out to the even larger than larger than life Orson Welles). The plusses of this period are 'The Leader of a Big-Time Band' from *Something for the Boys* and a song from the film *Something To Shout About* which exactly caught the darkening wartime mood, 'You'd be so Nice to Come Home to'. Porter's sole theatre hit came from *Seven Lively*

Arts,* and that long after the show had folded. Once again, he had found a simple but sophisticated marriage of subtle words and superior music in 'Every Time We Say Goodbye I Die a Little'. The gradual success of this song was not enough to bolster Porter's waning confidence. Nor was a Hollywood deification called *Night and Day*, which has become a collector's piece of absurdity; nor *The Pirate* with Judy Garland and Grace Kelly, which flopped for all its felicities. By now, *Bloomer Girl, On The Town, Carousel, Annie Get Your Gun, Finian's Rainbow, Brigadoon* and *Where's Charley?* had all confirmed that new ideas were finding a consistent place on the Broadway stage and that new voices were beginning to be heard.

It was against this background that Saint Suber, an ambitious stage manager, and Lemuel Ayers, a distinguished designer, approached Sam and Bella Spewak to make a musical of Shakespeare's *The Taming of the Shrew*. After first dismissing the idea, Mrs Spewak came back with a suggestion to treat it as a play within the context of a modern play. She insisted on involving Porter, to the dismay of her producers. When she approached the composer his reluctance and fear exceeded that of his detractors. He wriggled and squirmed to avoid the commission, coming up with enough reasons not to do it to fill one of his own laundry lists. His style would war with Shakespeare's. The plot was wrong; the premise was wrong; they had no star in mind. The director, John Wilson, was a producer; the producers, a stage manager and a set designer. The show was too high-brow. The public would not go for it. He could not afford a flop . . . he was working on a soap-opera musical . . . people like soap-operas . . . Mrs Spewak declined to take no for an answer. As so often in Porter's life, having found every excuse not to go along with the plan, once he allowed himself to be persuaded, he threw himself into the project with the desperation of a man who knew that he had to prove that time had not passed him by. As if to make it a challenge worthy of him, his legs started to play up at the same time. As the songs came from his pen the pain increased. 'So in Love', a mishap to the right leg; 'Another Op'nin', Another Show', another blood transfusion; 'I Hate Men', an ulcer; 'Too Darn Hot', an abscess; 'I Sing of Love', the ulcer and the abscess met over a nerve centre; 'We Open in Venice', more medication; 'Tom, Dick or Harry', a bite from a dog and part of a shinbone exposed; 'Where is the Life That Late I Led?', the skin around

---

* Rose's concept involved ballet, opera, Broadway, vaudeville, jazz, concert music and modern painting. Stravinsky was commissioned to write 'Scènes de Ballet' for Markova and Dolin. From Philadelphia Rose cabled Stravinsky, 'Your music great success could be sensational success if you would authorise Robert Russell Bennett retouch orchestrations stop Bennett orchestrates even the work of Cole Porter.' Stravinsky's reply was prompt. 'Satisfied with great success!'

the bone is gradually covering; 'Always True to You in My Fashion', he was writing to a friend: 'I have learned my lesson and from now on will always wear a guard on my right leg . . . My show is very exciting. I've written fifteen songs and have about five more to do. You'll like this score. It's so simple it sounds as if it had been written by an idiot child . . .' The Spewaks finished the book. Porter liked it; he sent them another song, 'I Am Ashamed that Women are so Simple', almost entirely culled from Shakespeare. They begged him to send *no more songs*. 'Brush Up Your Shakespeare' arrived almost by return of post.

In fine, traditional fashion, the money now became elusive. After a caravanserai of auditions, $180,000 was raised from 75 different backers. One producer's mother ran a ticket agency. Halfway through the first run-through the man approached Mrs Spewak. 'Mother says this is *schwatz*' (weak). 'Tell your mother to go home and sell tickets,' she very properly replied.

They moved to Philadelphia. The Porters were accompanied by a dozen boxes of Kleenex, a piano, a Dali, a Grandma Moses, a Picasso and three dogs. Their Cadillac had a flat tyre. Linda developed pleurisy. Her always troubled chest made her fight for breath as she took her place on the first night. The house could use the chic. Only a token group from New York had turned up for a passé Porter opening.

The next morning the verdict was simple. This had been an out-of-town first night and yet no major changes were necessary.

Linda's lungs became congested and she was despatched to the dry air of Arizona. Cole bought his usual 100 first-night seats and kept his invariable cool. However, as George Jean Nathan wrote, 'The musical show, in a word, is like the other fellow's wife or sweetheart. For one man who shares his taste there are always those who wonder what he sees in her.' Wisely, Porter refused to count his chickens. At the party afterwards, he entered bent over his stick. The news that *The Times* was a rave brought him erect. 'I never saw anyone enjoy good notices as much as Mr Porter,' an aide recalled. He had to search hard and long for a qualifying note; but he found it eventually in the *Saturday Review of Literature*. To Harold Clurman these were not Porter's best songs 'by a long shot'. The judgment was familiar, but the triumph was sweet. Four months later, it was eclipsed by *South Pacific*. One evening, Porter, stationed by a radio, heard 'Some Enchanted Evening'. 'Who wrote that?' asked his guest from out of town. 'Rodgers and Hammerstein,' he replied, 'if you can imagine it taking two men to write one song.'

Alas, the trick was never to be repeated. There were to be three more shows. *Can Can* and *Silk Stockings* totalled 1370 performances between them, *Out of this World* only 157. All three divided the critics. The list songs continued to be as sparky and erudite and flip ('Nobody's Chasing Me'), or as topical and name-studded ('Give Me the Land' cut from *Silk*

Stockings before it opened). The sentimental songs varied from the routine 'I Love Paris in the Springtime' to the lovely 'It's the wrong time and the wrong place, but It's All Right With Me', and the romantic laundry list which leads up to 'All of You'.

There were to be two original film scores, *High Society* and *Les Girls*. There was to be a television special, *Aladdin*. The rest of the life was a threnody. There was to be the death of mother. There was to be the death of Linda. He was to lose the fight to keep one of his legs. There was to be drink and bad temper and despair, and in the last months not even his appearance concerned him and then they knew that he must be dying.

The last song he was to write in the despised *Aladdin* was for the Emperor of China: 'Wouldn't it be Fun not to be Famous? Wouldn't it be fun to be nearly anyone, Except me, mighty me!'

It turned topsy-turvy the philosophy of a lifetime – except perhaps if you think of those last two lines and the last bitter, pain-racked, lonely years.

3

IRA GERSHWIN

'They Can't Take That Away From Me'

In 1894, the very year that Irving Berlin's family, journeying to the New World from Temun, caught their first glimpse of the Statue of Liberty, so did Ira Gershwin's father. No provincial cantor he, but a city slicker from St Petersburg. And where the poor, the huddled and also timid Balines had clutched little Issy to their bosoms and taken him a step back from the side of the churning ship, the thrusting Morris Gershovitz, for that was the family name, strode eagerly to the rail, the better to see this symbol of his new life past which, to lend it extra significance, his sweetheart Rose had sailed only a year before. He did not know where Rose might be living but, tucked snugly in his hatband, was the address of his uncle, Greenstein the tailor. Greenstein would know, he felt sure. Unfortunately, at that moment a gust of good American wind blew his hat away and deposited it in a watery grave – Greenstein's address and all.

But Morris was not without resource. Was he not the grandson of a rabbi? Was he not the son of Yakov Gershovitz, an army engineer who had served his Czar faithfully for 25 years, boy and man, and was therefore entitled to settle outside the ghetto in the periphery of fashionable St Petersburg? Was he not in his own right a manufacturer of tops for ladies' dainty boots, a man of action who, realising that he too would very soon be required to serve his Czar faithfully for the next 25 years or be sent back to the ghetto, had decided to get out quick? Was he not also, he reminded himself in this uncleless hour, a gambler? Safely on shore, hardly stopping to take a room in the Bowery, he was away to a pool hall, finishing the evening 30 cents better off than he had started it. A good omen, he said to himself, jingling the coins in his pocket with a bravura that would have given the part-time cantor Baline something to sing about, let alone Morris's grandfather the rabbi, safely buried in Holy Russia.

Nor did Morris's ingenuity fail him next morning. Diligent enquiry

Ira Gershwin (*ASCAP*).

in Russian and Yiddish – he had no English, nor was he to acquire much – led him to Brownsville in Brooklyn where the consensus of opinion was that Greenstein the tailor was most likely to be found. And opinion, for once, was right. Repossessed of his uncle, Morris repossessed himself of the lovely Rose who in no time at all became Rose Gershovitz instead of Rose Burskin.

Ira – or rather Issy, as he was known as a child – was their first-born. With characteristic family ambition, he assumed that he had been christened Isidore and it was not until he applied for a passport in 1928 that he discovered the name they had given him was Israel. Ira was his own invention – and he would have some cause to regret it. 'George Gershwin and his talented sister, Ira . . .' said the wags before long.

Born in 1895 he was followed by George (or Jacob as he started life) in 1898, Arthur in 1900 and Frances, ten years younger than Ira, in 1905. Removed in stages from their religious background, the Gershovitzes adopted a casual attitude towards their religion. By two generations they had removed themselves from the rabbi; by one generation from the ghetto. Morris and Rose had removed themselves from mother Russia and after Ira's barmitzvah they let that ceremony lapse for the other boys – perhaps the price, two dollars a place for 200 people at Zeitlans on Grand Street, was too much. The Gershovitzes had finally broken their direct link with a religion which had lasted in their family since the evening of the day when God first walked in the Garden and found that it was good.

But make no mistake, they were no ordinary family. No sooner had Morris's zeal and determination sought out and found Greenstein the tailor, than somehow it lost any sense of direction. It led him all over New York – 25 residences in Manhattan plus three in Brooklyn in twenty years. It led him through a bewildering variety of trades. And no one more bewildered than Morris. From the job he knew, foreman in a fancy-boot factory, he proceeded briefly, ingloriously and magnificently unprepared to be part-owner of a Turkish bath-house on the Bowery and then a 'Russian and Turkish' bath further up town, and then another Turkish bath back down town; part-owner of a restaurant on Third Avenue and 129th Street and then, down town again, part-owner of another restaurant on the Lower East Side.

Then foolishness turned foolhardy and he became the sole owner, nothing less, of a cigar store, a pool parlour, a bakery, a rooming-house, a summer hotel. Was there nothing to which Morris could not turn his hand and fail? Nothing. He became a bookmaker at Belmont the one month all the favourites won. And yet the Gershovitz children were always fed and clothed. Momma had her system – a simple practice of pawning and redeeming – tasks for which the industrious Ira was usually selected. The father's peregrinations lent the son a unique acquaintance with pawnshops all over the city and the pledge on Momma's diamond ring always yielded $400. It was this big-city – St Petersburg – knowhow which enabled the strong matriarch and the weak patriarch to survive – always attended by a servant, always precariously, often squabbling, leaving their children to roam the streets and acquire at first hand the slickness of the new town, and above all its language. How much does the richness and exuberance of American lyric writing owe to the fact that song writers at the turn of the century were the sons of immigrants, young men intoxicated by the innocent idea of making words work for them in a language which their fathers and mothers imperfectly understood?

Certainly Morris's struggles with the new language in his new world were epic. Though his two talented sons might write a song called 'Fascinating Rhythm', to him it was always 'Fashion on de River'. 'Embraceable You' from *Girl Crazy* became 'My song . . . sing my song . . . the song about me . . .', simply on the strength of the two lines 'Come to Poppa, come to Poppa do'. Occasionally, his gaffes worked to his advantage. Stopped by a traffic cop he said proudly, 'You can't arrest me, officer. I'm the father of Judge Gershwin.' At least that was what impressed the cop when he let the culprit off; what Morris's accent had not allowed him to say was 'I'm the father of *George* Gershwin.' Apart from setting himself up as an expert on opera, of which he knew nothing, Morris was often opinionated about his two sons' work of which he grasped little. His verdict on the *Rhapsody in Blue*, which George wrote and Ira named, was 'Of course it's a good piece. Doesn't it take fifteen minutes to play?'

As Rose, a rare reverse of the over-protective Jewish mother, encouraged her children to rely on themselves, Ira and George pursued their education at school and on the streets. From his haphazardly remembered kaleidoscope, Ira has recalled 'horse-drawn streetcars on Delancey Street, their stoves hot in winter; the trips with other kids to China Town to buy sugar cane at about a cent a foot; learning to swim in the mucky Harlem River; picking up some Italian phrases to serve as passwords in case you were ganged up on around Mulberry Street (a ploy which sometimes worked – and if it didn't you got at least a sock on the jaw and ran like hell); the laundry with a two-cent lending library side-line.' George, the younger, more wayward child, was the first to be attracted to music. With characteristic impetuosity he allowed himself to be summoned from a street fight by the sound of an automatic piano playing Rubinstein's 'Melody in F' in a penny arcade on 125th Street in 1904.

In 1910, when the Gershwins had settled for a short stay on Second Avenue over Saul Birn's Phonograph Shop, Rose installed their first piano. Two thoughts lay behind the purchase. Of course it seemed an appropriate instrument for the quiet, methodical, studious Ira; but, more important, Rose's sister had just bought a piano. No woman who had a servant, played cards for money with the actresses at the Jewish National Theatre on Second Avenue and on occasions allowed her husband to rent a private limousine to take her to the races, was going to see her sister score over her like that. Doubtless, Ira was despatched with the diamond to raise another $400. However, no sooner had the piano been hoisted up through the window of the second floor apartment than George settled himself at the keyboard and, without effort, played a popular tune of the day. Ira remembers 'being particularly impressed by his left hand' which remained a Gershwin trademark. George recalls the reluctant but conscientious Ira concentrating on the keyboard for a time: 'He actually covered about 32 pages of Beyer's text before resigning himself to his fate — words came easier than music.'

The words were indeed beginning to appear. Although George left the High School of Commerce when he was fifteen to enrol as a pianist and song-plugger for Jerome H. Remick and Co., thumping out numbers in a small studio at fifteen dollars a week, Ira was by this time publishing occasional drawings, verses and epigrams in the Townsend Harris Hall *Academic Herald* and editing, along with E. Y. Harburg, a column called 'Much Ado', modelled on Franklin P. Adams' 'Conning Tower'. In 1914 Ira had moved on to evening classes at City College and the column in the weekly *Campus* had become 'Gargoyle Gargles'. Then on 26 September he saw his first published squib in C. L. Edson's New York *Mail* column: '. . . Tramp jokes, writes Gersh, are bum company . . .'

If Ira had chosen his own first name he followed his brother's lead in settling on a surname. Morris Gershovitz adopted 'Gershvin' soon after his arrival in America. George, on becoming a professional musician, toyed with Wynn and Gerchwin but eventually fell into the habit of Gershwin, and Ira and the rest of the family followed suit.

George's new horizons, glimpsed at first through the windows of Remick's, expanded in the office of Harms, the publishers, where Max Dreyfus talked of publishing his songs and issuing contracts and paying retainers of $35 a week and royalties of three cents a copy. The outline of a rainbow appeared. In the rehearsal rooms at the Princess Theatre George began to play at rehearsals for his idol, Jerome Kern, and the two men whose names were indissolubly linked with Kern at the time, Bolton and Wodehouse. Finally, he sat on stage accompanying, not entirely self-effacingly, two solo singers, Louise Dresser and Nora Bayes, who occasionally sang his music. He was very near his first crock of gold. It was called 'Swannee'.

Ira's horizons obstinately refused to broaden. They held no hint of a rainbow. By day he worked as a clerk in a Turkish bath. At night he attended evening classes at City College and visited the movies and the music hall. Consistently he kept a journal, 'Every man his own Boswell' . . . 'To the Century with George and saw the *Century Girl,* a mammoth musical extravaganza . . . Music by I. Berlin and Victor Herbert, or vice versa.'

Above the Turkish bath lived an English playwright, Paul M. Potter, able to afford such uniquely salubrious accommodation as a result of having dramatised *Trilby.* To him Ira took three satirical paragraphs called 'The Shrine', which he had not been able to place. Out of many submissions so far his record of placings was still one sentence of five words (or seven if you count 'writes Gersh'). Potter directed him towards H. L. Mencken's *The Smart Set* and no sooner had he submitted the piece than he received an acceptance and a cheque for one dollar. Potter further encouraged him to explore the charms of native American argot which seems so exotic to the ears of visiting English playwrights. His lyrics were often to make a feature of the easy graceful use of slang expressions: 'Boy! What Love Has Done to Me', 'I Got Rhythm'.

However, back in 1917, Mr Potter's advice brought nothing but a new crop of rejection slips and Ira varied the Turkish bath routine with a short-lived job in Altman's department store (and this only after rejection by Gimbels); a brief term (three reviews) as a critic on the New York *Clipper* and a longer spell as treasurer for a travelling carnival, *Colonel Lagg's Greater Empire Shows.* The good colonel was Ira's good cousin Maurice Lagowitz. 'I'm afraid I was pretty much of a floating soul,' he has written of this period; but the nomadic life did not appeal and eventually he left the road and came back to New York to his father's Lafayette Street baths. 'I couldn't concentrate on anything. I haunted the movies; I read without plan or purpose. To tell the truth I was at a complete loss and I didn't care.' He was about 22 and although Rose was beginning to ask what had happened to his quiet purposeful academic instinct and his way with a pawnbroker and a diamond ring – a liberal education indeed – it is clear that he was simply marking time in the way that so many people do in their early twenties. Ira Gershwin 'dropped out' into the baths and one day as he was sitting there watching fat men imagining that they had become thinner and taking their money for it, 'I first thought of becoming a writer of lyrics . . .'

If George's moment of truth had happened in 1904, when at the age of six he heard the automatic piano leaping through the 'Melody in F' in the penny arcade in Harlem, then Ira's came some sixteen years later, after a long and difficult search, not unlike the slow, painstaking process by which words so often follow music on to paper. Add to this that it is never easy to live in the shadow of a famous kinsman, be it father, mother, sister, brother, uncle or cousin; but, fortunately, George was to become so protective of Ira in later years that no cloud came between the brothers. In the first days of their success, when George took a penthouse on Riverside Drive, Ira took one adjoining. In the heyday of the thirties, when George moved to even grander quarters on 72nd street on the East Side, Ira and his wife moved to the same street. When the Ira Gershwins set up house in Hollywood, George moved in with them. And, of course, it made work easier. When Ira had appendicitis much later, in the middle of writing *Oh, Kay!*, George looked to the unknown Howard Dietz rather than the established P. G. Wodehouse to supply the missing lyrics so that the focus should not be deflected from his older brother. When the question of who should work with Du Bose Heyward on his lyrics for *Porgy and Bess* came up, it was George who advanced Ira's cause and over the matter of payment it was George who grasped the nettle and secured a 50-50 split between the two lyricists.

But all these brotherly manoeuvres took time. Now that he had something to think about at the St Nicholas Baths, Ira was coming up with song suggestions like 'If You Only Knew What I Thought of You, You'd Think a Lot More of Me' and 'You May Throw all the Rice You Desire, but Please, Friends, Throw no Shoes'. Another lyric was to become the first George and Ira Gershwin song ever performed professionally, 'The Real American Folk Song (is a Rag)'.

For all the concern of the successful George, Ira was determined not to use his brother's name as a password. For these early works he called himself Arthur Francis, a title compounded of the first names of his younger brother and sister, and mercifully consigned to oblivion in 1924 when he was seen to have made his own way. 'All who knew me knew me as a Gershwin anyway.' The first performance of this first work was at the Trent Theatre, Trenton, New Jersey, in a show called *Ladies First*. The star was Nora Bayes, George accompanied her at the piano and Ira took a day off from the baths and journeyed, or tried to journey, to Trenton for the great event. Whether it was that he was lost in some day-dream of the beauty of his lyric decked out in Miss Bayes's voice, or whether he was already thinking of the lyrics he would one day write, decked out in the voices of other performers, or whether he was simply lost in admiration for the artistic rig in which he had decked himself out – 'purple shirt, dark blue knitted tie, and mottled green tweed suit' – history does not record. However, history has no doubt that he got off at the wrong station – Princeton instead of Trenton – got lost and only just made the theatre in time. The song was a success; but although Miss Bayes brought her show to the Broadhurst Theatre, 'The Real American Folk Song' did not stay long in her repertory, nor did it earn Ira a cent. It was promptly forgotten for twenty years, when it was resurrected and published in a Gershwin collection.

George's next nudge along the professional path came in 1920 when he heard that a producer needed a new song for Helen Ford in a show called *The Sweetheart Shop*. It was having a success in Chicago but it needed strengthening before it moved to New York. Overnight the brothers wrote 'Waiting for the Sun to Come Out', and George, passing off Arthur Francis as 'a clever college boy with lots of talent', an accurate if incomplete description, auditioned it so successfully that MacGregor, the producer, bought it for $250. New York liked the show less than Chicago and when George went to collect the money MacGregor asked to be let off the debt. George was magnanimous. 'I'm working,' he said, 'but the college boy really needs the money.' Ira received a cheque for $125, as well as $723.40 from sheet music and $445.02 for phonograph records – his first fortune and his first published song.

Meanwhile, the indefatigable George had also teamed his brother with Vincent Youmans, first in a revue called *Piccadilly to Broadway*, which failed to reach its advertised destination, and then for a musical, *Two Little Girls in Blue*. There was to be a second composer, Paul Lannin, whose father was more ambitious for him to get acquainted with every aspect of the hotel trade than with any aspect of music. Lannin was at that time learning to be a chef at the Garden City Hotel. Conferences were held there so that the vital collaborator could pop in from the kitchens in his chef's uniform to contribute. When the show opened at the George M. Cohan Theatre on 3 May, 1921, Ira's old paper, *The Clipper*, was loyal to its former, albeit pseudonymous dramatic critic. 'The lyrics by Arthur Francis are of the best, and seem to show that there are some lyricists who are still able to write a lyric which rhymes and also means something.' However, Youmans interfered with every aspect of the production and the show ran only because of the obstinacy of its producer, Abraham Lincoln Erlanger.

George secured Arthur Francis another interpolation the next year in *Little Miss Bluebeard*; it was 'I Won't Say I Will, I Won't Say I Won't', sung with appropriate French ambiguity by Irene Bordoni. However, it was not the bigger younger brother who brought Ira in on 'I'll Build a Stairway to Paradise', but the bigger younger brother's collaborator, B. G. 'Buddy' de Sylva. De Sylva had heard a lyric of Ira's – 'New Step Every Day' – which he thought might furnish a first act finale for *George White's Scandals of 1922*, on which he and George were working at the time. It was the last line which appealed to him, 'I'll build a staircase to paradise with a new step ev'ry day'. George, Ira and de Sylva toiled from nine till two one night to complete the new version. Ira earned enough from the song to keep himself for a year and the stage was set for the first Gershwin and Gershwin show; the brothers were to be represented on Broadway by eight shows in the next seven years. They were graceful, amusing confections, often with books by Guy Bolton and P. G. Wodehouse or Fred Thompson, musical farces which sometimes displayed sprightly wit or effective staging, but which were innocent of any ambition to pack a dramatic punch or to experiment inside the form.

Lady, Be Good was the first in the line. The score included the title song, 'Fascinating Rhythm' and 'The Half of it Dearie Blues'. At one point it also included 'The Man I Love', a song which was to find itself in and out of three of the Gershwins' Broadway shows before it established itself as a standard, independent of any showcase. It owed its final success to the amateur song-plugger Lady Louis Mountbatten who, having heard George play it, took an autographed copy back to London and forced her favourite dance bands to repeat it at every opportunity. The song was a source of both pride and irritation to its writers. Its eventual success was enormous but limited in that it cannot easily be adapted for a male vocalist. The Gershwins were never able to get maximum mileage out of it. They might have got away with:

> Someday she'll come along
> The gal I love . . .

but they were immediately on thin ice with:

> And she'll be big and strong
> The gal I love . . .

and were finally defeated when they came to:

> She'll build a little home
> From which I'll never roam . . .

Though perhaps in a later, more liberated age even this may become singable for a man – expecially one asking for the family domicile in part-settlement. There was an added irony in that 'The Man I Love' had earned the producers a $10,000 investment from Otto Kahn when George played it to the financier on a boat trip back from Europe where he had been to supervise the opening of another Gershwin show, *Primrose*. However, Mr Kahn's investment was well protected by the rest of the score and by the performances of the Astaires.

The triumph of *Lady, Be Good* enabled George to move the whole family into a large house on West 103rd Street and from then on pawnbrokers had looked their last on Rose's diamond ring. The mansion was carefully divided among the various members of the family and contained a built-in toy for Poppa Gershwin – a self-service elevator which he loved to demonstrate for his sons' friends, sometimes

even proudly donning a uniform for the occasion. It ascended as high as
the fifth floor which was George's terrain. Here he could work except
when the house was overrun by gregarious Gershwins and their friends.

Taking the lift down from the top, Morris would arrive at the fourth
floor where Ira and his wife, Leonore, after they married in 1926, were
accommodated. One more stop and he was among the rest of his family
sleeping on the third floor. The living and dining rooms were on the
second floor and when the lift finally hit the bottom it opened on to a
billiard room. S. N. Behrman has described a visit to the ménage. 'For a
long time I rang the doorbell and got no answer . . . finally I pushed the
door open and walked in. Three or four young men I had never seen
before were sitting around the hall smoking. Off the hall was a small
reception room which had been converted into a billiard room. I peered
in – there was a game in progress but I knew none of the players. I asked
for George or his brother Ira. No one bothered to reply, but one of the
young men made a terse gesture in the direction of the upper storeys. I
went up one flight and there I found a new group. One of them I
vaguely remembered from 110th Street and I asked him where George
and Ira were. He said he thought they were upstairs. On the third floor I
found Arthur, the youngest brother, who had just come in and didn't
know who was in the house, but on the fourth I got an answer to my –
by this time agonised – cry. I heard Ira's voice inviting me up to the fifth
. . . "Who under the sun", I asked, "are those fellows playing billiards
on the first floor?" Ira looked almost guilty. "To tell you the truth," he
said, "I don't know!" "But you must," I insisted. "They look perfectly
at home." "I really don't," he said. "There's a bunch of fellows from
down the street who've taken to dropping in here every night for a
game. I think they're friends of Arthur's. But I don't know who they
are." "Where", I demanded sternly, "is George?" "He's taken his old
rooms in the hotel round the corner. He says he's got to have a little
privacy."

Lady, Be Good! may have set the Gershwins up in their new home; its
successor, *Tell Me More*, did nothing to make them feel secure in it. It ran
for only 100 performances and there were no big hits – not until it opened
in London did it flourish. The advent of *Tip-Toes*, however, brought
joy to 110th Street before the year was out. Apart from 'Sweet and Low
Down' and 'That Certain Feeling', 'Looking for a Boy' beautifully
states the predicament of a diminutive heroine who, believing that 'love
affairs are all arranged in Heaven', is conveniently 'looking for a boy
'bout five foot six or seven'. The lyrics for *Tip-Toes* brought an
enthusiastic letter from Lorenz Hart:

When the other night . . . Joe Meyer told me a departing guest was
Ira Gershwin, I should have brushed aside your friends, grasped

you by the hand and told you how much I liked your lyrics of *Tip-Toes*, but . . . I had imbibed more cocktails than is my wont, and so . . . all I could say was, 'Zat so!' . . . such delicacies as your jingles prove that songs can be popular and intelligent . . .

Brother George's working pattern was now established. He interspersed his musical comedies with his serious composition. He had his triumph with the *Rhapsody* – all fifteen minutes – and he followed *Tip-Toes* with a trip to Europe in which he started to toy with his ideas for *An American in Paris* before returning to plan *Oh, Kay!* with Ira. The book had been conceived by Guy Bolton and P. G. Wodehouse during a country-house weekend in England. Its plot revolved thinly around Prohibition but provided a peg for topical gags like 'Don't criticise a bootlegger's English if his Scotch is all right', and for some of George and Ira's freshest songs – 'Someone to Watch Over Me', a title suggested by Howard Dietz, 'Maybe' and 'Do, Do, Do', a lyric which they completed in less than half an hour as a result of Ira's notion that they should be able to do something amusing with the simple repetition of the words 'do' and 'done'.

> Do, do, do what you've done, done, done before, baby,
> Do, do, do what I do, do, do adore, baby . . .

As proof that the chorus took 30 minutes to write, Ira Gershwin has offered the information that it was composed between the time that the future Mrs Ira Gershwin telephoned to announce her intention of coming to dinner and her arrival to hear the finished product. She confirmed in 1984 that the journey up town from 8th Street took less than half an hour.

They wrote the score with Gertrude Lawrence in mind and Bolton and Wodehouse insisted on Victor Moore as the bootlegger. When they tried out in Philadelphia Moore had a comic triumph early in the first act. On the second night he made his exit to similar laughter and applause. However, he was disconcerted to hear even more hilarity during Gertrude Lawrence's quiet scene which followed his. Rushing back to see what business she had imported to top his moment, he found that a stray mongrel dog had wandered on stage leaving the actress with nothing to do but watch it as it took its time crossing and leaving by walking through a fireplace full of an apparently roaring fire, against which it nonchalantly cocked its leg before departing. This business was not retained when *Oh, Kay!* opened at the Imperial Theatre where it ran for 256 performances.

Alex Aarons and Vinton Freedley had produced *Lady Be Good, Tip-Toes* and *Oh, Kay!* Largely on the strength of these successes they were now in a position to build a theatre of their own, which they named the Alvin after the first syllables of their first names. To complete this monument to themselves, they were anxious to open it with another Gershwin show starring the Astaires, and *Funny Face*, originally called *Smarty*, was the chosen vehicle. Unfortunately, this time the book – the responsibility of Robert Benchley and Fred Thompson – was a disaster and the producers, faced with failure, insisted on major revisions of both book and score before bringing the show in. 'How Long Has This Been Going On?' was one of the casualties; but by the time the Alvin opened its doors on 22 November, 1927, the score included 'He Loves and She Loves', 'High Hat' and ''S Wonderful', which survived a prudish reception in Philadelphia from a local critic who found it obscene. The line to which he took exception was:

You can't blame me for feeling amorous . . .

Conveniently for the Gershwins, they had another show, *Rosalie*, a Ziegfeld production starring Marilyn Miller, on the boil at the same time; and as soon as Aarons and Freedley threw out a song they were able to peddle it to Ziegfeld. 'The Man I Love' cropped up again, only to disappear summarily but 'How Long Has This Been Going On?' found its rightful place in the repertory.

Rosalie, which also featured some Romberg songs, was an even bigger success than *Funny Face* and George and Ira set off together for what was to be Ira's first visit to Europe. It was at this time that he had to check his birth certificate while applying for a passport and learnt that his given name was Israel, not Isidore. He appears to have taken the news in his stride.

On their return the Gershwins had two tasks. For George there was the business of completing and unveiling *An American in Paris*, for the pair of them there was a new show for Gertrude Lawrence, *Treasure Girl*. Ira Gershwin attributes its failure to the unsympathetic role in which Miss Lawrence was cast – a single-minded fortune hunter. Gershwin songs such as 'Feeling I'm Falling', 'I Don't Think I'll Fall in Love Today' and 'I've Got a Crush on You' did not have a chance to establish an immediate rapport with their audience.

Their next outing was even more unhappy. They fell foul of Ziegfeld as was the way of so many song writers.* The production was *Show Girl*. Ziegfeld rushed the play into rehearsal, calling on Gus Kahn to share the responsibility for the lyrics with Ira. The show was heavy on music, incorporating a fifteen-minute ballet, 'American in Paris', and a

* See Lorenz Hart.

spot for Duke Ellington and his band: 27 musical items all told. In between, the simple rags to riches story of a chorus girl, Dixie Duggan, tried in vain to get itself told. Ruby Keeler played Dixie Duggan and not even the presence on the first night of her new husband, Al Jolson, joining her from the stalls as she sang 'Liza', a minstrel number, could generate enthusiasm in the audiences which attended subsequent performances. Ziegfeld took the interesting line that it was the Gershwins' fault and, when they sued him for their money, he threatened to sue them for not writing a hit show. However, the brothers do not seem to have risen to this bait. In any case, they were too busy with the first of their three satirical operettas.

This trio of works consists of *Strike Up The Band*, tentative; *Of Thee I Sing*, triumphant; and *Let 'Em Eat Cake*, trailing. They constitute the most individual and most innovative work attempted by the Gershwins until they tackled *Porgy*. For all the felicities with which they had packed their individual songs in other shows, they had been firmly trapped by the bookwriters with whom they worked in the convention of the twenties musical. Nor do they seem to have found it unpleasant to conform. However, in 1926, encouraged by the producer, Edgar Selwyn, they made a first attempt at creating a more original show which tried to take on where Gilbert and Sullivan left off – and which was savagely critical of politicians, the League of Nations and war itself. The book was the work of George S. Kauffman* and in its first version, which folded in Philadelphia, it looked like proving Kauffman's adage 'Satire is what closes on Saturday night.' During that Philadelphia run, Ira Gershwin observed two old-world gentlemen, elegantly dressed, be-whiskered and sporting monocles and silver topped canes, arriving at the theatre. He turned to Kauffman muttering, 'It looks like Gilbert and Sullivan have come to fix the show.' To which Kauffman replied, 'A pity the jokes in your lyrics aren't as good as that.' The fixing process was to wait three years, when Morrie Ryskind was called in to tone down the cutting edge of Kauffman's book. But it was the imaginative work of the Gershwins, taking the whole drive of the show, its satirical barbs and its plot points, under the protection of their score, diversifying it with more ambitious musical forms than they had chosen to employ in the past, that gave it its character and success.

---

* Kauffman, born in Pittsburgh in 1899, had followed a comfortable pampered childhood with an apprenticeship on the Washington *Star* before becoming a drama critic in New York – first on the *Tribune* and then the *Times*. In the early twenties he tried his hand at playwriting and after an initial flop his mordant wit – as celebrated in off-stage asides as in his plays, written alone or in collaboration, won through. The musicals which he wrote, or directed, read like a role of honour: *Animal Crackers, Band Wagon, Cocoanuts, Face the Music, Guys and Dolls, Let 'em Eat Cake, Music Box Revues, Of Thee I Sing, Silk Stockings, Strike Up the Band.*

There was still some room for sturdy Gershwin ballads like 'Soon'; but 'The Man I Love' made its last appearance in a Gershwin book-show at this time and was thrown out once more before it reached New York. Encouraged by the reception of *Strike Up The Band*, the Gershwins, with Kauffman and Ryskind, tried again in the same vein, but with a different set of targets. Ira worked closely with the bookwriters from the inception of *Of Thee I Sing*. This time the satire was directed at graft and political chicanery behind the scenes of the White House. The libretto envisaged a candidate, 'the man the people choose', who was all things to all men and who accordingly, 'loves the Irish and the Jews'. 'Love is Sweeping the Country' is a campaign worker's song. 'Of Thee I Sing, Baby', the title song, caused some adverse comment initially because of the irreverent juxtaposition of the revered phrase and the slangy 'baby', but the idea of allowing a candidate to sing his campaign song to his bride-to-be was typical of the neat and endearing technique with which sentiment and satire were blended through the show.

By the time they tackled *Let 'Em Eat Cake* in 1933 the formula was beginning to wear thin. The characters who had become much loved cults in *Of Thee I Sing* had outstayed their welcome when put through their paces in the sequel, nor did the story show them in such a warm and affectionate light. The sequel itself was an anticlimax, lacking the freshness, surprise and originality of the earlier show. Kauffman, Ryskind and Ira Gershwin had won a Pulitzer for *Of Thee I Sing* – the first awarded to a musical, though the other outstanding architect of its success, George Gershwin, was ignored under the rigidly interpreted rules of the prize. The songs in *Let 'Em Eat Cake* are sprightly and inventive again, but carry with them a slight feeling of second time around; and audiences found the attitude of down-with-everything depressing.

Clive Barnes summed up the appeal of these three musicals in his review when *Of Thee I Sing* was revived in 1969. He did not find that the book had survived. 'It is not just bad, it is terrible,' he wrote, '. . . nor is this entirely a matter of changing tastes, except in respect that we do demand a new standard of wit and even literacy from our musical books nowadays . . . but . . . George and Ira Gershwin remain fresh as a daisy . . . this is an extraordinary advanced kind of musical comedy. The Gershwins were here actually straining towards proper, or more likely improper operetta, and had the courage to use arias, ensembles, even, as unlikely as it sounds, recitatives, and the musical aspect of the show . . . is as new as tomorrow. They don't write musical scores like that any more, but let's live in hope.' *Let 'Em Eat Cake* ran for 90 performances and it was to be two years before the Gershwins were ready to go even further with innovation in *Porgy*.

In the meantime, they did not desert their lucrative, conventional

careers. In 1930 – the same year as *Strike Up The Band* – they wrote *Girl Crazy*, another show for Aarons and Freedley. The book was a simple, old-fashioned affair originally destined for Bert Lahr, but played in the end by Willie Howard, cast as a New York taxi driver, Gieber Goldfarb, whose fare demands to be driven to Custerville, Arizona. Goldfarb insists on addressing all Indians in Yiddish. Ginger Rogers played the village post-mistress, and Ethel Merman (née Zimmerman), playing the saloon keeper, 'Frisco Kate', had one of the most sensational Broadway triumphs singing 'Boy, What Love has Done to Me!', 'I Got Rhythm' and 'Sam and Delilah', a highly individual western look at an Old Testament story.

Then there were 'Bidin' My Time', 'But Not For Me', 'Could You Use Me?', as well as 'Embraceable You', salvaged from an earlier attempt to write an oriental musical for Ziegfeld, *East is West*. (Poppa Gershwin was having his last chance – in the words of his oldest son – to 'thump his chest, look around the room and beam' at 'my song'. He died of leukaemia in 1932, mourned by all his children, who found his eccentricities endlessly endearing.) Added to this extraordinary clutch of songs and singers was a band led by Red Nichols which included Roger Edens, Benny Goodman, Gene Krupa, Glenn Miller, Jack Teagarden and Jimmy Dorsey. The show ran for 272 performances and was to be the last joint hit for its producers.

Meanwhile, the Gershwins had their first Hollywood experience. The invitation inspired a quick dash to the trunk to unearth 'Blah, Blah, Blah', from the abortive *East is West*, a title song, 'Delishious', which had been on the stocks for some time and one of their party pieces, 'Mischa, Jascha, Toscha, Sascha'. The violinists, Mischa Elman, Jascha Heifitz, Toscha Seidel and Sascha Jacobsen lent their names to a chorus which did not finally find a place in the film, but continued to be played whenever the Gershwins could find a captive audience. George Gershwin's keenness to play at parties was nicely summed up by George S. Kauffman, who said wearily, 'George's music gets around so much before an opening that the first night's audience thinks it's at a revival . . .'

As George Gershwin continued to programme his serious work between his Broadway shows, so Ira continued to collaborate with other composers, and in some cases with other lyricists. For *Garrick Gaieties of 1930* he worked with E. Y. Harburg on a song which they wrote with Vernon Duke, 'I'm Only Human After All', and in the same year he shared a credit for a song called 'Cheerful Little Earful' with the insistent Billy Rose* and Harry Warren in a revue called *Sweet and Low*.

In 1933, working together again, George and Ira managed a resounding flop, *Pardon My English*. Herbert Fields took the blame for the book, Jack Buchanan bought himself out on the tour, Aarons and

Freedley lost a fortune, one fleeing the profession and the other the country. However, the Gershwins salvaged some songs. As Ira has wisely pointed out, 'I've never known of any theatrical failure where, sooner or later, an author or stage manager or one of the backers, or some member of the cast, didn't reminisce to the effect that there were some pretty good things in it'. In *Pardon My English* lurked 'Isn't It a Pity', 'The Lorelei' and 'My Cousin in Milwaukee' – who had a 'voice that's rather squawky'.

However, the next year, while George began the long haul on *Porgy and Bess*, Ira collaborated with E. Y. Harburg again on *Life Begins at 8.40*. This time their composer was Harold Arlen* and the songs included 'You're a Builder-Upper', 'Shoein' the Mare', 'What Can You Say in a Love Song?' and, best known, 'Let's Take a Walk Around the Block'. But, by the time protective brother George had edged Ira, the protégé, into honing those of Du Bose Heyward's lyrics which required polishing, Ira was free to give *Porgy* his full attention. In some of the songs he simply admired what Heyward had written ('Summertime', 'My Man's Gone Now', 'A Woman is a Sometime Thing', 'The Buzzard Song'); in others he edited the words by making sure that they were singable ('Bess, You is My Woman'). In some he enjoyed a full-scale collaboration with Heyward ('I Got Plenty of Nuttin' ' and 'It Takes a Long Pull to Get There') and in yet other cases Ira was the sole lyricist ('There's a Boat Dat's Leavin' Soon for New York', 'It Ain't Necessarily So'). Heyward has left a vivid picture of Ira and George at work: 'The brothers Gershwin, after their extraordinary fashion, would get at the piano, pound, wrangle, sweat, burst into weird snatches of song, and eventually emerge with a polished lyric.' The admiration of the protégé for the protector, which was clearly the lifetime basis of their relationship, survives in Ira's own words: 'I can still shake my head in wonder at the reservoir of musical inventiveness, resourcefulness, and craftsmanship George could dip into. And no fraternal entrancement, my wonderment.' A wonderment incidentally

---

* Rose was a diminutive but dynamic impresario who also cherished ambitions to be a song writer and in many cases he insisted on collaborating with other lyricists or hiring them to streamline his raw material. His other 'collaborators' included E. Y. Harburg, Al Dubin, Mort Dixon and Charlotte Kent. When he produced shows by Cole Porter, Rodgers and Hart and Oscar Hammerstein he was not required to assist.

* Harold Arlen, one of the most talented Broadway and Hollywood composers, wrote with a variety of lyric writers. Apart from Harburg and Ira Gershwin – with whom he was to write the score for Judy Garland's *A Star is Born* – his principal early collaboration was with Ted Koehler. Together they wrote 'Stormy Weather' and 'Get Happy'. The lyric writer Dick Vosburgh has always wanted to produce an L.P. on which the comedienne Imogen Coca sings the songs of Ted Koehler simply so that he could call it 'The Coca-Koehler Song Book'.

which was not immediately shared by the critics nor, when *Porgy* closed after 124 performances, by a Hollywood which viewed the composer's operatic pretensions with the deepest suspicions.

After *Porgy*, Ira's first task away from George was the *Ziegfeld Follies of 1936* in which his composer was Vernon Duke. Josephine Baker, Fanny Brice and Bob Hope were in the cast and, according to Duke, he found 'Ira's writing methods . . . slow and soothing and very restful after E. Y. Harburg's strident screams and wild pacing of the floor . . . our work sessions usually began with a family dinner with Ira and Leonore, joined by Fanny Brice or Ellin Berlin. After a long and copious meal . . . I, on tenterhooks, would be dying to get to the piano . . . I would shoot expressive glances at the ever placid Ira . . .' Eventually, he 'would heed my desperate call, stretch himself, emit a series of protracted sighs, say something to the effect that "one had to work so-o-o hard for a living" and more in that vein, then interrupt himself to intone a magic word: "however . . ." This "however" meant that the eleventh hour had struck and a period of delicious procrastination was over. Ira, sighing pathetically, would then produce a small bridge table, various writing and erasing gadgets, a typewriter and four or five books which he seldom consulted – Roget's *Thesaurus*, Webster's *Dictionary*, a rhyming dictionary and the like – wipe and adjust his glasses, all these preparations at *molto adagio* pace, and finally say in a resigned voice, "OK Dukie . . . play that chorus you had last night." After wrestling with last night's chorus for half an hour, Ira would embark on an ice-box raiding expedition, with me, fearful of too long an interruption, in pursuit. There we'd stand in the kitchen, munching cheese and pickles, Ira obviously delighted with this escapist stratagem, I dutifully pretending to enjoy it too. Another sigh, another "however", then back to the piano. At 2 or 3 am Ira would put away his working utensils and victoriously announce to Lee that he had completed four lines for a new chorus.' Of the end product of the midnight oil, one of their numbers, a hillbilly-gangster-T-Man song-ballet, 'The Ballad of Baby Face McGinty', was dropped in Boston; Bob Hope and Eve Arden sang 'I Can't Get Started With You' into great popularity; and Fanny Brice had a moment satirising her hit, 'Mon Homme', in 'He Hasn't a Thing Except Me'. Josephine Baker's first night success was not reflected in the reviews and in Duke's opinion 'the score didn't come off too impressively in the theatre'. The show closed after 227 performances because of Fanny Brice's illness.

The next year George and Ira contributed another of their party pieces to a Broadway revue, *The Show Is On*. The director was Vincente Minnelli, who recalled their send-up of Viennese waltzes and included 'By Strauss'. The lyric rejected Berlin, gave no quarter to Kern or Cole Porter and dismissed Gershwin as 'pounding on tin'. This 'musical drivel' was dismissed as fit only for night-clubbing 'souses'. The waltz must be Strauss's. The verse of 'By Strauss' gave the Gershwins' publishers particular problems. It was unusually long and cuts were requested. George wrote on the brothers' behalf:

> I am very sorry that the verse to 'By Strauss' is so long that it requires an extra page in the publication copy; but then it's always been my policy to give the public a lot for their money. And I think it would be a good idea to put on the title page 'This song has an extra long verse so that you are getting more notes per penny than in any other song this season.' And if the song doesn't sell, I would like my grandchildren (if I ever have any) to see the trouble that their granddaddy took with verses. In other words . . . I would like the song printed as I wrote it, with no commas left out. Love and kisses, George.

The journey out to Hollywood was not easily arranged. Suddenly, to the studios, George Gershwin was not the hit song machine of *Lady Be Good* and *Girl Crazy*. He was a doubtful quantity, harbouring dubious operatic ambitions, presumably shared by his brother. In one exchange with an agent, George was stung into sending a cable denying that he and Ira were no longer in the popular song market:

HAVE WRITTEN HIT SONGS IN THE PAST AND EXPECT TO DO SO AGAIN IN THE FUTURE.

Finally, they signed a contract with RKO, closed up their Manhattan apartments , held a farewell party in George's, and on 10 August, 1936, flew from Newark to Glendale, California. Their first assignment was to write *Shall We Dance?*, originally called *Stepping Toes*, for Astaire and Rogers. Hollywood at that time seemed to contain more song writers than people, and to confound those who had doubted their ability to turn out hits, they wrote 'I've Got Beginner's Luck', 'Let's Call the Whole Thing Off', 'Shall We Dance?', 'Slap That Bass' and 'They All Laughed' – a title line that had lain dormant at the back of Ira's mind since he had read a correspondence-school advertisement in the twenties which began 'They all laughed when I sat down to play the piano.'

George Gershwin's health was giving cause for concern during this year and the title of another song which they were writing for *Shall We Dance?* seemed to presage his untimely end, only a few months away – 'They Can't Take that Away from Me'. 'Nice Work if You Can Get It' was based on an observation Ira had long cherished from a *Punch* cartoon in which two Cockney charwomen are discussing the daughter of a third who has become a whore – 'nice work if you can get it!' 'Things

Are Looking Up' and 'A Foggy Day' were to be the other enduring songs from their last full score together for the film *A Damsel in Distress*.

George Gershwin died of a brain tumour on 11 July, 1937 and Ira flew his body to New York where he was buried on a rain-spattered July day. He was already in the middle of a new score for *The Goldwyn Follies*, which included 'Love Walked In', and the last song the brothers wrote together:

> . . . In time the Rockies may crumble
> Gibraltar may tumble,
> (They're only made of clay)
> But – our love is here to stay.

Although Ira Gershwin had lived so much of his life in the shadow and under the wing of his younger brother, his professional life widened and diversified after George's death. He continued to work on some of his brother's themes notably 'Aren't You Kind of Glad We Did?' And he worked on film scores with other composers. With Jerome Kern in 1944 he wrote *Cover Girl* which included 'Long Ago and Far Away'. The next year he collaborated with Kurt Weill on *Where Do We Go from Here?*, a fantasy for Fred MacMurray who, trying to join the army, wishes himself into service first with Washington at Valley Forge and then with Columbus on the *Santa Maria*. 'All at Once' and 'If Love Remains' were pleasant conventional love songs; but there was more than a spark of originality in the 'Song of the Rhineland' for a band of Hessians remembering 'The Rhineland . . . a fine land . . . that wonderful pretzel and stein land . . . Where the beer is beerier and the soup superior . . .' and in 'The Nina, the Pinta and the Santa Maria' where the hero urges Columbus's crew on to the New World:

> You're just being dumb, not to know that you'll come
> To a land that's the world's panacea.
> No laurels you'll rest on if you don't keep west on
> The Nina, the Pinta, the Santa Maria . . .
>
> So think twice my friends, before you doubt Columbus,
> Just imagine what happens to Posterity without Columbus.
> No New York, no skyscrapers, no funnies in the papers,
> No automat nickels, no Heinz and his pickles,
> No land of the Brave and the Free. . . .

In 1949 he joined Harry Warren for *The Barkleys of Broadway* with Astaire and Rogers. And in 1953 he wrote *Give a Girl a Break* with Burton Lane, a bad film which contained one song which deserves to join the lexicon of show business anthems, 'Applause, Applause!'

Most notably he collaborated with Harold Arlen on *A Star is Born* for Judy Garland in 1954, finding again his old casual, colloquial style for two songs, 'Lose That Long Face' and 'Gotta Have Me Go with You'. But the most celebrated song strikes a different note from the rest of his lyrics. Harold Arlen has commented on Ira Gershwin's reluctance to write straightforward ballads; and certainly the ripple of humour, the instinct to toy with words, which pervades his work goes against any straightforward statement of emotion. He wrote a powerful, simple lyric for 'The Man That Got Away'; but even in that song he seems somehow to be on the edge of parody. Perhaps Harold Arlen's strong tune took him further than he would instinctively go, perhaps he was confident that Judy Garland's emotional performance would ensure that his tongue could not be seen hiding anywhere near his cheek.

Ever since this world began
There is nothing sadder than
A one-man woman looking for
The Man That Got Away. . . .

Meanwhile, he had not neglected the theatre. *Lady in the Dark*, a collaboration with Kurt Weill and Moss Hart in 1941, joins the list of musicals which at that time were preparing writers and audiences for the revolution of *Oklahoma!*. *Lady in the Dark* broke fresh ground in its treatment of psycho-analysis. Not only the subject matter, but also the technique of 'making the music and lyrics part and parcel of the basic structure of the play' are claimed by Moss Hart, who wrote the book, as new developments. 'One cannot separate the play from the music, and vice versa. More than that, the music and lyrics carry the story forward dramatically and psychologically.' Gertrude Lawrence played a disturbed magazine editor whose analysis was seen in musical dream sequences. Working with Weill inspired a new simple poetry in Ira Gershwin, especially in 'My Ship', a unifying theme for the whole play, looming in the unconscious of the leading lady throughout her sessions with her shrink. However, the score was not solely devoted to simple poetry. They presented Danny Kaye with a show stopper in 'Tschaikowsky'. The lyric was exhumed from a magazine which had published it in 1924, and listed forty-nine composers. 'The names that always give me brain concussion. The names of those composers known as Russian.' It became necessary to find another song in which the leading lady could follow Mr Kaye's performance. This Miss Lawrence did with 'Jenny' – who 'would make up her mind'. Both songs looked like being lost in rehearsal; but on the opening in Boston, Danny Kaye and then Gertrude Lawrence took their material by the scruff of the neck and scored first a great and then an even greater triumph.

The influence of *Lady in the Dark* was not immediately observed but, in Gerald Bordman's phrase, 'Years later, looking back . . . it . . . would be recognised . . . along with *Cabin in the Sky* and *Pal Joey* as an isolated beacon . . . in an otherwise dark period illuminating ways to the future.'

Ira Gershwin continued his collaboration with Weill in *The Firebrand of Florence* – a musical about Benvenuto Cellini based on Edwin Justus Mayer's earlier success *The Firebrand*. The show was a failure but the score was full of interest. The verse to 'Sing Me Not a Ballad', which provided a grand entrance for Lotte Lenya who was borne in on a sedan chair as Duchess of Florence, playfully rhymes 'Circe' and 'mercy', 'Venus, Cleo and Psyche' with 'my key' and finally:

> Give me a man who's strong and silent
> Inarticulate – but vi'lent.

The chorus develops with purposeful simplicity:

> Sing me not a ballad,
> Sing me not a sonnet.
> I require no ballad,
> Rhyme and time are wasted on it . . .

Building to:

> Just, oh just make love!

The trio, 'I Know Where There is a Cosy Nook' is an indulgent attempt to write a song based on Spoonerisms:

> I know where there's a nosy cook –
> My lord, you mean a cosy nook?
> Yes, yes, of course! A cosy nook for two
> And there we two can kill and boo.

And equally indulgent is 'A Rhyme for Angela'. The lovesick swain cannot find a rhyme for Angela though he can conjure up rhymes for other names no matter how improbable or unromantic. For example:

> Edith . . . possesses what every man needeth.

It is easy to feel that in this musical Ira Gershwin was following the example of one of his own songs, 'I Love to Rhyme'.

His last Broadway show was *Park Avenue* – his colleagues were Arthur Schwartz and George S. Kauffman; the premise was a sophisticated modern musical comedy intended to be a sharp and refreshing contrast to the current vogue for earnest costume musicals. The rich, modern Manhattan characters simply changed partners frequently. It sounds like a precursor of Sondheim's *Company*; but it failed to live up to the hopes raised by the announcement that the three distinguished collaborators were at work. Ira Gershwin's lyrics show no fangs; indeed, it is difficult to see why they should have been expected to, it was not his style; nor did they reveal the wounds that a more emotional, open lyric writer might have uncovered for the brittle subject in hand. His 'Don't Be a Woman if You Can' invades the same territory as Sondheim's 'The Ladies Who Lunch' – but without the same bitter relish. Even more striking is the similarity between Sondheim's 'The Little Things We Do Together' and Gershwin's 'There's Nothing Like Marriage for People'.

> Imagine signing a lease together;
> And hanging a Matisse together;
> Being alone and breaking bread together.
> Reading the *New Yorker* in bed together!
> Starting a family tree together!
> Voting for the GOP together!

Again, Sondheim's lyric has a more powerful snarl. Ira Gershwin blames the show's lack of success partly on its lack of charm. Closer to his taste must have been the more whimsical 'My Son-in-Law' for two rich, proud parents.

> Some day he'll come along,
> My son-in-law;
> His strong box will be strong,
> My son-in-law.

One anecdote – perhaps apocryphal – has survived from the production. Kauffman is said to have fallen in love with his leading actress before rehearsals started, to have built up her part and given her a contract approving any changes. The show went on tour. First the show went badly, then the relationship. By the time they got back to New York the show was in trouble and the affair was over. The time for rewriting arrived and it was contractually necessary to get the approval of the leading lady. By now she was installed in a penthouse with a new young man. The distinguished trio, Schwartz, composer, Gershwin, lyric writer and Kauffman, writer, director and recently created ex-lover, arrived to find the young man installed on the sofa and the leading lady bored by the idea of hearing the new songs. They had hardly played half a song before she approved the lot – plainly she was anxious to get back to her beau. She saw them to the lift and asked for their approval of the new man in her life. 'Isn't he divine?' she said as they waited uneasily for the lift. Ira Gershwin is said to have intervened diplomatically, 'Yes, he seems very nice, what does he do?' 'Oh,' she replied, 'he's in cotton.' At that moment the lift arrived enabling Kauffman to step into it saying sharply, 'An dem dat plants it is soon forgotten.'

Perhaps that is what the musical should have said; but claws were no part of Ira Gershwin's armoury. He closed his collection of lyrics with the opening statement of the article on song in the *Encyclopaedia Britannica*:

> Song is the joint art of words and music, two arts under emotional pressure coalescing into a third. The relation and balance of the two arts is a problem that has to be resolved in every song that is composed.

That complements his own opening disclaimer: 'Since most of the lyrics in this lodgment were arrived at by fitting words mosaically to music already composed, any resemblance to actual poetry, living or dead, is highly improbable.'

Thus with typical modesty he dealt himself out of the can-lyrics-be-poetry debate leaving only a superb, mellow, musical mass of work as uncalled evidence in the argument.

He died in California in the autumn of 1983, survived by his widow, Leonore. In *Lyrics on Several Occasions* Ira Gershwin adds a note to his lyric 'Let's Call the Whole Thing Off'. Writing in 1959 he pointed out that he and his wife had been married over 30 years and noted that 'my wife still "eyethers" and "tomahtoes" me, while I "eether" or "tomatoe" her.' This he defines as proof of 'phonic and marital tolerance on the parts of Mr and Mrs Ira Gershwin'.

4

LORENZ HART

'Where's That Rainbow You Hear About?'

Lorenz Milton Hart, five foot tall with a chunky body and a head too big for it, so hated his own appearance that he could not live with it. In front of a looking-glass, his self-confidence turned to self-disgust. Drink served to blur the edges of the reflection; but his talent was squandered and the line of bottles led down the years inevitably to the gutter, albeit a plush gutter. He was a homosexual, a near-dwarf and a drunk, three traits perfectly acceptable in themselves, but which, in the period in which Hart grew up, placed an intolerable strain on his sensitive nature.

His father was short, stout and bald; vulgar, exuberant and questionably honest. His mother was tiny and placid, delicate, sensitive and genteel. However, their lack of size did not hag-ride them – nor did his lack of inches affect their younger son, Teddy, three years Larry's junior and not much taller than he. When to be little was appropriate, little Larry Hart filled the house with laughter. As his friends grew taller and he did not, the habit of laughter remained; but the pain beneath it grew. His gnome-like appearance never appalled his friends, for he was everyone's favourite until the last day of his life, even those he most exasperated.

Oscar Hammerstein II has described him as 'skipping and bouncing . . . like an electrified gnome. I think of him always, as skipping and dancing. I never saw him walk slowly. I never saw his face in repose. I never heard him chuckle quietly. He laughed loudly and easily at other people's jokes and at his own, too. His large eyes danced, and his head would wag. He was alert and dynamic and fun to be with.'

When Hart's parents met in 1886 on the Lower East Side, his mother, Frieda, née Isenberg, had been in America less than a year; his father Max (né Hertz, in Germany) little longer. Max Hart's raucous personality and wealth of not entirely scrupulous schemes, and the bravura with which he carried them at least halfway to completion, corkscrewed the newly-weds from Allen Street up to East 106th Street, where his dreams of a fortune to be made out of deals in real estate had rather more attractive real estate to build on. It was here that Lorenz Milton mewed his first mew and puked his first puke in 1895. By the age of six he had refined the act and was writing verse and spouting it at his father's bidding to the intense delight of his father's friends. When Max Hart was not planning and plotting, or gambling, or selling insurance, or real estate, or dreams, he was entertaining. Devoted and discreet, Frieda Hart piled high a table which provided the parties with a centre-piece of delicious, nourishing, impeccably ethnic food – sometimes financed by her quiet pawning of her jewellery.

When the schemes and dreams and the family moved across the Park to 69 West 119th Street, the groaning board and the pawnbroker's tickets moved with them. It was a rich diet for the little boy with books at hand, visits to the German theatre, an adoring mother, and a noisy father, who gambled and indulged and shouted and womanised, and was not above, in moments of stress, urinating out of the front window.

At school, and more especially at summer camp, Lorenz Milton was nicknamed 'Shakespeare' and it was here that he turned up with a case stuffed full of books whereas other boys' lockers were filled with their regulation summer kit. Unabashed, he helped himself and borrowed freely – naturally from boys rather younger, and therefore his size. His small capering figure, the dark eyes often flashing under a long blonde *travestie* wig, enlivened the entertainments he devised for summer camp concerts and for the end of term entertainments which he later master-minded at Columbia, presented by, written by, directed by and starring himself. In the Columbia 1915 Varsity Show, *On Your Way*, a fellow actor was Oscar Hammerstein II, who was also twenty. In the audience sat a thirteen-year-old Richard Rodgers. It was three years before Rodgers and Hart would begin their collaboration.

In the meantime, Hart, like one of his idols, W. S. Gilbert, began by translating German lyrics. He ghosted some lyrics for Billy Rose and he was regularly employed to write more translations on salary for United Plays, a subsidiary of the Shubert* organisation. For these he received neither credit nor royalties, although Molnar's *Liliom, The Lady in Ermine* and *La Belle Hélène* were among the translations on which he worked. What Hart was looking for now was an escape from anonymity and, even more, for a composer-collaborator. He had already found an unofficial agent – a show-business-smitten dentist, 'Doc' Bender, who was to spend the rest of his life extracting his pound of flesh from Hart's success and Hart's unhappiness.

---

* Lee and J. J. Shubert – the Shubert Brothers – were powerful impresarios and theatre owners whose empire has grown since their deaths, when it was handed on to an energetic pair of New York lawyers.

Lorenz Hart (*Hulton Picture Library*).

By 1919, Richard Rodgers, a precocious sixteen, was about to write music for his brother's Social and Athletic Club concert. The search for a lyricist led from friend to friend in the tight little Upper West Side society and finally arrived at Lorenz Hart.

Rodgers and Hart met at the Hart home where, we need not doubt, Frieda was hovering with nourishing food. It was Hart's appearance that made the first impact on Rodgers: 'The total man was hardly more than five feet tall. He wore frayed carpet slippers, a pair of tuxedo trousers, an undershirt and a nondescript jacket. His hair was unbrushed, and he obviously hadn't had a shave for a couple of days . . . but that first look was misleading for it missed the soft brown eyes, the straight nose, the good mouth, the even teeth and the strong chin. Feature for feature he had a handsome face, but it was set in a head that was a bit too large for his body, and gave him a slightly gnomelike appearance.' Hart did not record his impression of the sixteen-year-old composer, but, as soon as he heard his music on the family upright piano, he paid him the compliment of taking him seriously. They shared enthusiasms, compared favourites, raved about Wodehouse and Bolton and Kern, the innovators of the day, and decided there and then to work together. Their score for the Akron Club revue was a success and they grew ambitious. They saw commercial possibilities in one song – 'Venus'. Taking advantage of an acquaintance with Dorothy Fields, daughter of the comedian-producer, Lew Fields, they – or rather Rodgers – auditioned for the great man. It was appropriate that, at their first professional audition, Hart did not show up. It was a pattern he was to pursue for the rest of his life. It is interesting that the recollections of Richard Rodgers and Phillip Leavitt, who introduced Rodgers and Hart, do not coincide here – Leavitt remembers accompanying both to Fields' house in Far Rockaway; Rodgers recalls going alone. It was not 'Venus' which appealed to Fields, but another song, 'Any Old Place With You'. He bought it. He incorporated it in his current Broadway Show, *A Lonely Romeo*. The song was published – the first Rodgers and Hart number to be published. Their first hit; and the first appearance in sheet music of the unmistakable rhyming signature of Lorenz Milton Hart: 'Portugal' with 'court you gal'; 'Corner ya' with 'California'; and calling each 'dude a pest' in Budapest.

The first Rodgers and Hart score for Broadway was not a Rodgers and Hart score. Commissioned by Lew Fields to write *Poor Little Ritz Girl* for reasons of convenience and economy, the fledgling collaborators set off for its Boston opening. Rodgers arrived, meticulously, on time. Hart, his small frame underlooked in the top bunk of a sleeping coach, had been shunted away into the train-yards. He just made the theatre for a triumphant opening. The triumph was not repeated in New York where the nearest and dearest of the Rodgers and Harts arrived with plenty of time to scan their programmes, and to learn that the work of their prodigies had been largely replaced by the 'interpolations' of Sigmund Romberg and Alex Gerber. Fields had merely followed the old Broadway maxim – 'if something is wrong change everything'.

Between 1920 and 1925, the great new Broadway team of Rodgers and Hart was only represented on Broadway by one show, *The Melody Man* (1924); and neither was happy about it. They collaborated on more university shows, on a straight play flop, and on a musical comedy *Dear Enemy* for which they could find everything but the money. In the case of the straight play flop, Poppa Hart was soliciting $1,000 from a fledgling impresario, Billy Rose (another smaller than average character) whose ambitions as a lyricist had already been furthered by collaboration with Hart who acted as a 'ghost'. Desperately frustrated, Rodgers was contemplating a future as a salesman of babies' underwear. Hart was chomping at the bit and chomping too on the large, if inexpensive, cigar which drooped permanently from his mouth. Each man's neurasthenia fed the other's; but a more promising diet was just around the corner. It arrived in the form of a telephone call in the spring of 1925. The cadet branch of the Theatre Guild was planning a revue to raise money to buy tapestries for the Guild's new theatre. Sketchwriters they had; lyric writers they had; a composer they lacked. A first approach found Rodgers unexcited. It sounded like yet another amateur show. His ambition tempted by babies' underwear, Rodgers had failed to hear the magic words 'Theatre Guild'. Once they realised who they were working for, Rodgers and Hart leapt on board. With them they brought 'Manhattan', which they had been auditioning unsuccessfully for years all over that very island, and 'Sentimental Me' – an early example of the fascination which unrequited, out-of-the-question love exercised for Larry Hart and which he expressed in lines like 'Love is much more painful than it looks'.

There was no unhappiness in the reception of *Garrick Gaieties*. Drenched with sweat from conducting the first performance, Rodgers rushed backstage to see Hart jumping up and down yelling 'It's going to run a year! It's going to run a year!' But it could not. They were due to give only one more performance. However, the Guild was reckoning without young Mr Rodgers, a child who was the determined father of a man if ever there was one. The show promoted itself from a one-Sunday engagement to a repeat; from the repeat to a series of matinées; from the series of matinées to a regular run which replaced the Lunts, by then running out of steam in Molnar's *The Guardsman*. There was some criticism of Hart's lyrics. In the *New York World* Alexander Woollcott noted that they were 'rich in sprightly elaborate rhymes and suffer only from the not unimportant qualification that they do not sing well.' Woollcott's reservation did not stop 'Manhattan' being singable for over

50 years. As Oscar Hammerstein has said, the essence of Rodgers and Hart's work together was its youth. 'They were a couple of New York kids, products of their own town and time.'

Suddenly that town was wide open to them. Everyone in it had time for them. They could write new shows. They could dust off their old rejects. In the first of these, *Dear Enemy* became *Dearest Enemy* for Broadway. In it another song perpetuates the theme from the heart of Hart – 'no one is ever going to love me.' He could hardly write that in his arms it was adorable without bemoaning the fact that it was deplorable that his love never was there. As yet the defeatism was lightly stated. Champagne was sparkling, the morning after was hardly a premonition – not enough to disturb adolescent hopes; but this adolescent was nearly 30 years old.

To set *Dearest Enemy* in its age group, it opened in 1925 the same week as *No, No, Nanette, Sunny* and *The Vagabond King*. The 'kids' arrived precociously on Broadway alongside Vincent Youmans, Irving Caesar, Rudolf Friml, Jerome Kern, Otto Harbach and Oscar Hammerstein II. Left to themselves they were never content to accept the traditional limits of musical comedy. Looking at it with hindsight it may be difficult to see subsequent shows – *Peggy Ann, A Connecticut Yankee* or *Chee Chee* – as trail-blazers; but for a twenties audience it was a new experience to be exposed to a plot based on Freudian dreams and fantasies, on a Mark Twain classic, or, most outrageously and least successfully, on the predicament of a potential eunuch. In the main, the mood of the songs was bright and brash and escapist.

Hart could happily compare arms which were martial to a cheek which was partial to a face. But his personal counterpoint of angst remained; and reminded him to keep to himself and weep to himself because,

> This funny world
> Can turn right around
> And forget you.

Still, he could sing that there was no one to care for him and that,

> Life is a loveless tale
> For a ship without a sail.

Innovation sometimes took the boys too far. *Chee Chee*, based on a novel called *The Son of the Grand Eunuch*, was about a man with an understandable reluctance to go through the painful process of qualifying for his father's grand but restricted function. To give him his due, Rodgers hated the idea; though not as much as the Irish critic, St

John Ervine, who wrote, 'The price of a stall for the first performance of *Chee Chee* was eleven dollars. That was exactly eleven dollars too much.' *America's Sweetheart* also attracted its critics – notably Dorothy Parker. She did not confine her scorn to the creators. She also savaged the leading lady: '. . . and there is, besides, Jeanne Aubert, whose husband, if you can believe the papers, recently pled, through the French courts, that he be allowed to restrain his wife from appearing on the stage. Professional or not, the man is a dramatic critic.'

As their professional lives grew busier, their personal goals began to differ. Rodgers, business-like, organised and energetic, grew more business-like, organised and energetic. He moved into his own smart quarters; he looked for girls. He sought a wife. He negotiated publishing deals. He set up shows. Above all, he led Hart to the piano and when he got him there blandished him with seductive tunes. This was the surest way to interest Hart, always restless, jumping about beside the upright over which he could hardly see – then, at last, at the sound of an alluring theme, writing furiously. Hart was not looking for work and only at Rodgers' insistence for words. He was certainly not looking for girls or a wife. He was looking for fun in parties and speakeasies, always with the dentist-agent-pimp Bender at his elbow.

Yet their work, when Rodgers persuaded Hart to get down to it, prospered as long as unsympathetic impresarios did not thwart them. Out of favour were Jack Hulbert, who imported them to England to write *Lido Lady*, which they despised, and Ziegfeld, who crossed them double. On the first occasion, for *Betsy*, Belle Baker, the leading lady, was dissatisfied with her Rodgers and Hart song, 'This Funny World'. Irving Berlin had written for her before. She asked him to do so again. He produced 'Blue Skies' on the day of the opening and it was inserted without Rodgers' or Hart's knowledge, let alone consent. It was the one certain smash hit of their show and Berlin stood to acknowledge the encores in the, to them, unpardonable spotlight which Ziegfeld had provided. Even the amiable Hart did not speak to Miss Baker for several years. Rodgers and Hart set off for Europe and a more congenial and enlightened impresario, C. B. Cochran. The show was to be a revue, *One Dam Thing After Another*. Taking a weekend off in Paris they were hurrying back from Versailles with two girls in a taxi. The taxi screeched to a halt narrowly avoiding a crash. 'My heart stood still!' said one of the girls. It was typical of the collaboration that Hart yelled, 'What a title!' and that the methodical Rodgers made a note of it. Back in London he produced a tune for Hart who had already forgotten the phrase, but completed the lyric in an hour. When the show opened, it failed to draw the town; but 'My Heart Stood Still' became the Prince of Wales' favourite song. Social circles were beginning to spin fast for Rodgers and he had been singing it at private parties before the opening.

Even the Prince's favour would not have helped had he not had to sing it painstakingly to a band leader at the Royal Western Yacht Club, Plymouth, who had never heard of it. It became THE SONG THE PRINCE LIKED in the headlines; the second instance of royal song-plugging in the twenties (the first was Lady Mountbatten's crusade for the Gershwins' 'The Man I Love', which was equally successful).

By the late twenties exuberance and indulgence, wild schemes and bankruptcy, amours and, paradoxically, devotion to his wife, and, finally, cancer, were taking their toll of Lorenz Hart's father's stout but redoubtable frame. Though Lorenz Milton had moved the family more comfortably to Central Park West and though he made his father an allowance of $250 a week, a lift to the penthouse failed to conserve his father's health. The money simply fuelled his irresponsible ventures. When he died in 1928 Larry Hart and his brother Teddy were at his bedside. He told them that he would die that night but that they were not to disturb their mother. 'Let her sleep, she doesn't have to know until morning.' His final words were, 'I haven't missed a thing.' After his death, the crowded hospitable house remained crowded and hospitable and Frieda Hart exerted some restraining influence on her devoted son, at least until he had packed her safely off to bed.

Present Arms, *Spring is Here*, *Heads Up*, *She's My Baby* and *Simple Simon*, their shows for the late twenties, represent routine Rodgers and Hart, sprinkled with vintage songs. Of the two vintage songs in *Simple Simon* (1930), one came late and the other escaped early. The song writers had been persuaded to work for Ziegfeld again only because of the prospect of writing for the comedian, Ed Wynn. 'Dancing on the Ceiling' was anathema to Ziegfeld. He wanted it out and out it went. He harangued his writers with all the sensitivity of a born impresario. 'Why can't you fellows write an ordinary song?' he shouted. 'Why are you always so fancy-shmancy?' They responded with 'Ten Cents a Dance' and set off for England to offer 'Dancing on the Ceiling' to Cochran for Jessie Matthews in *Evergreen*.

The Depression which sent Wall Street businessmen jumping off tall buildings sent Rodgers and Hart scurrying to one-storey Hollywood. It was hard to find a solvent producer on Broadway; but the movie companies had money to fling around and large sums found their way into, and even more speedily out of, Lorenz Hart's numerous pockets. It was a strange irony that while Wall Street was straitened the beloved dwarf should be capering in money. Wall Street suicides leapt to their destruction as Hart started to drown himself slowly in a sea of (now legal) liquor. The alcohol had never been hard to come by for Hart and his circle; but with the end of Prohibition the ingredients became safer, consumption increased and parties were more abandoned. Rodgers and Hart worked on *Love Me Tonight* for Maurice Chevalier and Jeanette

MacDonald, on *Hallelujah, I'm a Bum!* for Al Jolson. They wrote for *The Phantom President* with George M. Cohan and on *Mississippi* for Bing Crosby. Rodgers hated the atmosphere of Hollywood. Hart embraced it enthusiastically, taking a large house and filling it first with family — headed by Frieda — and then with friends. Frieda was once asked if the friends were not sometimes too much. 'Oh no,' she said, 'except', she reflected, 'one time, ven Paul Viteman came mit his whole band.' Her son picked up other people's bills all over Hollywood and lavished gold and silver presents indiscriminately; but especially on the Rocky twins, identical Norwegian dancers procured by the ever-present Bender. He sat at the feet of Jean Malin, the smartest drag act in the town; and he rarely stopped partying until it was time to turn out a lyric for shooting at seven the next morning. There is more than a suggestion of seven o'clock shadow about his first three atempts to find a lyric for the Rodgers tune that was later to become 'Blue Moon'. It only achieved its successful lyric some months later when Hart was back in New York and an enterprising music publisher asked for a version which was more immediately accessible. It was one of Rodgers and Hart's biggest sellers. It remained Hart's least favourite lyric; perhaps because the publisher suggested a change which resolved the chorus from the archetypal Hart phrase 'Without a love of my own', to the more optimistic 'Now I'm no longer alone'.

Hart and Rodgers next attacked Broadway in 1935. Their most brilliant five years began badly. Blandished by Billy Rose they wrote the songs for *Jumbo* — a circus extravaganza large enough to swamp the score. About this time, one contemporary lyricist said, 'Larry Hart can rhyme anything and does.' A later wit has suggested that above his bed hung a sampler with the rubric, 'Prepare to make thy metre.' In fact, through this period, bed and board at the Hart household were presided over by one Mary Campbell. By 1937, when she was interviewed by the *New York World Telegram*, Mary Campbell had coddled and bullied the surviving Harts — Frieda, Lorenz and Teddy — for nineteen years. She blamed Bender for bringing Lorenz home late; she blamed the late Hart senior for 'turning her to drink' (one rye highball which made her sleepy); she blamed Tyrone Power for raiding her icebox; and she trounced a French film star who failed to give her a tip by running after him and giving him a quarter. Could it have been Maurice Chevalier? Josephine Baker incurred her most memorable wrath. Miss Baker, a black girl from St Louis, long transplanted to France, had requested, '*Donnez-moi une tasse de café au lait, s'il vous plait.*' 'Honey,' replied Mary, 'talk out of your mouth, like you was born.'

Their great shows in the thirties included *On Your Toes*, which bravely invested in an unknown, youthful cast and a plot built around a vaudeville song and dance man devising a ballet for a classical company;

Babes in Arms; *I'd Rather Be Right*, an unhappy mistake which reunited Rodgers and Hart with George M. Cohan; *I Married an Angel*, a fantasy lifted from an idea they had had in Hollywood; *The Boys from Syracuse*, a risky but successful attempt to lift Shakespeare and put him down on Broadway, exploiting brother Teddy Hart's resemblance to another comic, Jimmy Savo; *Too Many Girls* – youth again; and *Higher and Higher*, a 1940 attempt to repeat the formula of *On Your Toes* without the same ingredients. They added a performing seal who stole the show and attracted most of the first-nighters' interest – especially a Frenchwoman who kept admiring 'zee phoque' in a loud voice which distracted fanatically phonetic Americans. Coincidentally, from this period comes one of his most arresting images:

> When love congeals
> It soon reveals
> The faint aroma of performing seals
> The double crossing of a pair of heels . . .

And side by side by these sad, beautiful lyrics, bound into the fragile, sometimes witty, books which framed them, sat the simple love lyrics, 'There's a Small Hotel', 'This Can't Be Love' and 'Where or When'; and the bright, bouncing, sassy, sophisticated rhyme-spinning, comedy numbers, 'Too Good for the Average Man', 'Johnny One-Note' and 'The Lady is a Tramp'.

Joshua Logan, who directed *I Married an Angel*, has handed down a first-hand account of the joys and the battles, the scares and the scars of working with Hart at this time. His initiation as director of *I Married an Angel* was to be despatched to Atlantic City by a stern, unsmiling Rodgers. His mission was to extract from Hart the second act, which he was showing no inclination to write. Hart had elevated the writer's block to a fine art and though, as Logan says, 'he had a still unmatched flair for telling jokes in rhyme gracefully, then being able to switch quickly into poignant poetry', on this occasion he was unable to persuade him to do either. By the end of the week they had played a lot of cards, smoked a lot of cigars, drunk a lot of drink and although Hart had made occasional references to 'the principal' – it was also his habit to refer to Rodgers as 'the schoolmaster' or 'the General' – 'a certain five-foot-eight character back home with a sour-apple face' – the threat had comfortably receded. Hart's charm defeated the work-hungry Logan; and when they got into the train to come home he meekly accepted a packet of scribbles which, when he handed them over to the unsurprised Rodgers, he realised were Hart's illegible, last-ditch stratagem to avoid work. The solution was two nights of midnight oil with the schoolmaster in charge – he and Hart pacing and Logan scribbling as he tried to keep up with their invention. What shocked Logan was the suggestion that in a play set firmly in old Budapest he found himself suddenly hurtled by Hart into a sequence set in New York's Radio City music hall. 'It's a divertissement,' the temporarily elated Hart assured him. 'We can't expect an audience to stay in Budapest all night.' 'How do we explain it?' Rodgers completed the lesson in escapist musical craftsmanship. 'The less you explain, the happier the audience are. Let's just do it.' 'Okay,' said Logan, defeated, 'but you'd better do it in the verse.' They did:

> You've got to come to New York,
> It would be such a pity
> For anyone to go through life
> Without seeing Roxy City . . .

With similar lack of logic, Hart wanted the number to involve the ballerina, Zorina, dancing a Balanchine ballet against a surrealist Dali-esque backdrop. Salvador Dali was about to take New York by storm when the innocent Logan, confronted by these beguiling madmen, asked what surrealism had to do with Radio City music hall? Hart's answer was short and to the point: 'Nothing, why?'

'Then why do you want it in the show?' The cigar did not even need to leave the corner of Hart's lower lip. 'So Zorina can dance and Balanchine can fry Dali's ass. What the hell are you trying to do? Make this Ibsen?'

Logan records another vivid incident during dress rehearsals in New Haven.

'Come with me . . .'

The irresistible invitation to the Roxy music hall continued, but the singer added the word 'now':

'Now, come with me.'

A tiny but vociferous windmill exploded at the back of the theatre.

'No, *now* – singers! *She's* a now-singer. Did you hear how she began my chorus? It's "Come with me", and she began "*Now* come with me!" No "*now*" – singers!'

Pacified by the apologetic soubrette the tiny windmill clambered on to the stage to guard against further 'nows' and transformed himself into a sleeping cherub, a diminutive caryatid supporting one arch of the proscenium. Time passed and Logan was drawing Walter Slezak's attention to the beauty of the set. Slezak agreed but found fault with the symmetry. 'What it needs', he said, 'is another little Lorenz Hart asleep on the other side.' The show was a hit, divertissement, asymmetry and all; and the critic, Brookes Atkinson, found the perfect epitaph for Hart and Rodgers: '. . . musical comedy has met its masters.'

They may not together have been the men to advance the cause of serious music drama. Hart's mission and his bequest were the introduction of originality, invention, literacy and wit. His last years, the years of decline, began with *Pal Joey*, which was produced in 1940. Ironically, it was perhaps Rodgers and Hart's most considerable, most daring show. It was based on a character in John O'Hara's short stories – a heel who hung around small clubs talking big – a character Hart could recognise and with whom he could sympathise. His entourage was full of these men.

'Bewitched, Bothered and Bewildered' is a litany for a witty, mature woman waking up to the fact that she's in love with a heel. According to Joshua Logan, Hart took a private delight in slipping *double-entendres* past the censorious.

> He's a laugh, but I love it
> Because the laugh's *on* me!

'Zip' punctured the pretensions of the intellectual stripper, Gipsy Rose Lee.

> Zip, I was reading Schopenhauer last night,
> Zip! and I think that Schopenhauer was right.

The whole score gleams with a hard realism which was a new departure in 1940. The press was not so sure. The *New York Times* viewed the subject-matter with distaste. 'Can you', its critic enquired, 'draw sweet water from a foul well?' Some ten years later, the same critic reviewed a revival of *Pal Joey*. This time he found that it 'renewed his confidence in the theatre . . . no one is likely to be impervious to the liveliness and versatility of the score and the easy perfection of the lyrics.'

The news came too late to be of much comfort to Lorenz Milton Hart; he had drunk himself to death hard upon the earlier rejection. One other show, *By Jupiter*, had some success; but the disappointment over *Pal Joey* led to further bouts of irresponsibility. Rodgers tried to persuade him to collaborate on *Green Grow the Lilacs*, the Lynn Riggs play which the Theatre Guild had produced and which they now wanted to turn into a musical. Hart could not see it. Perhaps he was right, but his decision drove Rodgers to Hammerstein and together they created *Away We Go!* or, as it arrived in New York, *Oklahoma!*. The wide open spaces were not for Lorenz Hart.

Freeloaders continued to crowd his apartment and cushion his life. On one occasion Hart invited a friend to dinner. The man enquired, 'About seven?' 'Hell!' said Hart, 'bring as many people as you like!' To a very small extent, his mother had exercised a restraining influence. When she died in 1943 his unhappiness built to hysteria. He returned from the funeral to a macabre wake, saying, 'There doesn't seem to be any reason for Uncle Willie to go home.' Uncle Willie was 92. Six months later, Uncle Willie did, indeed, make the journey to the graveyard again; but the funeral this time was Lorenz Hart's. After the triumphant first night of *Oklahoma!*, during which Hart lavished his generous congratulations on Rodgers and Hammerstein, Hammerstein went off to mount *Carmen Jones*, his long planned black version of *Carmen*. Rodgers threw Hart a lifeline, staging a revival of *A Connecticut Yankee*. By now, Hart had been admitted to hospital several times to dry out; but there was the extra incentive to work again, in that Vivienne Segal, his favourite singer, who had had an enormous success in *Pal Joey*, would be playing Morgan le Fay. There were new songs to write for her including the classic comedy number, 'To Keep My Love Alive'. The therapy did not provide a cure. Rodgers, as he had to do in some cases in *By Jupiter* and *Pal Joey*, had to finish some of the lyrics. He is credited with a couplet sung for a time in 'Zip':

Zip!
English people don't say 'clerk', they say 'clark',
Zip!
Anybody who says 'clark' is a 'jark'!

At the out-of-town tryout in Philadelphia, Hart was a sorrowful mess. On the Broadway first night, elaborate plans were made to keep him under control – if necessary out of the theatre. It was a cold, wet night and Hart had lost his overcoat once again. He had lost three in Philadelphia, hastily replacing them from a children's outfitters. He prowled the back of the orchestra and tried to sing along with his favourite singer. Finally, he was ejected from his own theatre. He disappeared into the damp, chill night and when he reappeared some days later he was admitted to Doctor's Hospital. He never recovered. He left a devoted brother and sister-in-law and the dangerous Bender who, his meal ticket finally cashed, faded into the shadows. When two biographers – Samuel Marx and Jan Clayton – asked Howard Dietz in 1975 if Bender was still alive, Dietz replied succinctly, 'Doc Bender was never alive.'

It was L. S. Lowry who said that a bachelor lives like a king and dies like a beggar. At least Lorenz Milton Hart left a legacy of dancing words. His last sentence is said to have been, 'What have I lived for?'

5

OSCAR HAMMERSTEIN II

'The Time of Your Life is Today'

Lorenz Hart's sister-in-law, Dorothy, has recorded a poignant moment during the handing on of the lyrical baton from Hart to Hammerstein, successive collaborators with Richard Rodgers. In Philadelphia, Hammerstein was trying out *Carmen Jones*. Rodgers and Hart were reviving *A Connecticut Yankee*. Hart was in bad shape. 'When we ran into Dick Rodgers in the lobby of the hotel,' Mrs Hart reports, 'Larry seemed fearful . . . he was obviously not up to the half a dozen new songs that were needed. After Larry and I talked to Oscar Hammerstein, I went to my room in tears. The contrast between the dignified Hammerstein, who had replaced Larry as Rodgers' collaborator, and Larry's pathetic demeanour, appeared to penetrate even Larry's befuddled mind. He seemed to cringe.'

Hammerstein's stance and philosophy had been hatched some 40 years earlier and honed over the ensuing decades with experiences both triumphant and bitter. His origins were a rare combination of the respectable and the theatrical. His father, William Hammerstein, who erred on the side of respectability, managed the Hammerstein's Victoria Theatre; but it was not his creation. That was the work of Grandfather Hammerstein who unquestionably redressed the balance towards theatricality. The shadow that looms largest down the generations of Hammersteins ('The Hammerstein family is to the American theatre what the Adams family is to American politics, and is equally worth the study,' Clifton Fadiman has written) is that of the creator of the dynasty, Oscar Hammerstein I.

At the age of twelve in Stettin Oscar I became addicted to opera. He never discovered a cure. The malady racked him through adolescence, and drove him from home. He sold his violin to get to Hamburg, New England and finally New York. His determination to foster the virus saw him through a year as a cigar maker at two dollars a week and then inspired him to invent a machine for the creation of cigars of uniform

Oscar Hammerstein II (*R*) with Richard Rodgers (*Hulton Picture Library*).

size. Marriage did not abate the fever and indeed his wife, Rose, a unique woman, encouraged him to invest in theatres. He wrote, he composed, he invested, he leased and he bought. Rose produced four sons and died. Hammerstein's grief, like all his emotions, was operatic, but in this case the aria was short. His obsession revived him and he started to build an opera house in the unlikely neighbourhood of Harlem. The Apollo still stands as one of his monuments. When the enterprise looked like failing, his answer was to do the same thing again on the East Side. He called it The Columbus. It prospered. Then, suddenly and surprisingly, so did his first theatre. He wrote, fought, boasted and all the time he built and expanded, throwing up operatic castles with the prodigality of a Ludwig of Bavaria on Broadway. He took his cautious sons into business and, rather than live at home with his new wife and daughters, he moved into his theatres – surrounded by the clutter of his art, his commerce, his litigation and his dust – and stood always in their foyers, wearing his top hat. ('Why do you wear it indoors, Mr Hammerstein?' 'Madam, I sleep in it.')

Above all, he fought the Metropolitan Opera in New York and Covent Garden in London, where he built another rival opera house. Combat was in his blood and bankruptcy always on the cards. To one creditor he wrote, 'Sir, I am in receipt of your letter which is now before me, and in a few minutes will be behind me. Respectfully yours, Oscar Hammerstein.'

For a grandson he was a heavy responsibility, especially as Oscar Hammerstein II did not encounter the legend that was Oscar I until he was seven. At that age, he was too shy to raise his eyes to meet those of his grandfather. His biographer, Hugh Fordin, quotes him as saying, 'I couldn't understand why he wasn't a pain in the neck to everyone as he was to me.' He was certainly a pain to Oscar II's father, William, in his administration of the Victoria Theatre. William hated going to his work. He disliked singers, actors and theatres; but he ran the Victoria at a large enough profit for his father to make regular raids whenever he felt like financing another grandiose opera scheme. The passion for the musical stage, if not for business, had skipped a generation. In 1902, still at the age of seven, Oscar Hammerstein II saw his first comic opera, *The Fisher Maiden*. The fascination never deserted him; but it bred severe misgivings in his father. Oscar I financed his New Manhattan Opera House with money from William's Victoria. Asked by a friend what he was opening with, he said, 'With debts.' His policy of luring Melchior, Tetrazzini, McCormack, Trentini, Calvé and Mary Garden forced the Met to throw in Caruso three nights a week. Then they suggested lunch.

Oscar Hammerstein I (*Hulton Picture Library*).

Hammerstein declined: 'Gentlemen, I am not hungry.' However, his funds ran out; but just before they did, the Met, unaware of his plight, made him an offer he could not refuse – $1,250,000. He set off to London to build his opera house at the end of Kingsway. 'Pleased to meet you, King,' he hailed King George V.

Oscar Hammerstein II's mother died in 1910 and his father married her sister, a lady with 'King George' tattooed on one arm and 'The Prince of Wales' on the other. The sadness the boy felt was deep, but the comfortable, untheatrical, middle-class life continued until his father rebelled against another of Oscar I's raids on the treasury of the Victoria. William resigned and stayed at home. It was a year of tragedy. Hardly had William Hammerstein, smarting under his father's behaviour, made Oscar II promise that he would become a lawyer and never enter the theatre, and no sooner had he demanded that his impresario brother, Arthur Hammerstein, swear that he would never encourage Oscar II towards show business, than he died of Bright's disease. The old man, now 67 and coming to the end of his ability to indulge his grand obsession, lost three of his four sons in the course of a year. Oscar II saw him alone for five minutes. They said nothing. It was the longest that grandfather and grandson had ever spent together.

As Oscar II read law at Columbia, his feelings for the theatre grew through college shows. He wrote and he acted. He was a contemporary of Lorenz Hart who reviewed him favourably in the school magazine: 'He proved to be thoroughly original and distinctly funny, and demonstrated his ability to "put over" a song.' At the same time, he met Richard Rodgers, the fourteen-year-old brother of a classmate. Hammerstein, the star, was gracious to Rodgers, the novice. In 1919 he was to collaborate with Rodgers on a song, 'Only Room for One More'. It was 24 years before they wrote together again.

In 1917, still studying law, he was rejected by the army and nearly rejected by his future father-in-law who, when he sought his daughter's hand in marriage, asked sternly if he was a virgin. Oscar II admitted that he was. 'You mean you're going to practise on my daughter?!' By persuasion rather than practice, Hammerstein swept away the objections, but decided that a career as a law student would not enable him to support a wife. He was determined to be a husband and determined to go into the theatre. He set aside his promise to his father and sought out his Uncle Arthur – now a successful producer of operetta, notably Victor Herbert's *Naughty Marietta* and Friml's *The Firefly*. Oscar II applied for a job. Uncle Arthur had not forgotten his promise to his brother. 'How can I face the memory of your father?' he demanded operatically. Oscar II switched on his legal eloquence. Uncle Arthur capitulated. At last Oscar II was allowed to assist the stage management for twenty dollars a week. The show was called *You're in*

Love and Broadway's newest assistant stage manager was married on 22 August, 1917, to Myra Finn. Hammerstein had two children by his first wife, but the marriage was not happy. Myra Hammerstein was selfish rather than supportive. Her interest in her husband's work was soon replaced by her interest in her social life. Hammerstein's determination to master every aspect of his craft left him little time to develop the craft of marriage. It was not easy to be at home on nights when he was stage managing a show, and on one occasion playing a stage manager in it, as well as auditioning, rehearsing, watching in the wings or from the back of the stalls, conniving to write extra verses for an opening chorus, and writing a play of his own. It was called *The Light*. It played seven performances outside New York. He always referred to it as *The Light That Failed*.

Oscar I attended the out-of-town opening but by now he was racked by illness and melancholy. He died in August 1919. The funeral was of appropriate magnificence. The obituaries were suitably grandiloquent. His death affected his grandson more profoundly than he had anticipated. He has said that he felt a 'posthumous victim of his grandfather's charm . . . it is ironic and sad . . . that I did not begin to understand or like my grandfather until the day of his death. But he was a strange man and so, perhaps, am I.'

Getting on with his own life, Oscar II was deep into his apprenticeship. He was to be the greatest force for change in the musical theatre. He maintained that dramatic construction was important, that characters should be three-dimensional, that songs should be carefully integrated into the plot – all the saws trotted out by every student and most practitioners of the musical form since *Oklahoma!* and some before. That he was ever to achieve this insight is the more remarkable, given the list of titles of the early plays and musicals on which he worked: *Furs and Frills, Sometime, Somebody's Sweetheart, Joan of Arkansaw* (later *Always You*), *Tickle Me, Daffy Dill, Queen O'Hearts, Wildflower, Mary Jane McKane, Gypsy Jim* and *New Toys*, subtitled 'a comic tragedy of married life after the baby arrives'.

The mentor who made manifest the message of plot, character and the integration of songs and jokes, which Hammerstein had instinctively felt, was Otto Harbach, a successful book and lyric writer who was twenty years older than his collaborator. 'Playgoers follow the plot' became Hammerstein's maxim and, if hindsight suggests that it was some years before he could be seen to be following it himself, then hindsight knows little of the naïve conventions of the musical stage in the twenties. In such a silly world he was trail-blazing. In 1924, Uncle Arthur sent Harbach and Hammerstein to Canada on a wild goose chase, to research an ice carnival rumoured to be held annually in Quebec. Uncle Arthur, who had a weakness for majestic effects, thought that the nightly melting of an enormous palace of ice, lit by flaming torches, might bring in the customers. Unfortunately, no such rite existed in Quebec; but Uncle Arthur was not to be disappointed and, rather than waste their expenses-paid stay at the Château Frontenac, the diligent bookwriters assembled enough local colour to come up with *Rose Marie*, in which there was no melting ice palace, but Mounties, redskins, a totem dance, the 'Indian Love Call' – and above all – a murder. Sophisticated New Yorkers laughed when they heard that this new Hammerstein show would feature something so distasteful. They were used to murder from the critics but not on the musical stage. A programme note proudly told the audience that 'the musical numbers of this play are such an integral part of the action that we do not think we should list them as separate episodes.' (Four years later, in 1928, Rodgers and Hart added a similar note to the programme of *Chee Chee*, so the idea was obviously catching on. Unfortunately, as *Chee Chee* only ran for 31 performances to *Rose Marie's* 557, the formula proved not to be foolproof.) *Rose Marie* brought Oscar Hammerstein his first big success and a justification for his growing ambition to develop the musical play. Economic pressures, blinkered producers, exasperating comedians and the general climate of the theatre were to produce temporary backslidings, but Hammerstein pursued this grail until the forties, when he saw it shining in his grasp with *Oklahoma!*. (The London production of *Rose Marie* also brought him the bonus of hearing an English rose auditioning for understudy to Edith Day ignoring the 'oo-oo-oo-oo' of 'Indian Love Call' and caroling, 'When I'm calling you, double O, double O . . .' These English auditions seem to be an occupational hazard or perhaps occupational reward for Americans bringing their shows to Britain. The Gershwins could swap two stories for Hammerstein's one. First there was the girl who sang:

> You say eyether and I say eyether,
> You say nyther and I say nyther;
> Eyether, eyether, nyther, nyther –
> Let's call the whole thing off . . .

which seems a pity in the face of such unanimity. The second girl was more musical. Instead of singing 'Do, Do, Do', she sang 'Doh! Doh! Doh!' under the impression that the composer and lyricist were referring to the first note of the scale.)

When Hammerstein returned from Europe in 1925, it was time at last to work with Jerome Kern. He already had Herbert Stothart, Rudolf Friml and Vincent Youmans under his belt. Romberg and Rodgers lay in the future. Rodgers has defined Kern as a man with 'his musical roots in the fertile middle European and English school of operetta writing

. . . who amalgamated it with everything that was fresh in the American scene to give us something wonderfully new and clear . . . a giant with one foot in Europe and the other in America. Before he died he picked up the European foot and planted it squarely alongside the American one.' Kern's working association with Hammerstein was long and happy. He had a reputation for being difficult. Hammerstein insisted that he reserved his toughness for people who bluffed. 'He could be reasonably tolerant of incompetence, but he could not stand incompetence masquerading as genius. When he met cheapness of any kind he was merciless and shattering.' Arriving to discuss a project with one notoriously difficult producer, he sailed in with, 'Good morning, Mr Goodman, I'm Kern. I hear you're a son-of-a-bitch. So am I!' Hammerstein and Kern met to work on a piece called *Sunny*. The collaboration soon had to drop ideas of plot, character and integration, apart from integrating a tap solo for Miss Marilyn Miller and a speciality for a performer known as Ukelele Ike, whose contract required that he delight his public only between ten and ten fifteen. Presumably he had made arrangements to delight other audiences before and after. The songs, written in collaboration with Otto Harbach, are seamless, but hardly serious.

Four shows lay between Hammerstein and *Show Boat*, his masterpiece in this period. *A Song of the Flame* was a story of love between a young Russian nobleman and a revolutionary girl. According to one synopsis, 'they modify one another's ideas and end married in Paris.' It included a ballet 'symbolic of Russia's long winter of adversity and the first blossom of victorious ideals. At first, repulsed and chilled by the snows of bitterness, the sunlight she brings with her melts them away.' It was only a modest success. George Gershwin, in his sole collaboration with Hammerstein, wrote some of the music; but he was also and more memorably occupied with *Tip-Toes* and his *Concerto in F* at the time. *The Wild Rose* and *Golden Dawn*, dubbed *The Golden Yawn* by Walter Winchell, followed. So, of course, did *The Desert Song* which added Romberg's scalp to Hammerstein's collection of composers. A sometimes frustrating man with whom to write lyrics – 'His grudging comment on a recently finished piece of verse was often only "it fits" ' – Romberg's brave, soaring, simple and, some said, recollected tunes and his instinct for romance before comedy, all appealed to Hammerstein and their later collaboration was to produce 'When I Grow Too Old to Dream'. Like the Gershwin show which had started out of town with the obviously uncommercial title of *My Fair Lady* and arrived on Broadway as *Tell Me More*, *The Desert Song* started life as *Lady Fair*. It did not suffer its sea change until Hammerstein, making notes on a train journey, arrived at a collection of images which included a 'Blue Heaven' and 'you and I', and 'sand kissing a moonlight sky' as well as

'The Desert Song singing a lullaby'. The new title was secured.

Hammerstein has recorded the genesis of *Show Boat* – a call from Kern. ' "How would you like to do a show for Ziegfeld – *Show Boat?*" "Isn't that Edna Ferber's new book?" "Yes," Jerry said, "I haven't finished it yet but I've already bought it from Ferber. Get a copy and read it right away." "Is Ziegfeld enthusiastic?" I asked. "He doesn't know anything about it yet," said Jerry.' When Ziegfeld was let in on the secret he professed delight. He had a new theatre and he needed a big show to open it. Unfortunately, before Kern and Hammerstein were ready, he found another play, *Rio Rita*, which he liked even more. Having opened *Rio Rita* and the new house triumphantly, he began to have doubts about *Show Boat*. Where was the spectacle? Where were the girls? The gags? What was all this serious stuff about disastrous marriages, racial discrimination and doom? As Ziegfeld prevaricated, Kern and Hammerstein fretted; but they also polished. Stephen Sondheim has described the keynote of Kern's music as 'hard-won simplicity'. He argues that the tunes 'stand up now because they deal with the essentials, not the decoration, and essentials are timeless.' Hammerstein vividly describes Kern at work. 'I have seen him take off his shirt and work in his undershirt, the sweat pouring off him, forgetting completely that I was there . . . the smooth and easy undulating melodies . . . were all created in this way. Smoothness is only achieved by scraping off roughness . . .' The same was true of Hammerstein – though probably not to the extent of losing his shirt, judging by Sondheim's description of him in his introduction to Hugh Fordin's biography. 'Oscar was elegant . . . not that he was a dandy, he just always looked perfect, patrolling that delicate territory between the casual and the formal . . . in fact, I think he was nattier *out* of doors – the sweatier, the nattier.'

Both collaborators were aware that they were striving for a new stature for the musical theatre. It showed in the care that they were eventually allowed to lavish on the staging (largely because of Ziegfeld's preoccupation with other shows and his chorus girls' hairstyles); in the determination with which they fought for every indispensable line and note; in the ultimate triumph (after the first night Uncle Arthur said tearfully that he finally felt justified in breaking his promise to brother William to keep young Oscar out of the theatre); and in the number of remarkable songs with which Kern and Hammerstein managed to bind the rich, picaresque collection of events together. From the simplicity of 'Why Do I Love You?' to the dark rumblings of 'Ol' Man River', which, depending on which account you believe, was added, either at the last minute in Philadelphia because one Jules Bledsoe needed a number and B. G. de Sylva, hearing some throw-away dance music, threw in his two cents and said, 'Slow it down and give it to Bledsoe'; or because Hammerstein, realising quite late that he needed a symbolic song evocative of the Mississippi, spotted some up-tempo banjo music in the score which he felt, slowed down, would save the hard-pressed Kern from hunting for a new melody; or, according to Miss Ferber, because, quite early on, Kern turned up in her apartment one afternoon and played the song and 'I give you my word my hair stood on end, tears came to my eyes ... this was a great song.' Hammerstein always insisted this was not written as a protest song. The protest crept up on it. (He only wrote one undeniable protest song, 'I Won't Dance, Don't Ask Me ...'.) 'Can't Help Lovin' Dat Man' presages an unconscious common theme in Hammerstein's lyrical philosophy – happy female acceptance of rampant male chauvinism. In *The King and I* it crops up as a list of the dreadful things a man can do to a woman only to be forgiven the moment he says 'Something Wonderful', and it reaches its most extreme form in *Carousel*, when the heroine points out the irrelevance of 'wond'rin' ' if the man is good or bad:

He's your feller and you love him.
That's all there is to that.

These lyrics appear to suggest that women can be beaten, ignored, neglected or trampled underfoot, secure in the knowledge that any pain or humiliation they may feel will miraculously vanish the moment their man crosses the threshold and carries them off to bed, where the probability is that he will spend the next three hours boasting how he got the corn to grow high as an elephant's eye.

It is a sad irony that around this time Hammerstein's first marriage was breaking up and that one of the first Mrs Hammerstein's complaints was that he would continually come home as late as can be. An unhappy lady, she did not share his enthusiasm for his work and, as for her favours, she had for some time been sharing them with other men. By now, Hammerstein had met an attractive Australian ex-actress, Dorothy Blanchard (actress, that is, to the extent that she had once understudied Bea Lillie and also played the role of smoke on an ashtray, while Jack Buchanan sang and blew smoke rings). She was young, charming, interested – and married – but they fell in love on board ship, and her account of her disillusion with the stage as a disappointingly innocent vocation inspired another *Show Boat* lyric, 'Life Upon the Wicked Stage (ain't ever what a girl supposes)'. By the time that *Show Boat* opened and in the weeks that followed, the lovers were suffering under the strain of enforced separation. As both were married they made determined efforts not to see each other. Hammerstein had a nervous breakdown and Hugh Fordin suggests that his distress crept into a line for an unused lyric in *The New Moon*, where he wrote of 'lying alone, gazing at the sky, wondering how and why I lost a world I used to own'. By the same token, 'Lover, Come Back to Me', a song that *did* get into *The New Moon*, seems appropriate:

> You've gone away
> This aching heart of mine is singing
> . . . Ev'ry road I walk along I've walked along with you,
> No wonder I'm lonely . . .

Here the chase for examples of autobiographical lyrics in Hammerstein's work should end, but for two exceptions. It is reassuring to observe that from the moment of his second marriage he began to write sincere, unforced and charming songs about happiness in wedlock, like 'The Folks Who Live on the Hill'. And on one occasion during his later and most autobiographical show, *Allegro*, (which he wrote with Rodgers), Fordin catches him drawing on the experience of his breakdown for an emotional climax. On the whole, though, it is Oscar Hammerstein's philosophy, not the incidents of his life, which permeates his lyrics. Sondheim characterises him as 'conservative but never reactionary . . . moderate . . . a true moralist . . . he chose to use parts of himself at certain times and not at others . . .' And when he found Sondheim, under lyrical instruction and under his influence, writing lyrics about robins and larks, he encouraged him to be true to himself. 'You don't believe that stuff ', he said. 'I do!'

Oscar Hammerstein had two more successes – *Sweet Adeline* (1929) and *Music in the Air* (1932) – before entering a period of almost unrelieved failure and some unhappiness. He was unsuccessful in London, on Broadway and in California. Financial rays of light pierced the gloom. There were lucrative film contracts; some generous pay-offs for contracts reneged on by studios; and a steady royalty from his established songs which often brought in upwards of $25,000 a year. Balm to the souls of most people; but to a man born and raised in the theatre the years were bleak. It was the era when New York writers were bought and despatched to Hollywood, cash before, on and after delivery. Hammerstein enjoyed it even less than others who gathered around their swimming pools moaning into their margaritas. He discussed shows with Kern. One was a musical version of Donny Byrne's *Messer Marco Polo!*. Hammerstein posed the question, 'Here is a story laid in China about an Italian told by an Irishman. What kind of music are you going to write?' 'It'll be good Jewish music,' Kern replied, which, as Hammerstein points out, meant no phony pretentiousness, no phony pastiche, but with Kern's own music coming out of him it would be good. Unfortunately, it never happened. They produced charming songs during this period; but no *Show Boat*, no *Desert Song*, not even a *New Moon*. The Hollywood atmosphere and the enforced absence from the theatre were anathema to Hammerstein. The films on which he worked had titles like *The Night is Young*, *Champagne and Orchids* (never completed) and *Give Us this Night*. They were mostly unrewarding, though *High, Wide and Handsome* was a success with critics if not with audiences. Theatrical forays to New York at a bad time for musicals did nothing to lift the gloom. Sensing professional rejection, Hammerstein sank deeper into himself. Surprised alone in the shade of a Beverly Hills house and asked where everyone was, he sighed bitterly, 'Maybe they heard I was coming.' At home, he was not a tolerant parent; but according to Sondheim, a near-adopted son, 'His expectations were high, never higher than when his children were concerned; he was the best surrogate father one could have wished for, always encouraging, always understanding, always gentle . . . his own children fared less well . . . sometimes the irony lurched into sarcasm, and when it did the victims were more likely to be his own flesh and blood children.'

He emerged from Hollywood in 1939 at his wife's insistence. She had set up a thriving and lucrative decorator's business; but she threw it up, deciding that Hollywood was sapping Hammerstein and that it was time to bring him home to Broadway. He leapt at the chance. The return brought only trouble. He began his comeback as a producer and came up with '. . . one play that never arrived in New York and three that closed after twelve, eleven and seven nights, respectively'; not encouraging. He tried another show with Kern – *Very Warm for May*. There was nothing wrong with 'All the Things You Are'; and 'All in Fun' demonstrates his ability, when challenged, to write a lyric with the elegant, easy, graceful, bittersweet sophistication which we usually associate with Cole Porter or Lorenz Hart. Someone once asked Hammerstein why he didn't write about 'sophisticated' people. He replied, 'Ah, you mean people who live in New York penthouses. I suppose it's because they don't interest me very much.'

However good the songs in *Very Warm for May* were, a meddling producer improved on a successful show just before it came into town. He improved it out of recognition and into failure. 'Very Warm for May; not so hot for November', was the most succinct critique. Hammerstein indulged in one of the bouts of letterwriting to the critics which had been a feature of his career. 1940 found him licking his wounds on Long Island, when he heard the news that Paris had fallen to the Germans. It had a profound effect on Hammerstein, who retreated into a womb of nostalgic memories of the town to write one of his most feeling lyrics, 'The Last Time I Saw Paris'. The simplicity, the freshness, the hard-won grace of the earlier lyrics remain; but there is suddenly an added richness of detail; a closer approximation to conversational speech than in most songs Hammerstein had written before and since *Show Boat*. This was part of the process of maturing, growing more confident and more ambitious; but it was also, significantly, one of the few songs for which he wrote the words first (Kern set them later) until his collaboration with Rodgers. With Rodgers he was to show an increasing freedom and a greater ability to characterise and to be colloquial. Shortly after Hammerstein wrote 'The Last Time I Saw Paris', the Germans invaded Russia. It did not inspire 'The Last Time I Saw Moscow'; but it did produce a memorable verdict on German strategy from George S. Kauffman. 'I think', he told the Hammersteins, 'they're shooting without a script.'

The stage is set now for the arrival of Master Rodgers, whom we left, aged fourteen, on the occasion of their first collaboration. Now, in 1940, he was 38, seven years younger than Hammerstein's 45. As Hammerstein pondered an adaptation of *Carmen* for black actors (*Carmen Jones*) Rodgers and Hart were looking for a collaborator to work with them on the book of Edna Ferber's *Saratoga Trunk*. Or, at least, Rodgers was looking. He was having trouble with Hart. Hart's eyes were fixed on holidays in Mexico and on the bottoms of innumerable tequila glasses. Ira Gershwin has suggested that at about this time Rodgers arranged two dinners which Gershwin construed as an exploration of the possibility of their collaboration; but he records that he was more interested in Los Angeles and in semi-retirement. So Rodgers turned to Hammerstein.

He had doubts about Hammerstein's humour, after twenty years spent working with a man who could tell better jokes in rhyme more deftly than anyone else before or since except Porter, or perhaps Sondheim. Rodgers' first approach to Hammerstein brought a cautious response. Hammerstein would prefer to wait until it was clear that Hart would not and could not continue to work. If such circumstances arose, he promised not to let Rodgers down. When the Theatre Guild suggested a musical adaptation of Lynn Riggs' *Green Grow the Lilacs*, Hart skipped it and set off for Mexico. The way was clear for Rodgers and Hammerstein to start their partnership. A film biography of Oscar Hammerstein II should finish with the first night of *Oklahoma!*, or *Away We Go!* as it was first known. The show altered the conventions of musical plays to an even greater extent than *Show Boat*; it ran longer, and physically it was harder to get a seat. In later years Rodgers and Hammerstein had equally big successes alongside some shows which did not hit the same jackpot; but the breakthrough came with *Oklahoma!* and with it the drama. Scott Fitzgerald has said 'there are no second acts in American lives.' He said it before Rodgers and Hammerstein started their collaboration.

The list of disadvantages under which the show laboured is endless.

Lynn Riggs' play had not been very successful in the first place. Did Rodgers know how to write with anyone but Hart? Was Hammerstein washed up? Could the Theatre Guild find the money? Who wanted to be bucolic? A series of backers' auditions produced nothing. Could they afford not to bring on the girls until halfway through Act One? Worse, could they start a show with a middle-aged woman on stage, churning butter, and a solo cowboy singing in the wings? Even if he was telling the audience that it was a beautiful morning? Hindsight is an unfair advantage. The lack of enthusiasm in everyone except those intimately involved on the project – the Theatre Guild, the writers, the director, Rouben Mamoulian, the choreographer, Agnes de Mille, the largely unknown cast – continued way after the opening in New Haven. Even then, the impresario, Billy Rose, departed at the interval prophesying doom if the girls were not brought on sooner; and there were others – children of the knockers of *Rose Marie*, who, nearly twenty years later, still stated definitely that you couldn't kill people in a musical. Just before the New York opening, Hammerstein wrote to his son, 'I *know* this is a good show. I cannot believe it will not find a substantial public. There! My neck is out.' To his wife, at their country home near Doylestown, a few hours before the opening on 3 March, 1943, he said, 'I don't know what to do if they don't like this. I don't know what to do because this is the only kind of show I can write.' As it happened, the response gave him the green light to write *Carousel*, *Allegro*, *South Pacific*, *The King and I*, *Me and Juliet*, *Pipe Dream*, *Flower Drum Song* and *The Sound of Music*.)

Just before the collaboration with Rodgers he had written *Carmen Jones*. Indisputably, Bizet's music came first but, paradoxically, Hammerstein injected the same excitement and drama and colloquial speech into his lyrics that he did when writing words for Rodgers to set. The answer is that he had found two perfect vehicles for his mature talents. With *Oklahoma!* and *Carmen Jones* running alongside, Hammerstein indulged himself in one of the few bold theatrical gestures of his off-stage life. Rather like the masochist who was so thick-skinned that he never knew when he was beaten, Hammerstein took an advertisement in *Variety* listing his last five disasters and spelling out how short their runs had been.

HOLIDAY GREETINGS

OSCAR HAMMERSTEIN II

Sunny River (Six weeks at the St James Theatre, New York)
Very Warm for May (Seven weeks at the Alvin Theatre, New York)
Three Sisters (Six weeks at the Drury Lane, London)
Ball at the Savoy (Five weeks at the Drury Lane, London)
Free for All (Three weeks at the Manhattan Theatre, New York)

Then he added a final sentence:

I'VE DONE IT BEFORE AND I CAN DO IT AGAIN.

The rest of Hammerstein's life was spent in putting the lessons of dramatic song writing, which he had learnt patiently and painstakingly over a long career, into craftsmanlike practice. He had been called a 'veteran' by one critic when he was only 28; by now he had earned the title. He had the scars to prove it. But he had also a philosophy which was simple and firmly held and which informed all his work and gave it that point of view without which the craftsmanship would have remained fretwork. Rodgers wrote of him in 1967, 'His view of life was positive. He was a leader, a man willing to do battle for whatever causes he believed in. He was not naïve. He knew full well that man is not all good and that nature is not all good; yet it was his sincere belief that someone had to keep reminding people of the vast amount of good things that there are in the world.' Frequently this has led to accusations of sentimentality – 'My Favourite Things' from *The Sound of Music* is a favourite target and Roger Woddis once spiked this fondness for sentiment in a neat parody directed at the excesses of popular tabloid journalism.

> Newly-wed couples and all their relations,
> Small fluffy chickens and gentle alsations,
> Grannies of ninety performing on swings –
> These are a few of my favourite things.

The combination of nuns and children was an irresistible target for sophisticates, and perhaps to start a show in a convent is to invite comment. There used to be a convent rule that girls must never wear patent leather shoes because boys would see their underwear reflected in them – though presumably, if the girls wore patent leather underwear as well, all the boys would see reflected in their shoes would be another pair of shoes. There is no such simple way out for a librettist, given the premise of an Austrian convent and golden-haired moppets.

By a curious coincidence, Rodgers and Hammerstein were approached to write the musical version of *Pygmalion* before Lerner and Loewe, and found the subject-matter intractable, while Lerner and Loewe were invited to consider the Trapp Family Singers as dramatic material before Rodgers and Hammerstein. On receiving Lerner's wire telling him of the offer, Loewe cabled back succinctly, 'Dear boy, what do you want me to write – yodel music? Love Fritz.' The wire was seven words less laconic than the one with which he had answered a similar enquiry about making *Gone With the Wind* a musical. From the phoneticism of the spelling this cable appears to have been dictated. It ran: 'Vind not funny, Love Fritz.'

Hammerstein's principle was to approach each dramatic problem freshly and to try to solve it on its merits. He could not unlearn experience; but he refused to let it become his master.

Rodgers and Hammerstein musicals have a signature – Rodgers' autograph is musical. Cole Porter is reported to have said, 'I can always tell a Rodgers tune. There's a certain holiness about it.' Hammerstein's signature is written in his emotions. He has said, 'The longer I write the more interested I become in expressing my own true convictions and feelings in the songs I write. When I was very much younger, I thought that if ever I made all the money I needed out of musical comedy, I would then sit back and turn to straight dramatic plays in which I could say whatever I wanted to say and state my reactions to the world I live in. Later on, however, I became convinced that whatever I wanted to say could be said in songs, that I was not confined necessarily to trite or light subjects, and that since my talent and training in the writing of lyrics is far beyond my attainments in other fields of writing, I had better use this medium.'

Hart first made the lyric a subject of conversation, a thing of wit and charm; Hammerstein added another level of serious appreciation, making it the stuff of drama and a vehicle for liberal sentiments.

It is no accident that the best-known story about Hammerstein, or rather Mrs Hammerstein, albeit apocryphal, concerns the pecking order of lyric and music. Mrs Hammerstein loyally denies the story, but she is supposed to have grown irritated at a party by repeated requests for the pianist to play 'Jerome Kern's "Ol' Man River" . . . play Jerome Kern's "Ol' Man River" . . . play . . .' Finally, she snapped: 'Jerome Kern did not write "Ol' Man River". Oscar Hammerstein wrote "Ol' Man River". All Jerome Kern ever wrote was "Da Da Dee Da . . .".' Mrs Hammerstein may be correct to deny the story; but there is a poetic truth about it which says much for the underestimated role of the lyric writer.

On 7 July, 1960, Hammerstein, over whom the threat of death had hung for some months, realised that it was to come very soon. Five days later, making notes for an autobiography, he wrote: 'Today is July 12th, 1960; my birthday. I am sixty-five. This is the accepted age of retirement. I do not want to retire, am in no mood to retire . . . someday I may leave the theatre. But I couldn't walk out suddenly. I would have to linger a while and take a few last looks. I would have to blow a few fond kisses as I edged towards the stage door . . . I would have to look around and sigh, and remember a few things, a few people – no, many things, many people . . .'

With moderation and dignity, Hammerstein prepared his family and friends for his death. A month later, on 22 August, 1960, he died.

6

DOROTHY FIELDS

'The Way You Look Tonight'

Some day When I'm awf'ly low
When the world is cold,
I will feel a glow just thinking of you
The Way You Look Tonight

Four lines which contain the essence of Dorothy Fields' work, simple, direct, warm and stylish. In a world full of lady novelists, women poets and, increasingly, female playwrights, Dorothy Fields is not alone as a woman and a lyric writer; but she is way out in front. 'I'm In the Mood for Love', 'I Can't Give You Anything but Love, Baby', 'Pick Yourself Up', provide a range of romantic, graceful, amused conceits of the twenties and thirties from the pen which, 30 years later, would conjure up brash, believable, but quite different songs to suit the quite different sixties; and a defiantly modern phrase in 'Big Spender', like 'I don't pop my cork for ev'ry guy I see'.

Seven other women established themselves as lyric writers during the period in which Dorothy Fields worked; but in range and size her catalogue dwarfs theirs. Anne Caldwell's career stretched from 1905 into the twenties, including *The Night Boat, Chin, Chin* and *Tip Top.* Rida Johnson Young had three huge hits in the twenties with *Naughty Marietta, Maytime* and *Sometime.* Dorothy Donnelly wrote *The Student Prince* and *Blossom Time.* Nancy Hamilton contributed principally to revues: 'A Lovely Lazy Kind of Day' is perhaps her best-known song. Betty Comden's list of shows with Adolph Green is long and impressive. It includes *On the Town, Wonderful Town, Bells are Ringing, Do Re Mi, Applause* and *On the Twentieth Century.* Carolyn Leigh after *Wildcat, Little Me* and *How Now Dow Jones* failed to fulfil all her formidable early promise. Gretchen Cryer (*The Last Sweet Days of Isaac*) has written principally for off-Broadway. More recently than these seven, Carol Bayer Sager contributed the lyrics for *They're Playing Our Tune*, to

Dorothy Fields (*ASCAP*).

Marvin Hamlisch's music. However, none of them has written songs which have secured quite the same hold on the imagination of the public or the same admiration from fellow professionals as those of Miss Fields. How much was this due to her own keen mind, her humour and the warmth that lay behind? How much rubbed off from her contemporaries, friends of her brothers with whom she grew up – Richard Rodgers, whom she has described as her first boyfriend, Lorenz Hart, Oscar Hammerstein and Cole Porter, who gave her her first rhyming dictionary, saying, 'You've got to stop this nonsense. Why knock yourself out trying to find the right words?' And how much was inherited?

Miss Fields was born in 1904 the daughter of Lew Fields, of Weber and Fields, the famous vaudeville double-act. She had two brothers, Joseph and Herbert, who became successful playwrights, and one sister, who did not. Dorothy arrived earlier than expected in Allenhurst, New Jersey, Lew Fields' summer home. Her very birth was attended by the celebrated actor, William Collier, and a sprinkling of Shuberts who were staying with her father for the weekend. They scurried through the streets looking for a midwife and returned with one who ran the news-stand at the local railway station. It was a highly theatrical arrival and it landed Miss Fields firmly in the direct line of a thriving theatrical tradition. Although her father tried to stifle her interest in a life 'upon the wicked stage' he had little luck. In his early upbringing and in his professional art lie the seeds of the down-to-earth side of Dorothy Fields' work which she blends with her own romantic and sophisticated touch. Her work is a proficient mixture of the glamour and illusion of the theatre on one side and its professionalism and hard work on the other.

Weber and Fields were both East Side urchins whose parents had emigrated from Poland. Weber's came via Birmingham, England, and Liverpool to bring up seventeen children in half a cellar. Fields' father, whose original name was Schanfield, was a tailor who lived in comparative opulence just below Fourteenth Street, and earned $25 a week – some weeks. The two ragged scraps first met at school – PS 42 on Allen Street. They earned survival money through a variety of jobs, selling ginger snaps on 129th Street in Harlem, giving piteous impersonations of tongue-tied lads or tending street soda water fountains selling a beverage called 'gump' at one cent for half a glass, two cents a full glass, three cents a glass with cream. At the age of eight, they put on blackface-charcoal obtained from an itinerant pedlar and tried out for Tony Pastor's new theatre on Broadway. They scored less than a triumph. They assailed every theatre which would hear them, waiting hours for auditions, confronting innumerable joyless faces as they began to pipe their act, 'Here we are a jolly pair'. At nine, Weber was still working in a cigarette factory by day and, when they finally achieved a booking, at the Chatham Square Museum, Fields played so many of the performances alone that Weber, finding at the end of the week that his pay packet was one dollar fifty to Fields' six-fifty, turned his back on cigarettes forever. They toured New York; they went out on the road; and, when people grew tired of their blackface routines, the children played much the same act washing off the charcoal and donning Little Lord Fauntleroy suits of velveteen and lace, with grubby silk sashes, '. . . Here we are a jolly pair'. They boasted three separate and distinct feats at the same time, 'Dancing in unison, keeping time to the music and tearing sheets of paper in "on-trick-ate" designs.' When a rival failed with his German comedy act, the jolly pair added that string to their repertoire running the new routine up overnight, '. . . Here we are a German pair'. They toured with 'Jo Jo, the Dog-Faced Boy'; and on one occasion with a fraudulent 'Jo Jo, the Dog-Faced Boy', whom they unmasked. For six years they toured the 'Museums' of New York and the hinterland. They added an Irish song and dance, a wrestling burlesque and a boxing burlesque. Their entrances became more varied.

Here we are a coloured pair . . .
Here we are a fighting pair . . .
Here we are an Irish pair . . .

For their Irish entrance, to get an extra laugh, they held their hands ostentatiously over their Jewish noses. Much of their comedy was dredged from immigrant life in the mean streets around them, a violent exaggeration of actual experience. Their most famous sketch was their pool table scene. 'All the public wanted to see was Fields knock the hell out of me,' was how Weber defined its appeal. Fields elaborated, 'I don't know why it was, but the audiences always seemed to have a grudge against him.' Fields was the dark, slicker partner. Weber played a dumb, Dutch incompetent. It was an obstreperous energetic era, which could not always make itself understood; and they typified it.

By 1896, when they were 30, they were able to secure a theatre of their own, the Imperial Music Hall on Broadway at 29th Street. They played sketches and burlesques based on contemporary serious drama. Lillian Russell was often their leading lady and it is claimed that they originated the classic exchange, 'Who was that lady I saw you with last night?' 'That was no lady, that was my wife.'

Other confrontations in their sketches included one Sigmund Cohenski declaring, 'Better my daughter should marry a book-keeper than a hero.' 'A book-keeper? I suppose you think the pen is mightier than the sword?' 'You bet your life. Could you sign cheques with a sword?' Then there was a soldier, who had been shot. 'Where?' asked

Weber. 'In the excitement,' replied Fields. And, 'Whoever heard of a dog called Abie or Mosie?' 'Maybe he was a Kosher spaniel.'

In retrospect it is not, perhaps, surprising that, when they grew up and Lew Fields had become a Broadway producer, the three stage-wise Fields children tried to keep his hands off his old gag book. However, he continued to lapse and to return to it until finally they burnt it.

In 1902 Weber and Fields, again setting a fashion for a double act, were not talking to one another off-stage. Weber supervised the front-of-house arrangements for their joint venture, Fields controlled affairs on stage. They continued to share the same dressing room, so that the façade of friendship was preserved, and, when a rumour of trouble got out, they stood amiably together in front of a peanut-stand on 29th and Broadway for four hours to scotch it. The rift sprang from the critical reception of one of their burlesques, *A Message from Mars*. In the year Dorothy Fields was born, they split and their music hall closed its doors. Eight years later, in 1912, they tried a reunion at the new Weber and Fields Music Hall built by the Shuberts on 44th Street. Their return generated great interest and all their old in-fighting; but the demand for tickets was not what it used to be and they never played together again for New York audiences.

From now on Fields concentrated on musical comedy. In 1911 he had five separate hits running at the same time and his children had regular boxes for Saturday matinées – along with more admonitions not to think of the stage as a career. However, 'we lived in an atmosphere of comedy – jokes, blackout lines, funny routines . . .' Miss Fields was assigned to keep her father's cuttings book. Everybody in the family was expected to collect jokes for father, entering them into an enormous black ledger to which the old man would have recourse when he was planning a new show. Although theatrical stories were commonplace at the dinner table, other performers were very rarely invited home and Mrs Fields counselled her offspring, 'You children must be extra polite to strangers because your father's an actor.' The gentilities of turn-of-the-century vaudevillians are Dickensian in their vehemence.

Dorothy Fields was educated at the Benjamin Franklin School for Girls, and English, drama and basketball were her specialities. Her father frustrated her two early attempts to become an actress. On one occasion she applied for and got a job with a company in Yonkers. Unfortunately, she never received the letter of acceptance which her father high-handedly intercepted. Then in her teens she went to another producer's office. He simply searched for a telephone, called her father and said, 'Your daughter's here. Come over and fetch her home.' When she showed an inclination to write lyrics, Lew Fields was firm. 'Ladies don't write lyrics.' Falling into the family routine, she countered, 'I'm no lady, I'm your daughter.' She married early. Her first husband was a doctor and she did some teaching and worked as a laboratory technician. She contributed her obligatory poems to Franklin P. Adams' column, 'The Conning Tower'. Then a composer, J. Fred Coots, who was much in vogue in the middle twenties, suggested that they should write some songs. She did not think much of their work together; but Coots in turn introduced her to Jimmy McHugh, a song writer and plugger with Mills Music, who was to become one of her principal collaborators. McHugh's earlier songs included 'What's Become of Hinky Dinky Parley Vous?' and 'When My Sugar Walks Down the Street', but, according to Maurice Waller's biography of his father, 'Fats', many of McHugh's tunes were purchased from Waller, for down-payments of $50. Later Waller, realising the fortune he had signed away, forbade his son to play 'I Can't Give You Anything but Love, Baby', on the piano at home, and one Sunday morning, when he heard 'On the Sunny Side of the Street' on the radio, he smashed his fist through a French window in exasperation. Whatever the truth, the words in both cases are indisputably by Dorothy Fields.

However, her career as a song writer did not start auspiciously. A feature of Mills Music Catalogue at the time was the instant song, designed to achieve overnight popularity commemorating a current event. When Caruso died in 1921 they paid a writer $50 to write a song called 'They needed a song bird in heaven, So God took Caruso away ...'. A little later Valentino passed on and another creative soul (or perhaps the same one) came up with 'They needed a new star in heaven, So God took Valentino away ...'. Miss Fields was to learn her basic craft writing songs of this kind. She was given her $50 to write a number which would anticipate Ruth Elder's flight across the Atlantic. She was told to deliver a lyric about 'Our American Girl':

    ... You took a notion
    To fly cross the ocean ...

Miss Elder failed to make it, so did Miss Fields' song; but she became what she has called 'Mills Music's fifty-dollars-a-night-girl'. When songs like 'Varsity Drag' were the rage, Dorothy Fields tried a similar theme calling it 'Collegiana', crowning the lyric with an internal rhyme which made 'every pedagogue go to bed agog doing Collegiana'. McHugh then introduced Dorothy Fields to the Cotton Club in Harlem. It was the tradition to open a new show on Sunday nights. In a room packed with invited celebrities it became a gala evening. On this particular occasion, Duke Ellington and his orchestra were to make their début and Miss Fields worked away at the lyrics for which she was getting sole billing. The Broadway musicals Lew Fields was producing had become as tasteful, expensive and out of the rut as had been his burlesque shows. They included *The Girl Friend, Hit the Deck* and *A Connecticut Yankee*. At his daughter's opening, he and his wife sat at a table with the columnist, Walter Winchell. It was a family table. Miss Fields' husband, the doctor, was there; her brother Joseph and his wife; her brother, Herbert. Unfortunately, the entertainment took an unfamily turn. Halfway through the show, the leading lady – in all Miss Fields' retellings of the story she remains anonymous – suddenly interpolated three 'of the dirtiest songs you ever heard in your life'. Winchell looked at Fields. Fields looked accusingly at his daughter. 'Did you write those lyrics?' he asked, hardly able to believe his ears. Miss Fields denied authorship indignantly. Winchell despatched the anxious parent to remonstrate. The owner of the club, a man called Block, partner of the gangster Owney Madden, spurred on by Fields' threat to punch his nose, made a public announcement that the lyrics for the offending songs had not been written by Miss Fields and that the music had not been written by Mr McHugh. The next outing for Fields and McHugh was different but similarly unpleasant. McHugh had a tune which, depending on whose version of history you believe, was either his or Fats Waller's. Miss Fields, happening to eavesdrop on a young couple window-shopping outside Tiffany's, heard the boy turn to the girl and say ruefully, 'I can't give you anything but love, Lindy.' When Lindy became 'baby' the song became universal.* It was a charming thought and it fitted the tune. Moreover, it suited a situation dreamed up by Harry Delmar, a producer ambitious to establish his place in theatrical history alongside Ziegfeld, George White and Earl Carroll. At the end of 1928 Delmar was planning not his *Follies*, nor his *Scandals*, nor his *Vanities*, but his *Revels*. The show had some success; but it was not the sort of smash that starts a series. Delmar gave 'I Can't Give You Anything but Love' to two newcomers. Bert Lahr, making his Broadway début, played a Brooklyn kid sitting on a tenement stoop with his sweetheart, Patsy Kelly. After one quick chorus which included a reference to the 'diamond bracelets' which 'Woolworth doesn't sell, baby', Mr Delmar started to give his public the real thing. Back flew the curtains and the ladies of the chorus appeared showing as much of themselves as was consistent with current standards of decorum and covering what was not consistent with rubies, diamonds, opals, amethysts and sapphires; having gone to all this tasteful trouble, Mr Delmar decided after the first performance that he didn't like the song and threw it out. Six months later, another producer, Lew Leslie,

---

* Bert Lahr ascribes the genesis of the title line to Lew Brown (of De Sylva, Brown and Henderson) who he says gave it to Fields and McHugh (John Lahr: *Notes on a Cowardly Lion*).

wanted to start another tradition – *Blackbirds*, for an all-black cast. An orchestra led by the financier, Otto Kahn's son, Roger Wolfe Kahn, had accompanied Adelaide Hall in the renaissance of 'I Can't Give You Anything but Love' in a nightclub. Now Mr Leslie put it into *Blackbirds* and both song and show were promptly panned. One critic picked it out for a special attack. 'There is a sickly, puerile song called "I Can't Give You Anything but Love".' There was little initial enthusiasm but Leslie threw in a midnight show on Thursday nights and suddenly the whole enterprise became fashionable. Another hit for Adelaide Hall has dated more dramatically. 'Diga Diga Doo' deals with a 'spot I know a, Place they call Samoa, by the sea . . .'. In Samoa, by the sea, by some extra-ordinary geographical trick, 'Zulu Man' who is 'feelin' blue', hears 'his heart beat a little', which introduces the catchy chorus:

Diga diga do, diga diga doo doo,
Diga diga doo, diga doo . . .

The sketches included a black version of Elinor Glyn's 'It', and the newly chic show ran for nearly two years – 518 performances.

Miss Fields had her first stab at a book show the same year. She and her brother worked for their father on a play called appropriately *Hello, Daddy*. They got a six-months' run out of it and no surviving songs. Fields and McHugh did better with *The International Revue* in 1930. The cast, which included Gertrude Lawrence, Harry Richman, Markova, Dolin and Argentinita, could not keep the show running for more than twelve weeks; but 'Exactly Like You' and 'On the Sunny Side of the Street' are both songs which deserved to survive and did. The simplicity of Dorothy Fields' lyrics, the directness, the elegance, the perfect choice of the casual word, made an ideal invitation to happier days in the middle of a depression. Rarely has the potency of cheap music, whether it was Waller's or McHugh's, been more powerfully deployed. Fields and McHugh also wrote the score for the last Lew Fields Broadway show – *The Vanderbilt Revue*. However, the show flopped and Fields, the consummate Broadway professional, broke with tradition by making his farewell appearance his farewell appearance.

It was time for his daughter to join the song writers' wagon train west to Hollywood. Here she continued her collaboration with McHugh and branched out to work with some of the extraordinarily long list of collaborators she collected in her lifetime. Fifteen composers at a casual count – J. Fred Coots, Jimmy McHugh, Herbert Stothart, Jerome Kern, Oscar Levant, Fritz Kreisler, Sigmund Romberg, Harold Arlen, Arthur Schwartz, Burton Lane, Morton Gould, Harry Warren, Max Steiner, Albert Hague and Cy Coleman. Fields and McHugh suffered no setbacks on their arrival in Hollywood. They wrote *Love in the Rough* for MGM and *Every Night at Eight* for Paramount. Songs like 'Cuban Love Song', 'Dinner at Eight' and 'Don't Blame Me' which had started out in a Chicago revue, *Clowns in Clover,* secured their position.

Dorothy Fields' collaboration with Jerome Kern began when the producer, Pandro S. Berman, who was preparing *Roberta* at RKO, asked her to spend a couple of days working on a specific problem. Kern had written a fragment of music, sixteen bars long, which Berman needed to introduce a fashion parade. Asked why he had not written more Kern replied that that was all he had to say. Dorothy Fields solved the problem of making the lyric functional and also turning it into a love song; the opening of the verse shows her at her most elegantly and inventively direct:

> Clothes must play a part
> To light an eye, to win a heart.
> They say a gown can almost speak,
> If it is chic . . .

And then the chorus, directed to be sung, as it is written, 'gracefully':

> Lovely to look at,
> Delightful to know
> And heaven to kiss.
> A combination like this
> Is quite my most impossible dream come true
> Imagine finding a dream like you . . .

Kern was so delighted that he asked for Dorothy Fields when he signed to write the score for *I Dream Too Much* with Lily Pons for RKO. Like Oscar Hammerstein, Miss Fields found it pleasant to work with Kern, who had a reputation for being difficult. He taught her the habit of getting up at six-thirty every morning to start work at eight: a habit which proved valuable in later life when she sometimes found the challenge of a new day hard to face without stimulus. On Kern's piano were a basket of pencils and a small bust of Wagner. If Kern or his collaborator was unhappy with the work in progress, Kern would turn the bust around the wrong way saying, 'Wagner doesn't like it.' Together they went on to write *Swing Time* for Ginger Rogers and Fred Astaire, including 'The Way You Look Tonight', an Oscar-winning song which continues Miss Fields' obsession with songs about looking and seeing ('Look Who's Dancing', 'If My Friends Could See Me Now', 'Just Let Me Look at You,' 'Look Who's in Love', 'Lovely to Look at'):

With each word your tenderness grows
Tearing my fear apart
And that laugh that wrinkles my nose
Touches my foolish heart . . .

'A Fine Romance' they described as a 'sarcastic love song':

You're calmer than the seals in the Arctic Ocean
At least they flap their fins to express emotion . .

In 'Remind Me', again she turns a romantic situation upside down to
give wit to a simple declaration of affection. 'Remind me not to find you
so attractive', the heroine pleads; and goes on to hope she will feel no
regret;

'. . . Don't let me kiss you, please remind me,
Unless, my darling, you forget'.

Dorothy Fields and Jerome Kern continued to collaborate on *Joy of
Living* for Irene Dunne, on *When You're in Love* for Grace Moore, and,
anti-climactically, on *One Night in the Tropics* for Abbott and Costello
and Allan Jones; and with Harold Arlen she wrote 'Today, I Love
Ev'rybody'; but by 1939 Miss Fields had had her fill of Hollywood and
returned to New York to write the lyrics for *Stars in Your Eyes*. The
music was by Arthur Schwartz, the script was J. P. McEvoy's. He was
interested in a book about leftists working in Hollywood— *Swing to the
Left* was the original title. Dwight Deere Wiman was the producer and
he brought in Joshua Logan to direct. Logan found the political theme
passé and got rid of it. What remained was an uncertain entertainment
with a couple of interesting songs that have not quite survived: the
lugubrious 'I'll Pay the Cheque' and 'The Lady Needs a Change',
inserted on the pre-Broadway tour to give Ethel Merman a bawdy,
comic opportunity. The cast was extraordinary including, apart from
Merman, Jimmy Durante, Tamara Toumanova, Nora Kaye, Alicia
Alonso, Maria Karnilova and Jerome Robbins. The show ran for 127
performances and the high spot appears to have been a duet for Merman
and Durante, 'It's All Yours', in which they attempted to throw each
other off balance with ad libs of the order of one quoted by Logan in his
book *Josh*. Durante, grabbing a telephone from the footlights, enquired,
'Hello, is dis de meat market? Well, meet my wife at six o'clock!'
In the early forties, Dorothy Fields, who had already worked on
screenplays with her brother Herbert, collaborated with him on the
books of three Cole Porter hits. *Let's Face It*, starring Danny Kaye,
opened in 1941 and ran for 547 performances; *Something for the Boys*,

starring Ethel Merman, opened in 1943 and ran for a year; *Mexican Hayride*, with Bobby Clark, opened in 1944 and notched up 481 performances. With these successes under her belt, her plan was to return to lyric writing. In 1945 she and her brother wrote the book for *Up in Central Park*. The music was by Romberg and her lyrics included a vigorous 'The Big Back Yard', a metaphor for Central Park itself, and 'Close as Pages in a Book'. She has her fair share of Romberg stories – on one occasion he accused Kern, who was wearing a chequered cap, of 'looking like a race-course trout'; and on another he yelled at an inexperienced rehearsal pianist, 'The trouble with you, Miss, is you haven't got enough shows behind your belt!' But what Dorothy Fields wanted by now was to write with Kern again on a project which was her own idea. Working at the Stage Door Canteen, she saw a soldier covered with medals. Her imagination leapt off at a tangent to the idea of a musical about Annie Oakley for Ethel Merman. She called Billy Rose to suggest the idea to him. He asked 'who wanted to know from a girl with a gun?' Miss Fields then mentioned it to Oscar Hammerstein who agreed enthusiastically to produce *Annie Get Your Gun* with Richard Rodgers. Jerome Kern came east to start work and, as he walked back to his hotel after lunch with Guy Bolton at the Astor, he was felled by a heart attack at the corner of Park Avenue and 57th Street. He died six days later in Doctor's Hospital. Dorothy and Herbert Fields, and their producers, Rodgers and Hammerstein, had to look around for another composer. When Irving Berlin accepted their invitation it meant that there was no longer a place for Dorothy Fields as lyricist. However, she and her brother provided a vigorous book and the combination of Berlin's score, Merman's bravura, and the solid construction of the piece produced a run of 1,147 performances and a legendary success.

Arms and the Girl was an anticlimax. The story of a patriotic American heroine who dons breeches to join the revolutionary army had none of the sharp professionalism for which the Fields, brother and sister, had become famous and the subject often pushed Dorothy Fields' lyrics over the edge of their customary simplicity into unaccustomed pathos. 'A Cow and Plough and a Frau' is no better than it sounds and the two songs of any character were given to Pearl Bailey, 'Nothin' For Nothin' ' and 'There Must be Somethin' Better Than Love'. With this exception it was as though Miss Fields had not quite woken up to what was going on in the theatre around her. *A Tree Grows in Brooklyn* was a different matter. Dorothy Fields and Arthur Schwartz worked with a book by George Abbott and Betty Smith, the author of the novel on which the musical was based. A strong, nostalgic, sentimental story wrought a subtle, colloquial change in the lyricist's work. Her previous lyrics, for all their virtues, had achieved a universal quality without reaching for the degree of characterisation which more recent musical plays were demanding. Now she was dealing with a simple Brooklyn family at the turn of the century and she found a different simplicity. This quality is shown most strikingly in 'He Had Refinement', a song for an abandoned, bigamous wife remembering the man who deceived her. Her love held firm and if she 'ever seen a prince, my Harry was him'; even familiar smells linger in her memory. He 'always smelt from peppermints, his person was trim . . .'. His gentility was the standard she clung to. He was 'so high bred'. 'He undressed with all the lights off until we was wed, He had refinement . . .' Then there are the joyful 'Look Who's Dancing' and the sincere 'Make the Man Love Me', for which, consciously avoiding what she called 'High flown poetic writing', she mined a rich vein of poetry in everyday speech. Once she had explored this new terrain of colloquial expression and character observation, Dorothy Fields never abandoned it. *By the Beautiful Sea*, a third collaboration with Arthur Schwartz, which followed in 1954, was not a financial success; but in *Redhead*, written with Albert Hague in 1959, she tried not only characterisation, but characterisation in Cockney, expecially in a music-hall pastiche, 'Erbie Fitch's Twitch'. The show's premise was the Jack the Ripper murders, a sort of John the Baptist for Sondheim's *Sweeney Todd*, except that its aim was charm and its triumph lay in Bob Fosse's choreography. It was the last show she was to write with her brother, Herbert, who died during the out-of-town tryout.

For her last two musicals, *Sweet Charity* and *See-Saw*, she had a new collaborator, Cy Coleman. In both she exploited her recently acquired mastery of contemporary slang, sometimes disappointing younger lyricists who had admired her early work and felt that she was descending into the market-place to her disadvantage. She was aware of the criticism; 'Many of my songs, of course, do use catch expressions . . . the point is that the song writer has to inhale the idiom, not the cliché, of the moment.' Inhaling the idiom gives a wonderful vitality to her lyrics for *Sweet Charity* – 'Big Spender' has become so commonplace that it is easy to lose sight of the detail she crams in. And 'Where Am I Going?' has a defiant strength.

> . . . Run to the Bronx or Washington Square,
> No matter where I run
> I meet myself there, looking inside me . . .

where the character sees only '. . . anger and hope and doubt'. The musical was based on Fellini's *Nights of Cabiria* and, in transferring it to the 'Fan-dango Ballroom' in New York, Dorothy Fields missed no opportunity to enrich her lyrics with her new vocabulary in 'If My Friends Could See Me Now'. In 'Baby, Dream Your Dream' she returns to a pair of lovers like those she heard outside Tiffany's 40 years earlier. Still he cannot offer her any more than love; he urges her to 'dream her dream; to close her eyes and try it'.

>. . . Dream of furniture;
>Dream that I can buy it . . .

One of the most affecting songs written for *Sweet Charity* was dropped in Philadelphia because the scene which encased it was found to be superfluous. It describes the early days of the heroine, the child of a travelling salesman who sold 'juvenile frocks . . . once and so often he'd bring home a box'. That was the box she'd fall on. Her dream is the pink taffetta sample, size 10, but after each visit, back it goes into the box. She longs to possess it, 'copied', as it is, 'from an import . . . real Parisienne'. Each visit brings the same disappointment when Papa has to catch his train, until her eleventh birthday, when Papa can't get home but heals her hurt by sending her the present by irrevocable parcel post.

See-Saw, again written with Cy Coleman, was Dorothy Fields' last Broadway show – based on William Gibson's *Two for the See-Saw*. The tone of its lyrics is tougher than had been her custom, but she was clearly as alive to the influences of the seventies as she had been to those of the early twenties. In 'Spanglish', she finds yet another new colloquial idiom among Puerto Ricans wrestling with the English language:

>Anglish is what we don' know
>Spanglish is langlish we know . . .

'Welcome to Holiday Inn' strikes a raunchier note – 'All through the night there's a friendly receptionist'. Two songs have achieved a measure of popularity, 'Nobody Does It Like Me', and the number which stopped the show, 'It's Not Where You Start, It's Where You Finish'.

Although *See-Saw* was not Dorothy Fields' best show, that song is an appropriate last hit for a lyric writer whose own career was a living contradiction of its opening lines: 'If you start at the top, you're certain to drop . . .'; and whose reputation is a continuing affirmation of the last line: 'You're gonna finish on top.' Miss Fields' work reveals growth and development over 50 years not easily matched. In 1973, in an interview in the *New York Sunday News*, she said, 'Any retirement plans? Are you crazy? Listen, honey, I've got songs coming out of me I haven't even thought about yet. I plan to write till I can no longer hold a pencil.' She died the next year at the age of 70, before she could enter her sixth decade as a song writer, still maintaining the high standards with which she had started out, still questioning them and still enthusiastically embracing new ideas.

7

HOWARD DIETZ

'Oh, Give Me Something to Remember You By'

The legend, 'Words by Dietz, Music by Schwartz', was for some 30 years as beckoning an invitation as you could see on the theatre marquees of Broadway. Dietz and Schwartz wrote occasional songs, they wrote musicals, they wrote movies; above all they wrote revues. Dietz called it 'high class vaudeville'. The form is no longer fashionable; but when Dietz and Schwartz applied their minds to it they wittily superseded the elephantine entertainments against which they were reacting – the *Follies* of Ziegfeld, the *Scandals* of George White, the *Vanities* of Earl Carroll – with light, sleek, elegant, mocking songs and sketches. Their revues were fast, frothy compilations of sharply written pieces which sometimes informed and, occasionally, contained a smattering of social comment. Above all they gave performers a chance to shine. The closest thing to that sort of revue nowadays is probably the nightly television news. And television has been a major force in outdating revue techniques. Television can provide immediate comment and instant quip more readily than the theatre revue. Revues tended to rely on charming and attractive personalities. Today, such performers find easier pickings in television. Moreover, in the playhouse, the revue does not compare with a book musical as a long-term investment. The instinctive talents of the performers for whom the great revues were tailored cannot easily be replaced when they tire of a long run or when a show tours. But these were not the problems which puckered the brow of Howard Dietz while he was refining the revue form during its golden age in the twenties and thirties.

In his preface to Dietz's delightful autobiographical book, *Dancing in the Dark*, Alan Jay Lerner defines its author as one of the last genuine theatrical exponents of charm. He remembers Dietz's lyrics from his schooldays in the thirties. 'I remember . . . as I sang them to myself as I walked down the street (which, incidentally, is what good popular music is supposed to make you do), that, aside from their obvious wit, rhyming legerdemain, style and at times philosophic tenderness, they were the most charming lyrics in the world. They had that special grace, that warm, elegant glow that hung a smile around you . . . Howard is the Fred Astaire, the Chevalier, the Colman, the Lubitsch of lyric writers.'

Born in 1896, Howard Dietz was a brave and witty man: a wit himself and both the cause and the remembrancer of wit in others. In the early 1970s, physically depleted by Parkinson's disease and by heart attacks, he insisted on introducing a programme which celebrated his work in Maurice Levine's *Lyrics and Lyricists* series at the YMHA on 92nd Street. 'I don't like composers who think,' he opened; 'it gets in the way of their plagiarism.' But, relishing another wit, he went on to quote his collaborator, Arthur Schwartz, who was once asked to write two songs a week for a long-running radio series, *The Gibson Family*. 'Won't it take a lot out of you, Arthur?' enquired Dietz. 'Yes,' replied Schwartz, 'but it'll take a lot more out of Bach, Beethoven and Brahms.' A beleaguered Dietz himself coined the famous phrase, 'A day away from Talullah is like a month in the country.' A bright remark by a drama critic, Kelcy Allen, holds its place in Dietz's memories. Allen's victim was a ticket speculator called McBride. At a disastrous performance of *Macbeth*, Dietz heard Allen cap Shakespeare's line, 'Lay on, MacDuff', with a quick, 'Lay off, McBride.'

Applying for a position with a very small advertising firm, the young Dietz was asked if he had read Dr Johnson's *Rasselas*. He enquired what that had to do with the job. 'I want men who have some truck with culture,' replied his potential employer. Dietz looked around the empty shoebox of an office. 'You don't seem to have many men,' he muttered. Taken on, he helped his employer, Philip Goodman, branch out into theatrical production. 'But I have never written a play,' said the first author wooed by Mr Goodman. 'Neither has Mr Goodman,' said Dietz. 'You both start without the handicap of knowledge.' A Jewish friend sent her small daughter to an exclusive school. Fearing trouble the headmistress cautiously enquired if the mother would mind if her daughter was told stories about Christ at Christmas. The mother considered it and gave her verdict — 'I don't know any stories about Christ that my little Elizabeth ought not to know.' From his film production days he remembers Samuel Goldwyn agreeing that his secretary could destroy files from ten years back. 'Yes,' Goldwyn said, 'but keep copies.' And Goldwyn again, pronouncing the name of the Belgian playwright Maeterlinck 'as if it were a delicatessen item'. As Goldwyn's publicist, Dietz was bright enough to tell the world about George Bernard Shaw's famous brush-off. 'I am afraid we will not get together, Mr Goldwyn. You are interested in art and I am interested in business.' He was present when Oscar Levant was asked if the music of

Howard Dietz (*Hulton Picture Library*).

George Gershwin, who was famous for dominating parties by playing his own songs, would be around in 100 years. 'If George is around, it will,' said Levant. Ruefully, Dietz recalls his early days on the fringes of the Algonquin set: 'I didn't eat at the Round Table; I watched the Round Table eat. Although I rubbed elbows with the famous wits and playwrights, they didn't rub elbows with me.' Another friend turned Catholic; 'I should have realised he had fallen in love and religion went with the bride.' After dining and drinking too well at a meal, in the days when the idea that right wines should go with the right food was new to many Americans, did Dietz say, 'Don't worry, the white wine came up with the fish', or did another wit, Herman Mankiewicz? Dietz claims the line as his own. When he was promoted to dizzy heights as a senior film publicist, the head of MGM did not approve of Dietz's casual attitude to office hours. 'You come in late,' he said. 'But I go home early,' Dietz replied reasonably. Ernst Lubitsch called him 'The man who writes hit shows on MGM stationery'.

He has described his metamorphosis from publicist into lyric writer in his book *Dancing in the Dark*. '. . . I saw newspapermen at work so I became a correspondent. I saw advertising men at work so I became an advertising man; publicity people at work, I went in for publicity. I saw painters at work, so I bought some canvases and covered then with oil. I saw musical shows I liked and I became a lyric writer . . .' He followed the classic lyricist's line of having eccentric immigrant parents but, more originally, he disliked his father, a jeweller, born in Russia, who sported an alien accent and a penchant for punishment – the punishment of others, of course. 'I always had the feeling that my father wasn't my father and he always had the feeling I wasn't his son.' Young Howard preferred his mother and his verdict on the marriage is succinct. 'She was too good for him.' The ill-matched couple moved their four children around Manhattan, '. . . from Yorkville to Harlem, to Washington Heights, to West End Avenue, to Riverside Drive . . . inheriting neighbourhoods as they became passé.' With some relief young Howard watched his father move out. Dietz Senior still visited his wife occasionally to take her to the opera, mainly to spread the news that he had heard Caruso among his friends and relations. Decades later, mother's last words were, 'The ten years since your father died have been the happiest of my life.'

As Howard Dietz grew up the cinema was an extra, older brother. *The Great Train Robbery* and the Kinematograph, the Nickelodeon and the one-reelers, John Bunny – an early silent star so popular that on his death his pictures were withdrawn lest the shock of seeing him move on the screen prove too much for his mourning public, the stereopticon, with women in provocative poses or prizefighters looking punishing, filled his spare time. For his early theatrical experiences, Dietz paid 25

cents a time which was his whole weekly allowance. Meanwhile, he had
begun to write for school magazines at Townsend Harris Hall, the
preparatory high school for City College. He played truant from home
without anyone back there being very clear that he had gone to live in
Greenwich Village, working as a copy boy on *The New York American*
after school and during vacations. Later, he combined attendance at the
Columbia School of Journalism with more work on *The American* and
submitted light verse to that cradle of American lyricists, 'The Conning
Tower' column which moved from *The Herald Tribune* to *The Evening
Mail*, landing up at *The New York World*, and where Ira Gershwin, E. Y.
Harburg and Lorenz Hart looked, as eagerly as Dietz, to see if their
contributions appeared. His pseudonym was 'Freckles'. Not content
with his early published work, he read omnivorously, ploughed into
Ibsen, scaled Shaw, 'toyed with vegetarianism, became a snob'. He won
his first wife Elizabeth Bigelow Hall and, independently, $500, by
winning a competition to write the best commercial for Fatima
cigarettes. At the celebration for this second triumph were Oscar
Hammerstein of Rodgers and Hammerstein and Lorenz Hart of Rodgers
and Hart. Young Master Rodgers was still in short pants.

It was this victory which introduced Dietz to advertising. And since
Samuel Goldwyn was a client of the firm for which he worked, Dietz
had the job of designing his trademark. He derived Leo the Lion from
the symbol of Columbia University and threw in *Ars Gratia Artis* as a
bonus. In 1917 Dietz's budding career as an advertising man was
interrupted by naval service and naval service was in turn interrupted by
a brief, first flirtation with Broadway. For $250 he was commissioned by
Louie Wyle, a small-time agent whose name and business practices were
synonymous, to write a title song for a dancer, Lina Abarbanel, who
was getting a sketch together to play in vaudeville at the Palace. The
title of the sketch was *Philopena*, the lyric was satisfactory and, when he
heard that his work was playing the Palace, Dietz longed to witness his
triumph and collect his cheque. At last he arranged a 48-hour pass and,
leaving just enough time to catch the train back to the Hampton Roads
base in Norfolk, Virginia, he turned up at Wyle's office. The welcome
he got was warm. 'Take a seat,' said the impresario to the sailor; 'I'll get
to you as soon as possible.' The sailor muttered that he had very little
time but took a seat and the impresario retired to his office with a
purposeful air. After a disconcertingly long wait the sailor forced entry
into the coop of an office. The bird had flown through a second door
and there were no further theatrical interruptions of naval routine.

Discharged from the service, Dietz gravitated to Goldwyn and
secured a job by sitting in his office writing letters to the newspapers
saying what a wonderful picture company the wonderful Goldwyn
Picture Company was. He promised his wife that he would hold the job

until he published a book or finished a play. Four years after the débacle of *Philopena* he made another inauspicious move towards Broadway, contributing dialogue for W. C. Fields and a song for a show called *Poppy*. Unfortunately, Dorothy Donnelly, the official librettist, declined to give Dietz a credit and the producer declined to give a royalty. Undismayed he persisted and landed a chance to collaborate with Jerome Kern. Kern telephoned out of the blue. He had read Dietz's contributions to 'The Conning Tower' and he invited him to contribute lyrics to a new show, *Dear Sir*. Dietz took the train to Bronxville, where Kern lived surrounded by his first editions. Hardly believing his luck, he listened as Kern played over a cornucopia of songs. 'Some numbers I wrote for a few English shows that didn't come off, or rather didn't get on.' Clutching a bundle of music, Dietz hurried away with a date to meet Kern again in two days' time. He was uncertain whether he was expected to write lyrics to all the songs he had under his arm by the time he returned, or just one. He didn't like to ask and settled to write them all by Friday.* Picking the tunes out on the piano with one finger he worked at the Herculean task. One of the numbers was all that is left of the only recorded collaboration between Jerome Kern and Noël Coward – in its original form it was called 'If You Will be my Morganatic Wife'. It gave Dietz a start and he produced for American ears the rather more accessible 'If We Could Only Lead a Merry Mormon Life' – which raised the thought that 'polygamy' might 'make a pig o' me'. Encouraged, he completed the other lyrics. When he returned to Bronxville he was grateful for the Mormon song. Kern sat thoughtful and unsmiling as he played through the early numbers and Dietz kept producing more from the pockets into which he had stuffed them, still unsure how many he was expected to have produced for the great man. It was not until the Mormon song that he could relax on a compliment. 'That number alone will make the score great,' said Kern. He also liked a second song, 'My Houseboat on the Harlem', where 'the breezes sweep along the shore and tell us what they cook next door'; but the euphoria of securing Kern's praise wore off in the face of an embarrassing two-week run, and the two men never worked together again.

In 1924 Howard Dietz received a letter under a lawyer's letterheading. Arthur Schwartz introduced himself as a composer who was giving up the law to spend all his time at his music, a resolution to which he has not entirely kept. He complimented Dietz on being the only lyricist in town to compare with Lorenz Hart and suggested a collaboration. Dietz was evasive. He pointed out that he had written his first show with an

---

* Is this the origin of 'Do you want the song good or do you want it Friday?'?

established composer and suggested that Schwartz should take his first steps with the help of a well-known lyric writer. 'In that way we will both benefit by the reputation of our collaborators, then when we both get famous we can collaborate with each other.' Neither achieved fame before they were flung together. Dietz had two more unrewarding Broadway experiences to which to look forward. Ira Gershwin having surrendered to his appendix when he and his brother were preparing *Oh, Kay!*, Dietz stepped into the breach. George Gershwin turned protectively to the unknown Dietz, rather than the celebrated P. G. Wodehouse who was already writing the book, so that the focus of attention for the lyrics should remain on brother Ira. Dietz supplied the lyrics for 'Heaven on Earth', and the verse of 'Clap Yo' Hands'. Ira Gershwin recovered in time to rewrite Dietz's lyric, 'That Certain Something You've Got' as 'Oh, Kay, You're OK with Me', and to take over a title suggested by Dietz, 'Someone to Watch Over Me', and turn it into the best song in the show. Once again Dietz did not make a fortune out of his work. 'I was proud to work with the great Gershwin, and I would have done it for nothing,' he has written, 'which I did.'

Dietz tried again in 1927, contributing to the eighth musical to open on Broadway in the May of that year, *Merry-Go-Round*. As a summer revue it had some success and ran until the fall. Among the Dietz numbers was one with a tune by Jay Gorney (later to write the music of 'Brother, Can You Spare a Dime') for four ambulance-chasing lawyers, which *Variety* reviewed as the 'snappiest number in the show'. The lawyers were Messrs Moskowitz, Gogeloch, Babblekroit and Svonk. The song was in the best tradition of musical attacks on lawyers, from *Trial by Jury* to *Chicago*; but for Dietz, once again, the pickings were small.

It was 1929 before the still unfamous lyricist and Schwartz, the still unfamous lawyer-composer, collaborated. Their professional marriage was arranged at Tony Soma's, the same West Side café – or as Dietz defined it, 'speakeasy' – on 49th Street, in which the inspiration for 'April in Paris' was to strike Vernon Duke. Dietz, alert at the bar, heard Tom Weatherly, a 'man-about-Broadway', and Dwight Deere Wiman, a 'solvent theatrical producer', discussing a project to be called *The Little Show* – small, topical, tasteful, witty. Uninvited he wandered across to explain to them the foolishness of expecting to make money out of a small Broadway show. He cited his own recent experiences; and waxing enthusiastic quoted a poem he had just written;

Sing a lament for the plays that fail –
A dirge for the shows that fold,
A tear on the bier of the flops of the year
And the tickets that couldn't be sold . . .

Instead of taking his advice they asked him to write the lyrics, promising a cast which included Fred Allen, then a rising comedian, Clifton Webb and Libby Holman, who had had a success in *Merry-Go-Round*; the producers spoke of their up-and-coming composer, Arthur Schwartz. Dietz took them down to his home in the Village and showed them his previous correspondence with Schwartz. Undismayed they brought the pair together. Busy double lives made the short, sharp spurts required for revue-writing convenient. Dietz compares the full-length musical to 'the novel, whereas the revue is the short story'; he has described his working method with Schwartz as taking a series of hotel rooms – 'hostileries' as he calls them, on account of the irritation they caused their neighbours with late-night work sessions. 'We worked on borrowed time waiting for the manager to knock on the door.' Schwartz speculated that perhaps the other patrons did not like his tunes. Dietz agreed, pointing out that no-one ever complained about his lyrics. They broke the ice of their collaboration with a parody. Taking a popular hit, 'Woman Disputed, I Love You', they produced an ode to a department store – 'Hammacher Schlemmer, I Love You'.

> Your business deserves devotion that is loyal –
> I love you just like a fellow loves his goil . .

A song which has endured from *The Little Show* is 'I Guess I'll Have to Change My Plan'. Dietz wrote the lyric in response to a direct demand from Clifton Webb for a white-tie-and-tails number . . . 'full of suave romantic frustration . . .'. It started a vein of such songs for Webb whom Alexander Woollcott described as 'the general futility man'. Dietz countered by calling Woollcott 'Louisa M. Woollcott'. The tune was one which Schwartz had composed some years before as a summer camp song with a lyric by Lorenz Hart – 'I Love to Lie Awake in Bed . . .'. In *The Little Show* the song did only moderately well; but it had a vogue in England thanks to a cabaret act, De Lys and Clarke. They called it 'The Blue Pyjama Song' (there was one reference to blue pyjamas). When they returned to New York to perform it at the Place Pigalle, Dietz and Schwartz went along to see the act. Disingenuously, Schwartz asked who had written the song with which they were having such a success. 'I don't know,' said De Lys, 'it dropped in from nowhere. Someone like Noël Coward.' 'I think it's the best song someone like Noël Coward ever wrote,' said Schwartz, modestly. His publisher was no better. He called Schwartz to ask if he had heard this new song sensation. 'Dietz and I wrote it,' said Schwartz; 'you published it three years later and I want to congratulate you on the effortless way you go about making a song hit.' 'Moanin' Low', the big hit of the show, was especially designed for the singer, Libby Holman. Schwartz had difficulty finding the right bluesy tune for the torrid saga of love, theft, betrayal and strangulation which Miss Holman and Clifton Webb acted out on and around a bedstead; and Dietz, hearing the right sound in an improvisation by one of the featured pit pianists, Ralph Rainger, quickly found the powerful lyric. Dietz and Schwartz missed the first try-out performance in Asbury Park because their train broke down. They were greeted by despondent producers who had decided to close the show at the end of the week. The next night – for no very obvious reason – the entire atmosphere changed. When *The Little Show* came to the Music Box it ran for nearly two years. Dietz and Schwartz were established as a team. Together they wrote some 500 songs. 'After about 500 lyrics, you get to know the composer,' Dietz has written; 'if you can stand it that long you must like him.'

After *The Little Show*, they wrote six revues and four musical plays together. The revues were *The Second Little Show, Three's a Crowd, The Band Wagon, Flying Colors, At Home Abroad* and *Inside USA*. Wiman and Weatherly, their first producers, wanted to establish *The Little Show* as a title without conceding any dependence on its three leading performers, so for them Dietz and Schwartz wrote *The Second Little Show*. On the other hand, both composer and lyricist realised the value of Allen, Holman and Webb as a trio, so at the same time for a different producer, Max Gordon, they constructed *Three's a Crowd*. Mr Gordon got the 'best of the bunch' of material and *The Second Little Show* ran only eight weeks. Among the unknown talents Dietz tried to engage for the cast was Ethel Merman, but his producers did not share his enthusiasm. Instead, as their audiences were dwindling, she burst on to Broadway in *Girl Crazy*. For *Three's a Crowd* Dietz and Schwartz went through Schwartz's trunk and Dietz stopped at a fast foxtrot which Schwartz and the English lyricist, Desmond Carter, had written in London for *Little Tommy Tucker*.

> I have no words to say how much I love you
> That's my excuse, I have no words,
> I've got a cottage and a room with a view
> And H & C but I've no words . . .

Dietz slowed it down and wrote a lyric for Libby Holman to sing to Fred MacMurray, making his Broadway début, dressed as a sailor and showing only his back to the audience, as she sang 'Oh, give me something to remember you by . . .'

Dietz and Schwartz reached their peak as writers and devisers of revues with *The Band Wagon* in 1931. The cast included the Astaires, Tilly Losch, Helen Broderick and Frank Morgan. The production depended on a refreshing use of revolving stages – another of Dietz's ideas – and, from the opening number, the songs were good and used the carefully designed staging to the greatest effect. 'New Sun in the Sky' provided an optimistic note in Depression days, while 'I Might as Well be Miserable With You' mocked the Depression mood directly; but the song which is most firmly associated with *The Band Wagon* and its writers was 'Dancing in the Dark'. For a time Dietz despaired of finding an interesting staging. Finally, John Barker sang while Tilly Losch danced with herself in a series of mirrors. 'Time and applause', writes Dietz, 'have taken the dullness out of it.'

When Dietz and Schwartz unveiled their next revue score, *Flying Colors*, in the following year a note of sameness seemed to be creeping into their formula – although Schwartz's tunes were popular and Dietz's lyrics are still full of playful wittiness, sophisticated innocence, naïve knowingness and open-eyed awareness. 'Alone Together' shares a dark, brooding mood with 'Dancing in the Dark' so nearly that John Mason Brown called it 'Dancing in the Schwartz'; and instead of 'New Sun in the Sky', anti-Depression optimism was supplied by:

When there's a shine on your shoes
There's a melody in your heart.

'Smokin' Reefers' embraces a different attitude to marijuana from that currently held and a different attitude to black and white from ours.

It's the kind of stuff that dreams are made of,
It's the thing that white folks are afraid of . .

Above all, it dates from a time when acceptance, not militance, was the order of the day. Nowadays, of course, sentences for marijuana users are not as long as they used to be, and, indeed, people who smoke the stuff seem not to be so worried by serving a long sentence. They run into trouble when they have to speak one.

Seeking to break the pattern of their revue successes, Dietz and Schwartz wrote *Revenge with Music*, a musical which yielded two enduring hits and a profit although it was an artistic failure. Dietz risked asking C. B. Cochran what he thought of it. The answer was crisp. 'It's dire.' Dietz had recently visited Spain. For his book he followed in the footsteps of Manuel de Falla and Hugo Wolf, who had based a ballet, *Tricorne*, and an opera, *Der Corregidor*, on Alarçon's novel *El Sombrero de tres Picos*. The Governor of a Spanish province (Charles Winninger), tries to seduce a miller's wife (Libby Holman). In revenge, the miller (George Metaxa), woos the Governor's lady (Ilka Chase), with a good deal more success. Dietz records his disappointment at the effect singing lessons had had on Libby Holman's voice; others have laid the blame at the door of Dietz and Schwartz, suggesting that the premise of the show was operetta, that Dietz's lyrics were uneven and that Schwartz's work, though often graceful, lacked the rich flamboyant effects which Romberg or Friml might have supplied for this sort of subject. One of the hit songs which did capture the mood was 'You and the Night and the Music'; and a charming but bland song revived from their radio series, *The Gibson Family*, 'If There is Someone Lovelier Than You', was integrated successfully, partly because of George Metaxa's exotic accent and an appropriate orchestration. The next season saw Dietz and Schwartz back on familiar ground with a revue, *At Home Abroad*, but a revue connected by a skeletal story line – a world cruise undertaken by Otis and Henrietta Hatrick. En route they encountered Beatrice Lillie, Ethel Waters, Eleanor Powell, Reginald Gardner, Eddie Foy Jnr and Herb Williams. In 'Get Yourself a Geisha', Miss Lillie extolled the virtues of Japan, finally insisting 'It's better with your shoes off.' She moved on to her sort of Paree:

> . . . Un soupçon of sad, un soupçon of glad,
> Zee onion soupçon –
> Not bad!

Ethel Waters presided over a Hottentot kingdom in a lyric long since overtaken by emergent Africa:

> . . . The heathens live upon a bed of roses now
> And Cartier rings they're wearing in their noses now . . .

Having established her domination,

> I gave 'em that Hotcha . . . je ne sais quoitcha . . .
> . . . the jungle now has lots of chic to it,
> A touch of cloisonné and Lalique to it,
> And who put all this drawing-room technique to it?
> The Hottentot Potentate.

As well as their comedy numbers, Dietz and Schwartz also supplied 'Love is a Dancing Thing'; but once again they were not on top form and the revue survived a modest six months. They were to have one more try at a musical, before going their separate Broadways for eleven years. In 1937, *Between the Devil* opened at the Imperial Theatre with a bigamous Jack Buchanan switching between Evelyn Laye and Adele Dixon as his two simultaneous wives. 'I didn't make it hilarious enough,' Dietz concludes. 'Jack Buchanan tried to provide what the script lacked but Jack, left to his own comical inventions, was as funny as a blow with a cosh.' The lyric writer was, however, pleased with two lyrics he gave his potentially unsympathetic leading character to justify the irresistible attraction he had for two women. There is the persuasive 'I See Your Face Before Me' and the poignant goodbye, 'By Myself', perhaps Dietz and Schwartz's simplest and strongest love song.

Dietz's professional divorce came at about the same time as a change of personal partners. His first marriage petered out and he married Tania Guinness. The English newspapers, discovering that in adolescence he had spent a summer working in a creamery, ran headlines which announced LABOURER WEDS HEIRESS. In fact, Dietz was Vice President in charge of promotion for MGM and had, more specifically, the job of launching *Gone with the Wind* on his plate. He masterminded the opening in Atlanta; one woman rang Clark Gable's hotel asking to be told his room number. When Dietz refused to authorise its disclosure, she changed her tack and asked to book the room the moment Gable left, adding, 'Don't make up the bed.' In 1940, Dietz attempted to tidy up a Shubert show *Keep Off the Grass*, starring Jimmy Durante, but without much success.

During the war, he found himself in the Coastguard with Vernon Duke. They put together a show called *Tars and Spars*, a naval answer to Berlin's *This is the Army*. Vernon Duke has described their collaboration in *Passport to Paris*.

> Howard shone at everything he undertook; he never 'dabbled' in a new hobby, but applied himself to it with ferocious energy. He tackled bridge, golf, tennis, croquet and swimming fairly late in life and was soon out-playing and out-swimming his younger companions, trained for such pursuits in childhood. A brilliant executive, generally considered the best publicist in the film industry, he was also an inventive and facile lyric writer. We should have been a great team, for we had many traits in common, such as facility, adaptability and a 'sophisticated' outlook; but we just didn't 'pan-out' as a combination, probably because we had too much in common. No two people were less alike than Richard Rodgers and Lorenz Hart, than George and Ira Gershwin, than (the classic example) Gilbert and Sullivan; yet they complemented each other, the qualities lacking in one were abundantly present in the other.

Dancing in the Streets was the first Dietz and Duke professional show – based on a novel by John Cecil Holm, the author of *Three Men on a Horse*. It opened in Boston in the same week as *Away We Go!* – not yet renamed *Oklahoma!*. The meagre business done by *Away We Go* contrasted with full houses for *Dancing in the Streets* at the Shubert

Theatre; but *Dancing in the Streets*, starring Mary Martin, was withdrawn for rewriting and *Oklahoma!* went on to make all three Dietz and Duke musicals outdated. The next, *Jackpot*, lasted only 69 performances at the Alvin Theatre. *Sadie Thompson* was a musical version of *Rain*, designed for Ethel Merman. Unfortunately, Miss Merman did not like Dietz's lyrics and her husband was keen to rewrite them. According to Duke 'the lyrics were chic while she wanted them "sock"'. Dietz insisted that she sing the songs as written. Merman, in rehearsal, would get to a song and say 'number over' rather than deliver the original lyrics. Her agent attempted to mediate. He examined the Dietz lyrics and then those by the husband, Robert Levitt. He pointed out to Dietz how much better were Levitt's versions; only then did Dietz tell him he had switched portfolios and that the agent had given the nod to Dietz's original words. Merman left after a week and June Havoc replaced her – three of the big Merman songs had to be dropped. 'The Love I Long For' survived and became a hit thanks to a Harry James recording. But set, choreography and the generally dated feel of the show made it inappropriate to the forties. The revolution in musicals had happened and *Sadie Thompson* was one of its victims.

In 1947 Arthur Schwartz came back from Hollywood where he had been writing and producing films. On the way home he drove across America and in the course of the journey conceived the idea of building a revue about America around John Gunther's bestseller, *Inside USA*. He produced it himself. Once again Bea Lillie was the star, joined by Jack Haley. The best-known romantic song, 'Haunted Heart', seems once more to strive for the same theatrical effects as 'Dancing in the Dark'. The lighter lyrics read better today. In 'Rhode Island is Famous for You', for example, after a straight list of states and their characteristic products, Dietz's imagination takes off in a classic piece of whimsical light verse, creating an America in which 'Pencils come from Pencylvania, vests from Vest Virginia', and so on.

It was at this time that Dietz married Lucinda Ballard, the clever costume designer. She 'came romantically into my life as Tania, who had been gently and lovingly leaving me for years, finally left.'

And now I'm yoked
To the fair Lucinda
Divorce and such
Are out of the winda.

For Dietz his renaissance in this period was not to be in the theatre. It was not to be, as it was with Berlin, Harburg, Porter and Hammerstein, with a new Broadway show. He was to write two more musicals with Schwartz, but the vehicle which gave them their greatest post-war

success, and a new hit song, was a film. Appropriately, it was a
retrospective Dietz and Schwartz revue, connected by a slight backbone
of plot, and finally called *The Band Wagon*, after a planning period
during which the title was *I Love Louisa*. The new song – the only one of
the many which they wrote for the score to be included – was that
second anthem of show business, 'That's Entertainment'.

> . . . It might be a fight like you see on the screen
> A swain getting slain for the love of a queen
> Some great Shakespearean scene
> Where a ghost and a prince meet
> And everyone ends as mincemeat . . .
> . . . The world is a stage
> The stage is a world of entertainment.

In his book on the Arthur Freed unit at MGM, Hugh Fordin suggests
that the song was written in half an hour.

Dietz translated two opera librettos, both for the Metropolitan
Opera. His *Fledermaus* was well received; the *Bohème* had only seven
performances. There remain the two Dietz and Schwartz post-war
musicals. *The Gay Life* was based on Schnitzler's Anatol dialogues.
Despite Alec Wilder's verdict in his book, *American Popular Song*, that
this was the best Dietz and Schwartz score since the thirties, its sounds
lack lustre today and Dietz puts the blame squarely on his leading man,
who, he says 'couldn't . . . . . . speak English, which was a handicap'. He
is wryly amusing about the fate of *Jennie*, a vehicle for Mary Martin.
Unfortunately, while they thought they were writing a funny show
about a small-town gym instructress, their star had visions of playing 'a
tragedy queen' in a thinly disguised biography of Laurette Taylor. Miss
Martin and her husband were also the producers, which gave them the
whip hand. Worse was to follow. Miss Martin objected to the lewdness
lurking in the lyrics of a charming song, 'Before I Kiss the World
Goodbye'. The lines of which she disapproved were:

> Before I go to meet my maker
> I want to use the salt left in the shaker . . .

Miss Martin had her way where Miss Merman had not. She stayed and
the lines went. By the time that *Jennie* was in rehearsal and on the road,
Parkinson's disease had attacked Dietz. He went in and out of six
operating theatres in one year and came back with his stomach 'looking
like a Picasso'. He attributed a partial recovery to the drug L. Dopa.
Then he added two heart attacks to the list of obstacles to be overcome
with courage and wit and gaiety. To return to Alan Jay Lerner's

estimate of the charm which pervades Howard Dietz's work: '. . . when I finally met him and we became friends, I quickly found out where all that charm came from. He is a walking reservoir of it.' In the autumn of 1983 death excused him from the exercise of more willpower and finally robbed his friends and his family of his charm and wit.

8

E. Y. HARBURG

'Somewhere Over the Rainbow'

Howard Dietz has suggested that most of the classic song writers are not primarily concerned with protest, with the notable exception of E.Y. – popularly known as 'Yip' – Harburg, who, he said, never stopped asking why, if birds can fly over the rainbow, why, oh why, can't he? But protest was in Harburg's soul and not to protest about such a radical restriction on the freedom of the 'individle' would have been uncharacteristic. He was, paradoxically for so committed a writer, only a part-time song-smith. With the other part of his rhyming time he was also a politician, an activist, a liberal philosopher, a crusader for the rights of women, a man of peace and an ecologist – someone, that is, who fights to ensure that we leave enough of the planet Earth for future generations to destroy. Years after *The Wizard of Oz*, Noël Langley, who wrote the screenplay of the movie, was to say, 'Yip was out of *Alice in Wonderland* . . . he didn't understand about people on this planet. He thought he should correct it so we could all lead ideal lives.' Not a bad ambition and a belief which Harburg held and promoted for 80-odd years.

In *At this Point in Rhyme*, a collection of light verse which he published in 1976, when he had just reached 80, he wrote:

> At forty I lost my illusions,
> At fifty I lost my hair,
> At sixty my hope and teeth were gone,
> And my feet were beyond repair.
> At eighty life has clipped my claws,
> I'm bent and bowed and cracked;
> But I can't give up the ghost because
> My follies are intact.

E. Y. Harburg (*L*) with Ned Sherrin.

And, under the title 'Seated One Day at the Organ':

When our organs have been transplanted,
And the new ones made happy to lodge in us,
Let us pray one wish be granted –
We retain our zones erogenous.

Over the 50 years or so which elapsed between Harburg's first
attempts at light verse and his first collected edition, he published
hundreds of verses cushioned by other people's music, songs written for
revues, films and musicals. At the same time he embraced liberal causes
with the same enthusiasm President Nixon showed for the tape recorder
– he couldn't get enough of them and he couldn't switch off. Harburg
had a social conscience – almost as rare a thing in a song writer as it is in a
politician. If, as in Oscar Hammerstein's world, the corn grew high as an
elephant's eye, Harburg would have wanted to make sure that people
got a fair rate for cutting it. And this espousal of good liberal causes
grew directly from his background. The aura of poverty gave off no
rosy glow for Harburg. He resented it. He fought it and he emerged
from it with his character as a poet and a fighter fully formed. Some
business expertise which he had picked up along a by-way still clung to
him as he invaded the thief-infested thickets of Broadway and Tin Pan
Alley.

He was born on 8 April, 1898, in New York City, the son of poor
Russian immigrant parents. To get out was the prime incentive for a
slum kid from the East River, an area at that time of docks and derelicts,
of dangerous street gangs and drunken sailors. It was a melting pot of
arriving Russians, Italians and Irish. Italian gangs on Mulberry Street
faced the Irish whose home base was above Fourteenth Street. The
keener survival instinct of the Harburgs tugged them in the direction of
the settlement houses like the Henry Street settlement. Children were
looked after and encouraged. Social directors kept an eye on them and
provided a stimulus. Literary clubs, athletic clubs, amateur theatrical
clubs were available for a kid with a bright and enquiring mind. He
found himself involved in plays and he found that he was excited. He
discovered an ability to act and to write for himself. The period
conditioned Harburg's attitude to life. It was not easy to hide poverty
when periodically the furniture was out on the street; hindsight later
told him that it was exciting; it was real, and he said he had more fun
than he ever had in Hollywood. Life was a daily improvisation; but if
his contemporaries wanted to succeed on a level of street-fighting and
feuding his own instinct led him off the street and into the classroom. He
has said, 'The schools were better then too. I went to PS 64, on Avenue
B and Ninth Street. Great teachers – they were aware of the poverty

conditions of the kids that they were teaching.' He was already writing.
He may only have been writing parodies; but he felt that writing gave
him a status, '. . . an identity . . . suddenly you could hear a bleacher full
of little gangsters singing your song . . . that's how it started.' One of his
teachers at PS 64, Ed Gillesper, encouraged this instinct. If Harburg
wrote something for the school newspaper, his English teacher would
tell him to read it aloud in front of the class. With the wrong teacher and
the wrong pupil the results could have been disastrous; but Mr Gillesper
knew his extrovert, and the excitement of hearing his peers laugh at his
prose was heady wine for Harburg. 'I'd tell myself, I want to repeat this
experience!'

While he was writing his parodies for the boys in the bleachers, who
followed the Tompkins Square Park baseball team, he was also writing
poems for his high school paper. Attached to City College, 'which was
free', was Townsend Harris High School. There Harburg could cram a
four-year course into three years. At the going down of the sun he could
supplement the family income by lighting street lamps; and in the
morning he could deliver newspapers to the same purpose. In the days
when streets were lit by gas-light, his lamp-lighting chore earned him
$3.06 a week. It was the first decade of the twentieth century. The task
was spread, as far as his legs were concerned, over three or four miles of
streets. His brief included not only the job of turning on the lights at
sundown, but, in the morning, that of extinguishing them – at around
four; then he delivered the papers. It provided food. It helped the
family. It saw him through college. His brother Max, head of a college
physics department, his idol and sixteen years his senior, died when he
was twelve. Max was his inspiration. Feeding the family became
Harburg's responsibility. He cherished an ambition to be an actor, but
the family would not hear of it since an actor was required to act on
Jewish holidays.

His work on the Townsend Harris school newspaper led him towards
a new sophistication – he began to write light verse (some 50 years later
he published his first volume*). High school had introduced him to W.
S. Gilbert. Moving on to City College with his contemporary,
neighbour and friend, Ira Gershwin, they began to submit their work to
The World – specifically to Franklin P. Adams' column, 'The Conning
Tower'. On the occasions when Harburg's work was accepted – his
fellow authors might be Dorothy Parker, Marc Connelly, George
Kauffman and Edna St Vincent Millay – he got no money. For that he
still had to rely on the Edison Company and the local newsagent, until
Life and *Judge* began to take some poems. They paid. Meanwhile, the

* *Rhymes for the Irreverent*, Grossman, New York, 1965.

proximity of Ira Gershwin in class – G sat next to H – and their shared tasks fostered their friendship. Harburg remembers the Gershwins as better off; 'they had restaurants.' Benignly he also recalls the younger brother, George, dropping out of school – 'George didn't care too much about education.' More dramatic was the arrival of the Gershwin family's new Victrola. Recordings gave Harburg his first opportunity to listen to Gilbert's lyrics enhanced by Sullivan's music. 'Up to that time I thought he was simply a poet!' Hearing *Pinafore* was a turning-point in his life – just as hearing Harburg and Burton Lane's* *Finian's Rainbow* was later to be a turning-point for a writer of another generation, Sheldon Harnick. 'I couldn't sleep at night. It was that music – and the satire that came out with all the emotion that I never dreamed of before when I read the thing in cold print.' After a year at City College, Ira Gershwin left to join his father, who was now operating the Turkish bath while Ira worked the till. Harburg, however, went on to take a Bachelor of Science degree and, rejecting poetry as a career, went into business. 'Poetry was work for a dilettante – nobody made a living at that . . . money is made by the sweat of your brow. This is the old Puritan ethic . . . you've got to do something real nasty, dirty, get callouses on your hands or on your soul.' For about seven years he travelled in South America. He spent one year writing for a newspaper in Montevideo. Then he returned to New York. He applied himself to electrical appliances with another classmate, Harry Lifton, whose father was a professor at Yale. The twenties were a good decade if you were in the electrical appliance business, and they prospered. Electricity made him a lot of money; his occasional verse gave him a local celebrity. His colleagues, sensing the temptation that fame born of versifying held for him, bound him to an exclusive contract which demanded that he concentrate only on business. All this time he had been watching the high school drop-out, George Gershwin, increasing in reputation and facility, and the slower progress of his brother, Harburg's erstwhile classmate, Ira. Before the pressures of choosing between electrical appliances and versification became too heavy for Harburg, the Depression made up his mind for him. Suddenly the world of business was a bubble and poetry was the only practical solution. As his firm went bankrupt Ira Gershwin sent him a rhyming dictionary with a two-word inscription, 'Start rhyming.' 'I had my fill of this dreamy abstract thing called business and I decided to face reality by writing lyrics . . .

---

* Burton Lane's career as a Broadway composer began with Earl Carroll's *Vanities* of 1930 and other revues on which he collaborated with Harburg. After these initial successes he moved to Hollywood and wrote mainly for the movies until he returned to New York with *Finian's Rainbow* – his big hit with Harburg – and *On a Clear Day* – his sixties' success with Alan Jay Lerner.

the capitalists saved me in 1929 . . . I was left with a pencil and finally had to write for a living.' Ira Gershwin's other good deed to Harburg was to introduce him to Jay Gorney, the composer who, some years before, searching for a lyricist, had turned to F.P.A.'s 'Conning Tower' column and discovered some poems he liked above the signature 'Freckles'. Freckles had turned out to be Howard Dietz, who was also doing duty as MGM's publicist. The partnership between Dietz and Gorney flourished until Gorney too went into movies – rival movies – and became head of the music department at Paramount Pictures at their Astoria Studio – the studio which by a curious irony was 50 years on to be the home of *The Wiz* – the remake of Frank L. Baum's *The Wizard of Oz*, which managed without Harburg's lyrics, to Harburg's displeasure.

From Roosevelt to Nixon
From *The Wizard* to *The Wiz*,
My God, it can't be possible!
But oh, my country, 'tis!

Back in 1929, Gorney, having lost Dietz as a collaborator, turned to 'The Conning Tower' again and this time it was verses over the signature 'Yip' which attracted him. Ira Gershwin added his recommendation and simultaneously Harburg found himself in the theatre and in movies. Even so, while he wrote songs with Gorney at night, he sold watches during the day.

Their first five songs found a place on stage in Earl Carroll's *Sketchbook* in 1929. Ira Gershwin kept on selling Harburg. Vernon Duke, recently arrived in America from Europe where he had been known by his real name, Vladimir Dukelsky (George Gershwin translated it) describes his first meeting with Harburg in his autobiography, *Passport to Paris*. 'It was at Ira's that I met stocky, aggressive E. Y. Harburg, then writing with Jay Gorney . . . I was shown a song the two had written for the Earl Carroll *Sketchbook* entitled "Kinda Cute" – it was just that – and returned the compliment by playing a half-dozen tunes, one of which struck Ira and Harburg as a possible hit. They began "writing it up" then and there and the ultimate result was "I'm Only Human After All".' Duke played 'I'm Only Human After All' whenever he auditioned his music. He looked on it as his 'American song'. It went briefly into the *9.15* revue in 1929 and smartly out again. Harburg and Duke began to work together for Paramount at the Astoria, toying of all things with the screen version of Rodgers and Hart's *Heads Up*. They were not involved in the final product; but they did manage some short films including a song for a young brunette 'with a raucous speaking voice . . . who was just beginning to throw her not inconsiderable weight around!' She was Ethel Merman. The song Harburg and Duke

had written was called 'Old Devil Sea'. Duke continued to audition
'I'm Only Human After All', and eventually he auditioned it into the
third *Garrick Gaieties* – the first edition after the defection of Rodgers and
Hart. It was Harburg's first hit. A month later he and Gorney
contributed largely but unmemorably to Earl Carroll's *Vanities*. Harburg
notes that Earl Carroll's gimmick was the phrase 'through these portals
pass the most beautiful girls in the world.' Seeing the girls in the clarity
of rehearsal conditions and then seeing them carefully lit and made-up
on stage made Harburg realise for the first time how empty was the
boast and how valuable theatrical showmanship. Next, with Lewis
Gensler, Harburg had some songs in *Ballyhoo of 1932*, a half-cock revue
which represented Bob Hope's first important appearance on
Broadway. It also showed Harburg that he could write comedy songs.
Having added an element of satire he felt more at home. He was back to
his musical roots with Gilbert and Sullivan.

1932 was, however, to be the first real lyrical high spot in Harburg's
career. Jay Gorney brought him a tune which had gone nowhere with a
torch-song lyric which Harburg remembers imperfectly as being
roughly on the lines:

> I will go on crying big blue tears
> Till I know that you're true.
> I will go on crying big blue tears
> Till all the seas run blue . . .

This was not what the tune said to Harburg. To him it suggested a man
who had made a significant, unquestioning gesture towards building his
country and fighting for it. The man looked back on his contribution
with pride; but now he found himself denied the opportunity to work –
on the breadline without dignity. They used to tell him he was building
a dream with 'earth to plough or guns to bear'; he was always there,
'right there on the job'. Now suddenly he was out in the cold in a world
where the dream had collapsed and the system had fallen apart. Harburg
phrased his agony and his frustration eloquently in a song which has
contined to speak to posterity for that decade:

> Once I built a rail-road,
> Now it's done.
> Brother, can you spare a dime?

Harburg's protagonist was asking, without self-pity, 'I produce; why
don't I share?' The lyricist's achievement was to manage to say it
without becoming maudlin. Small wonder that his song divided the two
Shubert brothers, J. J. and Lee Shubert, who were producing the revue,

Americana, in which it appeared. As is often the way of great brothers and great impresarios and even more especially of great brothers who are also great impresarios, the brothers Shubert did not speak to each other. Mr Lee Shubert heard the song first. He liked what he heard and sent for Mr J. J. Through a third party J. J. was asked to listen to it. 'Tell him I don't like it,' said Mr J. J. 'He says he doesn't like it,' said the third party. 'Ask him why,' said Mr Lee. 'He says, "Why?" ' said the third party. Mr J. J. tried to rationalise his dislike of the lyric. 'It's too sorbid (sic),' he managed. The objection was not strong enough to keep the song out of the show.

'Brother, Can You Spare a Dime?' is the clearest early statement of Harburg's political standpoint and the strongest practical example of his firmly held belief that a song writer has a commitment to humanity. He was writing at a time when the WPA's (Works Progress Administration) Arts project was earnestly concerned with achieving a cultural revolution in America. Americans were learning that they had had a culture all along, but that 'it had simply been overlooked.' They were beginning to make up for lost time, to track it down, record, restore and celebrate it. Aaron Copland was going to American folk sources for *Billy the Kid* and *Appalachian Spring*; 'Moses and Ralph Sayer, studio painters before the Depression and after, went into the streets to paint derelicts and breadlines,' Harburg has said. Robert Sherwood was moving from European boulevard comedies to American subjects. 'This cultural revolution would have happened without the WPA Arts project. Its causes – the Depression and America's isolation in a menacing world – were more compelling than anything Washington could legislate . . . but the WPA brought the American artist and the American public face to face for the first time.' While the WPA was taking missionary entertainment, frequently heavy-handed and high-minded in its execution, to the masses, Harburg was able to introduce an important, unfrivolous, heart-searching examination of the American predicament into the tinsel texture of a Shubert revue. If the Federal Theatre called its documentary plays *Living Newspapers*, Harburg had managed to publish a vivid pamphlet packing many times the punch, and reaching a wider audience.

Some 50 years later, mid-Watergate, Harburg was asked to rephrase the song for *The New York Times*.

Once we had depression
But with a dime
A guy wasn't out of luck.
Now we've got inflation, drugs and crime.
Brother can you spare a buck?

Once we had a Roosevelt.
Praise the Lord!
Life had meaning and hope.
Now we're stuck with Nixon, Agnew, Ford.
Brother, can you spare a rope?

He was always aware of the power of a song. In his lecture at the YMHA in New York, for Maurice Levine's series, *Lyrics and Lyricists*, Harburg examined the importance and the potential of words wedded to music. 'How would God have managed had he not invented words?' he asked playfully. Where could we be if He had not come up with the word 'light'? Darkness would have continued to cover the earth and the 'heavens would have been one vast infirmary of broken Angels' wings . . . suppose God had had only the time for "Let there be light . . ." the miracle could never happen and we would all still be in the dark.' 'Music,' said Harburg, 'which is an extension of our emotions, comes naturally. It is the vested interest of the heart, a very ancient organ. The Word must be worked at and memorised for it is the vested interest of the frontal lobe, a rather recent development.' Speaking in 1970, Harburg pointed out how much further along in the evolutionary pattern music is than words by comparing 'Beethoven's Ninth Symphony with Agnew's last speech'. However, he found that words can give destination to music and music gives wings to words:

Together they go places . . . words make you think a thought. Music makes you feel a feeling. A song makes you feel a thought. Together they stand ready to soothe not only the savage breast, but the stubborn mind . . . a new idea can find a soft spot – even under a hard hat. The greatest romance in the life of the lyricist is when the right word meets the right note; often however, a Park Avenue phrase elopes with a Blecker Street chord resulting in a shotgun wedding and a quickie divorce. Music is the relentless censor of the false thought and the wrong word . . . songs have been the not-so-secret weapon behind every fight for freedom, every struggle against injustice . . . give me the making of the songs of a nation and I care not who makes the laws . . . to be a lyricist you've got to be a euphoric masochist . . . a book, a play, a painting, must be sought. A song seeks you. What is more it catches up with you. It is ubiquitous, insinuating. It beseeches you in your kitchen, your elevator, your supermarket, your dentist's chair. It can be dangerous. A song can degrade your culture, debase your language; can pollute your air and poison your taste or it can clear your thoughts and refurbish your spirit. It is the pulse of a nation's heart, the fever chart of its health. Are we at peace?

Are we in trouble? Are we floundering? Do we feel beautiful? Do we feel ugly? Are we hysterical? Violent? Listen to our songs. The wielder of so sensitive, so eloquent a medium of communication has responsibilities. The lyricist like any artist cannot be neutral. He should be committed to the side of humanity. He should be concerned for the rights, dignity and potential of his fellow men but he should also be able to express these ideas with a proper concern for the rights of the human ear, the potential of the human brain and the dignity of the human language . . . I grew up when America had a dream and its people a hope — song writing flourished, reflecting the exuberance of growth, the promise of abundance, the vigour and optimism of many new strains of immigrants . . . whether we were struggling against the shackles of slavery or the shackles of scarcity, hope was there. The songs evolved with the sweetness that hope always lends the minstrel.

By 1933 Jay Gorney had departed for Hollywood,* but Harburg was working with Harold Arlen as well as Vernon Duke. With Arlen he interpolated a song into *The Great Magoo*, a Hecht and MacArthur play, which Billy Rose was producing, about a Coney Island barker. Rose wanted something to suit the man's cynical character; but he also wanted a love song. Cynicism did not play a large part in Harburg's make-up.

It's only a paper moon,
Sailing over a cardboard sea,
But it wouldn't be make-believe
If you believed in me . . .

Lehman Engel has defined the plot of the song. 'It looks at life honestly and realistically. We are all perishable inhabitants on a temporary planet, acting a movie called life. Tomorrow the scenes are struck, and the actors gone.' But the impermanence of the paper moon, the cardboard sea, the canvas sky and the nylon tree are unimportant when the saving grace of love exists. 'Without it life is a honky-tonk parade'; but it's not make-believe if someone believes in it.

Harburg is not only a polemicist, he knows about love too:

Our days will be oh, so ecstatic,
Our nights will be oh, so exotic,

---

* After her marriage to Jay Gorney, Mrs Gorney married Harburg, whose first wife had left him. It is the proud boast of the second Mrs Harburg that she never married a man who did not write 'Brother Can You Spare a Dime?'.

For I'm a neurotic erratic,
And you're an erratic erotic.

And

Oh, innocent victims of Cupid,
Remember this terse little verse;
To let a fool kiss you is stupid,
To let a kiss fool you is worse.

However, in his love songs Harburg professes to find difficulty in saying 'I love you' head on. 'For me, the task is never to say the thing directly . . . to say it – in a curve, so to speak. For example, in "Fun to be Fooled" I was saying, "We are all being fooled by it – but it's a lot of fun." Again, in "April in Paris" – it's not simply about being in love in Paris, but about *wanting* to be in love anywhere.'

I never knew my heart could sing,
Never missed a warm embrace,
Till April in Paris . . .

Harburg wrote 'April in Paris' with Vernon Duke. He was finding the business of working with a variety of composers stimulating. 'I liked Vernon's facility. He was fast and very sophisticated . . . Vernon brought with him all of that Noël Coward/Diaghilev/Paris/Russian background . . . with my pumpernickel background and his orchid tunes we made a wonderful marriage.' Wonderful, yes, but not without its tricky moments.

The song was written for yet another revue, *Walk a Little Faster*. The producer, Courtney Burr, had a brilliant new set designer, Boris Aaronson ('who looked as if he had just stepped from an Assyrian frieze and wore twentieth-century coat and trousers under protest'). He had created a wonderful Parisian scene, an imaginary Left Bank café behind a transparent gauze curtain. Unfortunately, there was neither song nor sketch to go in front of it. Duke claims to have hit upon the title, 'April in Paris', in a restaurant, West-Side Tony's. After several double scotches had produced maudlin memories of Paris from Monty Woolley and Robert Benchley, Duke went to a tattered upright piano on the second floor and wrote the melody there and then. Harburg, who had never been to Paris, went out shopping for some travel guides and, poring over them at Lindy's with occasional glances at the Winter Garden, completed the lyric a week later. On the first night the song created no stir. However, the singer, Evelyn Hoey, had laryngitis. 'Her rendering', Duke wrote, 'rarely rose above a hoarse whisper,' which cannot have helped. Though Alec Wilder has called it 'the perfect theatre song ... if it's not perfect, show me why it isn't ...', Duke records disagreement with Harburg after the New York notices. 'My lyricist left in a huff, claiming that "April in Paris" should have been a "saucy jingle" in the first place.' Later Harburg began to feel that Duke's music lacked an essential sense of theatre and he turned increasingly to Arlen – with whom, in the sixties, he paid another musical visit to Paris, producing a beautiful lyric for Judy Garland, who sang it for the soundtrack of an animated cat film, *Gay Purr-ee*. This time Paris was a lonely town:

> . . . The chestnut, the willow,
> The colours of Utrillo
> Turn to grey, grey hues.
> The band playing Bizet
> Along the Champs Elysées,
> Sounds like way down blues . . .

If Harburg felt that Duke lacked a sense of theatre, Duke felt that Harburg lacked poise. He has written that he flew into a rage very easily. 'Upon demonstrating a song of ours, "Speaking of Love", he wound up with the last lines: "Speaking of love. I'll be your nincompoop, just be my *in*come poop, Speaking of Love." When Dorothy Parker, listening with her deceptively demure air, asked sweetly, "Dear Mr Harburg *what* is an *in*come poop?", Harburg let out an agonised yell, delivered a poignant address on the subject of Park Avenue Parasites and stormed out of the room.' He was a busy man in the autumn of 1932 and could well afford to take such verbal duels in his stride. Besides 'Brother, Can You Spare a Dime?' and 'April in Paris', Harburg was also represented on Broadway by 'Let Me Match my Private Life with Yours', a song inspired by Mayor Jimmy Walker; and at one point *Ballyhoo of 1932*, *Americana* and *Walk a Little Faster* were running simultaneously.

In 1934 Harburg was again involved in two revues, the 1934 edition of the *Ziegfeld Follies,* the first after Ziegfeld's death – fronted by Billy Burke, the Widow Ziegfeld, and backed by the Shuberts – and *Life Begins at 8.40*. For the Ziegfeld show Harburg, still working with Duke, contributed 'Water Under the Bridge', 'I Like the Likes of You', 'Suddenly' and 'What is There to Say?'. On this revue the relationship was stormy. The show, which starred Fanny Brice, was in trouble from its Boston previews. By the time it reached Washington the Duke/Harburg numbers were in danger. 'I don't know whether the fact is well known,' writes Duke, subjectively, 'but whenever a show is in trouble, the first one to be blamed is the composer . . .' – many a book

writer would disagree – '. . . a battalion of ambitious song writers was
dogging Lee Shubert's footsteps, and I had sombre visions of other
people's hits blossoming on the dead carcass of my discarded music . . .
no sooner did we arrive in Washington than Harburg, who had been
singing "What is There to Say?" with infectious ardour, if not in tune
(he would start the chorus near the piano in the right key, then gradually
progress to the opposite end of the room, getting away not only from
the piano but from the tune as well as he progressed, waving his arms
expansively and crouching bear-fashion at the climaxes) descended on
me in another fit of rage. In a torrent of ill-punctuated words, he abused
me for producing decadent, "unmanly", affected music instead of the
good, simple American tunes expected by the people . . . I, with equal
heat, refused point blank to cut "not only my own throat but also the
score's".' Duke paints a vivid picture of the scene at the Willard Hotel
the next day with three Shubert hacks all seated in suites on the same
floor pounding away at rival pianos trying to come up with alternative
tunes. He took a train back to New York and his reconciliation with
Harburg did not take place until John Murray Anderson came in to
redirect the show and restore the collaborators' songs in their original
form.

   Life Begins at 8.40 reunited Harburg with Ira Gershwin and Harold
Arlen. Apart from yielding 'You're a Builder Upper', 'Fun to be
Fooled' and 'What Can You Say in a Love Song', the score included
'Let's Take a Walk Around the Block' – another charming, yearning,
Depression song. More important, it teamed Harburg with Bert Lahr
for the first time. Harburg has said that Lahr's voice, along with
Groucho Marx's, are the two favourite voices for which he has written.
For Groucho, he and Arlen were to write 'Lydia, the Tattooed Lady':

   On her back is the battle of Waterloo,
   Beside it the wreck of the Hesperus crew.
   And proudly above
   Waves the Red, White and Blue!

   For Lahr, Harburg and Arlen sought to extend his comic range. They
wrote songs which confirmed their growing versatility as well as Bert
Lahr's. 'Things' is 'a beautifully inarticulate song', a take-off of a
Metropolitan baritone who in the person of Lahr, standing regally in
front of a Steinway grand, his hand resting pompously upon it, becomes
in everything he does, as Arlen put it, 'absolutely asinine'.

   When I was but a little lad
   I used to think of Things.
   The only joy I ever had

I had because of Things.
But now that I'm to manhood grown,
Fond memory always brings
The utter, utter, utter
Loveliness of Things.

Harburg finished another sketch, based on the three-cornered affair in
Coward's *Design for Living*, with the couplet:

Duets are made by Bourgeoisie – oh;
But only God can make a Trio.

And in 'Quartet Erotica', Lahr was cast as Balzac lamenting alongside
Rabelais, de Maupassant and Boccaccio their loss of popularity since
dirty books had become commonplace:

A volume like *Ulysses*
Makes us look like four big sissies.

When the refrain arrived at Rabelais, de Maupassant, Boccaccio and
Balzac, Lahr never ignored the explosive opportunities offered by the
first syllable of Bal-zac. It was a happy productive period for Harburg,
but Hollywood was beginning to beckon him and Arlen. However, in
1936 for *The Show Is On*, they collaborated to produce another song for
Bert Lahr, 'Song of the Woodman', a parody of Chaliapin and one of
the great comic moments in revue. Lahr had sketched out a general idea.
They developed it brilliantly; 'I always wrote Bert's material easily,'
Harburg told Lahr's son, John. 'Bert always had artistic hopes and
feelings; but the life he was given squelched that. His comedy was
always conscious of a lack of privilege. He wants to be an artist . . . he
knows he can never attain it . . . the audience laughs with him, while
he's slipping on an intellectual banana peel.' At one moment Harburg
parodied Browning's 'Pippa Passes' – there is a marvellously bathetic
section where he lists the uses of wood:

What do we chop, when we chop a tree?
A thousand things that you daily see.
A baby's crib, the poet's chair,
The soap box down in Union Square.
A pipe for Dad, a bat for brother,
An extra broom for dear old mother . . .

Harburg went to work with Universal Pictures in Hollywood. When
his and Arlen's separate contracts were up they moved together to

Warner Brothers where they wrote scores for Al Jolson's picture, *The Singing Kid*, and for *Gold Diggers of 1937*. Then they came back to New York to develop Harburg's idea for *Hooray for What?,* a satire on the armaments race designed as a vehicle for another popular low comedian, Ed Wynn. The not entirely satisfactory state of the world was, as always, much on Harburg's mind. The farcical motor of his plot, played as a conventional musical comedy, was the accidental invention of laughing gas with which Wynn, playing his usual clown figure, was to save the world from destruction at the hands of another Mata Hari. 'Down With Love', 'Moanin' in the Mornin'' and 'I've Gone Romantic on You' were the popular songs and 'God's Country' ('Every Man His Own Dictator') asserted the advantages of living in a land which could offer its people Gypsy Rose Lee and Popeye rather than Mussolini and Oswald Mosley.

Back in Los Angeles, Harburg and Arlen tackled the work which was to bring them the most lasting fame, *The Wizard of Oz*. Harburg sets his treatment firmly in the thirties. He asserts that he was not simply providing songs for Frank L. Baum's story. In the film he found a metaphor for the Roosevelt era. 'In the sphere of politics', Harburg suggests, 'Roosevelt was an artist . . . an artist is essentially a person in search of beauty. He cannot abide ugliness, either in a bad script or a bad society. He is always willing to rewrite, even if his subject is the social system . . . in spite of Depression he gave us inspiration – new light that gave the people social security, old age pensions, unemployment insurance, and that sweet new feeling of togetherness. On the screen his sunny leadership was reflected in so fanciful a medium as *The Wizard of Oz!* "Let us have freedom from want", he pleaded, "and time for learning and for arts"; and so the scarecrow longing for knowledge sang:

> "My head I'd be scratchin'
> While my thoughts were busy hatchin'
> If I only had a brain!" '

Harburg reads F.D.R.'s Good Neighbour policy into the Tin Man's line 'If I only had a heart!'; and from the phrase, 'The only thing we have to fear is fear itself', it was a short trip to the Cowardly Lion's chorus:

> And I could show my prowess,
> Be a lion not a mou-ess,
> If I only had the nerve.

Bert Lahr's enthusiastic delivery of Harburg's more fanciful rhymes drew the critique 'Mr Lahr's Lion is fion' from the *New York Times*.

Harburg saw his work on *The Wizard of Oz* as an attempt to reflect 'the glow that one man's humanity cast over the nation'. It was his lightest, most poetic statement of the liberal principles which pervade his work. Nowhere was the hope that enabled the nation to survive the decade more lyrically stated than in 'Somewhere Over the Rainbow . . . where the dreams that you dream really do come true . . .'. Arlen and Harburg were both excited by the commission to write *The Wizard of Oz*. It was a bonus in the frequently frustrating world of Hollywood. They had an opportunity to write more of the film in music than they had had before; and when they had to find the song that would take Dorothy out of Kansas into Munchkin Land, they were able to supply the key image of the rainbow. Arlen's tune did not sound right to Harburg when he first heard it. He thought it altogether too 'important' for the little girl. He characterises the way Arlen played it as 'too symphonic'. Arlen pleaded the tune's cause and eventually Harburg relented – as long as they could find a bridge to the song which spoke for the little girl. He remembered a distinctive rhythmic trill which Arlen used to whistle when calling his dog: the notes of the whistle became the middle of the song and its rhythm informed the whole treatment.

From Harburg's image of the rainbow sprang the device of exploding from the sepia prologue into the bright colours of Munchkin Land – a rainbow country in Dorothy's mind, in contrast to the monotone of Kansas. Even so, at the first screenings, there was a move to cut 'Over the Rainbow'; and the song writers had to enlist the aid of Arthur Freed, who was working with Mervyn LeRoy as an associate producer at that time, and finally of Louis B. Mayer himself. With hindsight, Harburg divides the credit for the song's extraordinary success between the fact that it was in a good picture and Arlen's tune '. . . You're talking about a big giant of a composer writing the hell out of a great tune . . . and I happened to take a hitchhike on his coat-tails . . .'; and finally on the tragic, emotional quality which Judy Garland possessed and the curious identification which grew up between the heart-breaking song and her own ruined life. She was, of course, only a second choice. The studio had wanted Shirley Temple.

After doing 'Lydia, the Tattooed Lady' for Groucho Marx in *At the Circus*, Harburg and Arlen had a rest from each other. Harburg teamed with Burton Lane for their first show together, a vehicle for Al Jolson's return to Broadway, *Hold on to Your Hats*. The score was serviceable, Martha Raye scored a success with two songs, 'Life was Pie for the Pioneer' and 'She Came, She Saw, She Can-Canned'; but Jolson decided after twenty weeks that a cold New York winter did not promise him the sort of weather to which he wanted to become re-accustomed and when the show still had several months' life left in it, he departed for warmer weather and the horse-racing which he was missing sorely. Back in Hollywood, Arlen and Harburg teamed up again – ironically on the film of *Cabin in the Sky*, a subject which Harburg had rejected for Broadway because he did not think it would suit Vernon Duke's music; Duke, who believed Harburg's rejection stemmed from his not finding sufficient social significance in the book, adds a final bitter note in his autobiography. 'It may be pertinent to note that in 1943, when the MGM film version of *Cabin in the Sky* was produced with Minnelli directing. Harburg thought the venture significant enough to interpolate two songs into it, with Harold Arlen supplying the music. (I, being in the armed forces, was unavailable.)' With Burton Lane, Harburg wrote for Sinatra ('Poor You') and with Earl Robinson, 'The Free and Equal Blues', which reflected his growing involvement in active politics.

However, back on Broadway, the usual forties scene change was taking place. *Cabin in the Sky*, *Pal Joey*, *Lady in the Dark* and eventually *Oklahoma!* were lending their new perspective to the look of musicals. In California Harburg came upon a play by Lilith and Dan James about Mrs Bloomer, set at the time of the Civil War. Harburg wanted more emphasis on women's rights and Negro rights and to this end he brought in Sig Herzig and Fred Saidy to work on the book. *Bloomer Girl* ran for 654 performances and its score distils a strong essence of Harburg. The passionate, poetic plea for freedom in 'The Eagle and Me' has made it one of his most durable classics, and the image he employs in the bridge of the song, 'Ever since that day, When the world was an onion', is one of his most beguiling.

The case for the emerging woman is powerfully and wittily argued in 'It Was Good Enough for Grandma':

> . . . It was good enough for Grandma
> But it ain't good enough for us.

Back in Los Angeles, Harburg and Jerome Kern wrote the score for *Can't Help Singing* for Deanna Durbin but, politically unpopular in Los Angeles at this time, Harburg was happy to return to Broadway once again in 1947. He had been playing with two ideas for plays: one about a leprechaun who could award three wishes; the other about a Southern senator who was magically changed into a Negro. The breakthrough came when Harburg saw the possibility of combining both plots. With Fred Saidy he set the play in the imaginary state of Missitucky, amid poverty conditions in Tobacco Road country:

> My feet want to dance in the sun.
> My head wants to rest in the shade.
> The Lord says, 'Go out and have fun',

But the Landlord says,
'Your rent ain't paid.'

In 'When the Idle Poor Become the Idle Rich', he examines both the
volatile nature of American society and the respect afforded to the rich:

When the idle poor become the idle rich
You'll never know just who is who
Or who is which.

To Missitucky the authors bring Finian, an Irishman, newly arrived and
anxious to bury a crock of gold at Fort Knox. The satirical argument is
that burying the gold there will ensure that it will grow, for to what
other purpose could the United States Government have planted all its
gold in a hole in the ground? Harburg went on to argue that a world
that makes greed for gold a priority is a ridiculous world. He still
wanted people to get tools for production rather than handouts. The
attack on the idiocy of racial intolerance through the Southern senator
was secondary; but, perhaps, in 1947, more easily identifiable and more
daring.

If the satire in the book now seems oversimple the vivacity of the verse
and the zest of Burton Lane's music are irresistible. The simple folk
poetry of 'How are Things in Glocca Morra' is cleverly used for Finian's
daughter, who is trying to make her father homesick for Ireland. For
good measure, the score also contains 'Old Devil Moon', and 'When
I'm Not Near the Girl I Love, I Love the Girl I'm Near' for the lustful
leprechaun – 'My heart's in a pickle I'm not too particle', capped by:

When I can't fondle the hand I'm
Fond of
I fondle the hand at hand.

There is also the Biblical masterpiece, 'The Begat':

The Lord made Adam,
The Lord made Eve,
He made 'em both a little naïve . . . .

Not so naïve, however, that they could not beget Cain and Abel:

Who begat the rabble at the
Tower of Babel . . .

Working down through civilisation, Harburg finally gets to:

. . . Fat filibusterers begat
Income tax adjusterers begat
'Twas Natchaler and Natchaler to
Begat
And sometimes a bachelor, he begat . . .

Then there were 'Look to the Rainbow' and 'If This Isn't Love' and the triumphant, 'That Great Come-and-Get-It-Day'.

Four years later, Harburg brought a new bag of songs and a new set of targets to Broadway. The show was called *Flahooley*, and this time the plot, which dealt with sensational sales generated by a doll that laughed in a market glutted by dolls who cry, was attacking reactionary McCarthyite pressure groups and Big Business. The most charming song is 'The Springtime Cometh'; but the show only lasted eight weeks. As if he had not sprayed enough shot across contemporary institutions and abuses, Harburg compiled a veritable shopping list of causes for his next show, *Jamaica*. 'For Every Fish' strikes a philosophical note in its verse:

Man, he eat the barracuda,
Barracuda eat the bass,
Bass he eat the little flounder,
'Cause the flounder lower class.
Little flounder eat the sardine,
That's nature's plan.
Sardine eat the little worm,
Little worm eat man.

'Push de Button' considers the doubtful advantages of city life on 'a little island on the Hudson . . . where . . . everyone big millionaire, with his own co-operative castle rising in de air-conditioned air'.

Push de button;
Up de elevator!
Push de button;
Out de orange juice!
Push de button;
From refrigerator
Come banana short-cake and frozen goose!

* Jule Styne – one of Broadway's most versatile and prolific composers – was born in London in 1905. He moved to Chicago with his family when he was eight. His successes range from *High Button Shoes* written with the lyric writer, Sammy Cahn, through *Bells Are Ringing* (with Comden and Green) to *Gypsy* – possibly his masterpiece, a collaboration with Stephen Sondheim.

Again, in 'Monkey in the Mango Tree', Harburg asks whether progress is synonymous with evolution:

> 'Don't you make a human out of me!'
> Said de monkey
> In de Mango tree.

And 'Leave the Atom Alone' says just what it seems to say – 'Don't get smart alecksy, with the galaxy.'

There remain two Harburg scores. For *The Happiest Girl in the World*, he married Aristophanes' *Lysistrata* to Offenbach tunes. The rhyming requirements of the music took him back towards his Gilbertian roots and the plot gave him ample opportunity to deal wittily with the absurdity of war and the responsibility of women to do something about it. The show includes one of his funniest songs, 'Never Trust a Virgin', ('. . . a hussy who is fussy 'bout her status quo . . .').

Jule Styne refers to the other enterprise, *Darling of the Day*, as one of his 'saddest shows . . . the saddest ones are the ones that have the greatest potential and then are screwed up.' Styne had seen this adaptation of Arnold Bennett's *Buried Alive* as his *My Fair Lady* and was insistent that Harburg join him as lyricist. 'There's only one man, Yipper Harburg. He's erudite. He knows painters. He can give me sophisticated lyrics.' The progress to curtain up was strewn with bodies of replaced book-writers and directors. Once up it only stayed that way for four weeks.

One of Harburg's most endearing qualities was his faith in the shows which went wrong, or at least, did not fulfil their early promise. He and Styne continued to work on *Darling of the Day* after it had closed and he always seemed to be taking out *Flahooley* or *The Happiest Girl*, cutting them down and seeing whether losing a charcter here or there might not make a revival economically possible, and musing on whether the public might not now be ready for such a show.

John Lahr has written that 'America is the only society which defines itself by a dream, not a reality. With his lyrics, E. Y. Harburg has given body and weight to his vision of social harmony, equality and human resilience.' Harburg called himself a 'minstrel' and a 'lyrical historian'. He said, 'I have tried to write songs that are rhymed chronicles of a crazy but exciting world spinning aimlessly around a small, unimportant galaxy.' Lahr also called him the only lyric writer 'on the Broadway treadmill to get comic with the cosmic'. His range was vast. He could be considered or he could be explosive; he could be acid or he could be emotional; he could be frivolous and sombre, whimsical and wise. He carried his rebellious torch for over 80 years, and probably found himself speaking more directly to an audience more ready to hear his message at the end than ever before.

His first book of verse was dedicated to his wife Edelaide with whom he had a long, happy marriage. He wrote:

These rhymes are unblushingly dedicated
To Eddy by whom I've been eddycated.

One of his verses has an air of finality about it:

For a halo up in heaven
I have never been too keen.
Who needs another gadget
That a fellow has to clean?

No matter how I probe and prod
I cannot quite believe in God.
But oh! I hope to God that he
Unswervingly believes in me.

It is easy to believe in **Mr Harburg** and his assured place in the song writer's Psaltery.

9

NOËL COWARD

'Why Must the Show Go On?'

Of the six men who made up that one consummate Man of the Theatre, Noël Coward — playwright, composer, actor, singer, director, lyric writer — it was the dramatist, particularly in the narrow but demanding field of high comedy, who was the most accomplished. As immediate heir to the tradition of Congreve, Wilde and Shaw, Coward had no equal. But the lyric writer and the composer in him will be remembered not because they challenged the skills of the American lyric writers and composers in these pages; but because of their determination to entertain and the wit and grace with which they achieved it, aided by the actor singer in Coward who put over their material. There would be other performers who acted better and had better voices, other directors who could fill a stage with more bravura; but in Coward the whole is so much greater than the parts.

He came from a different tradition from the others. It is a polite English tradition of Gilbert and Sullivan and Daly's and the Gaiety; of Lily Elsie and Gertie Millar; Camille Clifford and Gabrielle Ray; of Lionel Monckton and Paul Rubens; 'The Country Girl', 'The Shop Girl', 'The Quaker Girl', 'The Geisha Girl' and, daringly, 'My Mimosa Maid'. It is Teddington and Battersea and South Side, Clapham Common. It is a father and four singing uncles in the choir of St Alban's Church, Teddington-on-Thames, alongside four singing aunts, all accompanied by a fifth uncle at the organ; Aunt Hilda had the glamour, she was known as 'The Twickenham Nightingale'; and all was gentility and darned gloves and honey still for tea, and not a slice of gefilte fish in sight.

Arthur Sabin Coward, a walk-on cast as 'a father', made little of the part. Russell Arthur Blackmore Coward was an off-stage character, 'a first-born', who died of meningitis before our star appeared upon the scene. Eric Coward, 'a younger brother', is a role no more than outlined, even though he changed his billing to Erik with a 'k'. He is written out – Ceylon, a tea-planter – in Act Two and dies offstage before the Act is over. Violet Agnes Coward, née Veitch, is a 'stage mother', who encourages, prods, pushes, protects, bludgeons, idolises, infuriates, and would steal the drama from anyone less compulsive than her son, the star. She is the 'character' in Coward's life. She it was who shoved him towards his first professional appearance – not that he was reluctant to make it. Already in the chrysalis stage he had the temperament of a star. Determined to get and make his way, wilful, petulant to the point of screaming tantrums when crossed, eagerly assimilating dancing and singing and all the books he could steal from the Army and Navy Store, a spic and span urchin, 'I didn't gnaw kippers' heads in the gutter as Gertrude Lawrence quite untruthfully always insisted that she did.' He first met the fifteen-year-old Miss Lawrence when he was thirteen and they were travelling together to Liverpool to appear in a play; 'She gave me an orange and told me a few mildly dirty stories, and I loved her from then onwards.' By then his mother had manipulated him into his professional début in *The Goldfish*, described as 'A Fairy Play in Three Acts with a Star Cast of Wonder Children'. This Wonder Child played Prince Mussel and earned an infuriatingly good notice from the *Daily Telegraph* which congratulated, among other 'tiny artists', 'Miss Noël Coward'. Next, Mother netted him an engagement with the distinguished actor-manager, Sir Charles Hawtrey, where he picked up his basic training in light comedy. Alas! It was not to be of much use to him in his next appearance, in Miss Ruby Ginner's ballet, *An Autumn Idyll*, since in this romantic work he took the part of a mushroom partnering a pink toadstool, dancing but dumb. By the time he met Miss Lawrence, the growing experience of the stage-child included an appearance in variety at the Coliseum, where he stood in the wings watching and learning from the great stars of vaudeville; playing a clever little tot in *Where the Rainbow Ends*; and, encouraged by Hawtrey and applauded by Mother, directing, for the first time, his diminutive colleagues in a play one of them had written, *The Daisy Chain*. Directorial experience under his belt, he took his place confidently in a patriotic play at the Palladium, *War in the Air*, handling the line, 'Please God, Bless Mummy and Daddy and Violet and make me a great big aviator one day', with aplomb.

In the circumstances, his formal education was irregular, but Mother had managed to edge him into the Chapel Royal School at Clapham, though he was denied a place in the choir because his voice was unsuitable. 'Nonsense,' Mother protested passionately. 'Has he not moved the Queen of Portugal to tears?' An education of another sort, outside Mother's curriculum, took place in a railway carriage where a clergyman stroked the little chap's knee and give him sixpence. The process of learning the facts of life which the Lord had thus started on the

Noël Coward with Elaine Stritch (*Hulton Picture Library*).

Southern Railway, Miss Lawrence completed on the London, Midland and Scottish. To appear in *Peter Pan* was a feather in his cap. Already it was an essential stint for any stage-child worth his photograph at the back of the casting directory. The photograph grew bigger as he toured as Charley in *Charley's Aunt* and walked on when he felt like it in crowd scenes in *The Best of Luck* at Drury Lane where a friend had a speaking role. Egged on by Mother and by his appearance in two musicals, *The Light Blues* and *The Happy Family*, he wrote his first lyric. In the first three lines the authentic Coward voice can be heard:

> Ordinary man
> Invariably sighs
> In vain for what cannot be . . .

Indeed, seven years later when André Charlot was to commission Coward's first revue, *London Calling!*, the voice was not as sharply distinctive. In the meantime, the embryo Man of the Theatre had appeared in *Polly with a Past* and *The Knight of the Burning Pestle*; acted with Edith Evans, C. Aubrey Smith and Claude Rains; met and made life-long friends of the Lunts and Gladys Cooper and Elsa Maxwell; walked on in his first film, D. W. Griffith's *Hearts of the World* starring the Gish girls; travelled to America and Paris and Italy; penetrated the country houses which were to be the scene of so many of his plays; encountered Edward Molyneux who was to dress his modern pieces and Gladys Calthrop who was to clothe his period musicals; and seen two plays of his own mounted in the West End. He starred in *I'll Leave It to You* at the New Theatre, until it foundered amidst encircling gloom as Lady Wyndham, who was presenting it, cut the lighting by half as an economy measure. In *The Young Idea* (which produced a complimentary letter from George Bernard Shaw, '. . . I have no doubt you will succeed if you persevere . . . and, above all, never . . . see or read my plays . . .'), he played the lead again. Once more, a short run enabled him to be ready to write, compose and direct most of *London Calling!* 'Mr Coward cannot compose', wrote the *Sunday Express*, 'and should sing only for his friends' amazement.' The one song which has survived from this show, 'Parisian Pierrot', was introduced, not by Coward, but by Gertrude Lawrence. Coward was unable to perform in his next revue, *On With the Dance*, being otherwise engaged. The two years in between had been by no means fallow; he had written three plays, *The Vortex*, *Hay Fever* and *Fallen Angels*. He had journeyed to New York and he had worked obsessively to get his plays produced. It was *The Vortex* which catapulted all of them and as many more as he could write, or for which he could delve into his desk, on to the stage. By the time he arrived at *On With the Dance*, Herbert Farjeon, in *The Sphere*, was able to paint a

picture of Coward's frenzied activity which chimes familiarly with
Robert Benchley's picture of Cole Porter at work in Paris some years
later.

> It must be hard work throwing off a couple of lyrics before
> breakfast, setting them to music by eleven o'clock, finishing the
> big scene in Act II, before dashing off to the Ivy Restaurant,
> appearing in a matinée, talking business with Mr Curtis Brown
> (his agent) between Acts I and II and letting off gas to an
> interviewer between Acts II and III, sketching a new revue and
> practising the latest step before the evening performance,
> gathering copy and declaring that everything is just too
> marvellous or just too shattering at the Midnight Follies or the
> Gargoyle; as I say, it must be hard work, and I hope that Mr
> Coward will not suffer from a nervous breakdown as a result of it.

The nervous breakdown was much more likely to be caused by C. B.
Cochran, the distinguished impresario for whom Coward was
working for the first time. To start with, Cochran doubted that Coward
could write the whole score and called in a composer, Philip Braham,
who had contributed to *London Calling!*. Coward outwitted him by
writing sketches in which the songs were so closely integrated that no
one could write them but him. The unfortunate Braham ended up with
three numbers. For the Manchester try-out he was given two days' leave
of absence from *The Vortex*. The audience had to make do with an eager
but apprehensive John Gielgud.* Coward found more trouble awaiting
him in Manchester. It needed a battle royal to detach Cochran from the
simple billing 'A C. B. Cochran Revue' – a simplicity which has always
appealed to impresarios – and to preserve in the show that one song
which has survived it, 'Poor Little Rich Girl'. They fought out the
contest in Cochran's hotel suite. The impresario, a rotund gentleman,
chose his own weapons, dripping wet bath towel and bare chest; but
Coward, city-suited and straight off the train, won in the end. It was
sung by the star of the show, Alice Delysia, to a youthful Hermione
Baddeley, who seems subsequently hardly to have heeded her advice to
'take care' and 'beware!'.

Success did not notably change Coward. He had had quite enough
confidence before it overtook him; however, sadly, pride was followed
by a plunge. Hard upon the success of *Fallen Angels*, *Hay Fever*, *Easy
Virtue* and *The Marquise* and his performance in *The Constant Nymph*,

---

* Not so apprehensive that he could not sum up Coward as 'dreadfully precocious and
rather too keen to show off at the piano'.

Coward allowed *Home Chat*, *This Was a Man*, *The Rat Trap* and, above all, *Sirocco* to sabotage his reputation. Not only did its leading lady, Frances Doble, famously address the booing first-night audience with the only speech she had memorised, 'This is the happiest moment of my life'; but Mother, deaf in a stage box, leant forward and asked in ringing tones, 'Is it a failure, dear?'

At least Coward was able to salvage one moment for his next revue, *This Year of Grace*. In a series of short parodies summing up the current London theatre scene he needed only one line to hit off 'Any Noël Coward play' – 'This is the happiest moment of my life.' In his review, St John Ervine raved of the London production from A almost to Z (he ran out after W):

> *This Year of Grace* is the most amusing, the most brilliant, the cleverest, the daintiest, the most exquisite, the most fanciful, the most graceful, the happiest, the most ironical, the jolliest, the most kaleidoscopic, the loveliest, the most magnificent, the neatest and nicest, the most opulent, the pithiest, the quickest, the richest, the most superb and tasteful, the most uberous, the most versatile, the wittiest . . .

When Beatrice Lillie and Coward took the show to New York, Robert Benchley found a different set of superlatives:

> It is the kind of revue that one might dream of writing for a completely civilised world and so long as people crowd in to see it . . . we are prepared to retract everything we have ever said against Mankind . . . unless someone in America is able to do something that approximates Mr Coward's feat we shall always feel that it was a mistake to break away from England back there in 1776 . . .

Certainly *This Year of Grace* contained more good things than Coward's two earlier revues. Of course, his obsessions with feeling blue, with the blues, with saxophones, syncopation and jazz were becoming mannered. There were no fewer than 21 references so far; and that without counting 'Cocktails'; but good revue reflects the surface of contemporary manners and Coward was a faithful reporter of the chic little West End fish bowl in which contentedly he swam, and his best lyrics contained just those same strictures with which Delysia had admonished Baddeley in 'Poor Little Rich Girl', this time to the tunes of 'Dance Little Lady' and 'World Weary' (for the New York version).

Coward, 'the drug drenched, long cigarette holder punctuating, silk dressing-gown clad menace to society and corrupter of youth', was rapidly manifesting himself as Coward the moralist. Not that he was advertising the fact. As he told the London *Evening Standard*, 'I may say I have a frightfully depraved mind. I am never out of opium dens, cocaine dens and other evil places. My mind is a mass of corruption.' Of course, being Coward, there was a sunny side to his wit:

> I am just an ingénue
> And shall be till I'm eighty-two . . .

And there was in the show one simple, attractive, durable song with a simple, attractive, durable tune, 'A Room With a View'.

For Coward the most attractive view might have been due north to his family's south. North was his father, illogically situated in South West One, entertaining Jane Cowl, the uncommunicative star of his son's play, *Easy Virtue*, and encouraging her towards conversation and nourishment simultaneously: 'Here, have a tongue sandwich, that'll make you talk.' But Father was a beginner when it came to Mother. She was having immortal longings. 'How much better', she wrote to him, 'to have gone when you still loved me . . .' Cole Lesley – Coward's friend, secretary and executor – has rationalised the family feuds. 'One could say that they had a talent for quarrelling; perhaps this is why family quarrels are such a marked characteristic of every one of Noël's comedies.' Family feuds apart, 1928 to 1934 were, as Lesley points out, Coward's 'Golden Years'; *This Year of Grace, Bitter Sweet, Private Lives, Cavalcade* and *Words and Music* contain most of the songs for which he will be remembered. Never again, to paraphrase *Private Lives*, would his cheap music be so potent. *Bitter Sweet* was born out of a gramophone recording of *Die Fledermaus* played to Coward and his favourite designer, Gladys Calthrop, on a Kentish summer evening. By the time they had reached Wimbledon Common on the drive back to town, a world of Hussars and Viennese débutantes and waltzes had thrust itself hectically into their imaginations. Coward could hear it, Calthrop could see it. In two concentrated stints of work, Coward put the play on paper. He wrote the first act while sharing a cabin with Cochran on a voyage back from New York. Act Two and the romantic conclusion were achieved while he was recovering from an operation for piles in Lady Carnarvon's nursing home. The score was more elusive until, when he was trapped in a traffic jam between a matinée and an evening performance of *This Year of Grace*, in which he was appearing in New York, the theme for 'I'll See You Again' popped up in his mind forcing itself through the clamour of taxi horns and irate drivers. 'After that,' Cole Lesley reports, 'the remainder of the score came effortlessly.' Perhaps too effortlessly. Robbed of the richness of Miss Calthrop's clothes and Ernst Stern's settings, and looked at in the cold light of print some 50 years on, the treasure chest of Coward's lyrics contains isolated gems and some pinchbeck and theatrical paste. A diamond, of course, with 'I'll See You Again'; a Cabuchon ruby for the 'very rough and tumble' life of 'a humble diseuse' in 'If Love Were All'; a mere sequin for 'Tokay'; and a zircon for 'Zigeuner'. However, in its jewelled production, *Bitter Sweet* took London by storm and ran for two years. Peggy Wood played it in London. Evelyn Laye had turned down the role. She resented Cochran and Coward's decision to employ Jessie Matthews in *This Year of Grace*, Miss Matthews having recently 'stolen' her husband. Later, she mended her heart and pocketed her pride in time to triumph on Broadway. Alas, the triumph was short-lived. Wall Street Depression and European elegance were not the formula for a long run. Ziegfeld, true to form when dealing with song writers, urged Coward to sprinkle the show with sex in the shape of Ziegfeld girls. Coward refused. 'They wanted me to alter everything and I wouldn't . . . now . . . (Ziegfeld) is saying that the theatre will never die as long as there is a genius like me in it.'

Hard on his hit, Coward embarked on one of those glamorous world tours on which songs and plays came to him unbidden, and were instantly made welcome. *Private Lives* turned up in Tokyo. 'Someday I'll Find You', the song which pervades the play, took a little more seeking. 'Mad Dogs and Englishmen' worked itself out in Tonkin, half-way between Hanoi and Saigon. 'I sang it triumphantly and unaccompanied to my travelling companion, Jeffrey Amherst, on the verandah of a small jungle guest-house. Not only Jeffrey but also the gecko lizards and the tree frogs gave every vocal indication of enthusiasm.'

1930 found Coward playing *Private Lives* in London, conceiving *Cavalcade* and finishing off the year at home in Kent writing four songs for *Cochran's 1931 Revue*. 'Any Little Fish' is charming, but 'Half-Caste Woman' is Coward at half-cock. However, it had some success both in London and on Broadway for Ziegfeld. He was still inclined to preach to the Bright Young People of the bright new decade, but the sermon contained one of his neatest couplets:

Though Waterloo was won upon the playing fields of Eton,
The next war will be photographed, and lost, by Cecil Beaton.

The rest of the song is a sketch for the marvellous 'Marvellous Party'. By now the decks were cleared for *Cavalcade*, a pageant of English history from 1900 to 1929, staged on the grand scale. In it Coward mingled authentic music hall numbers and the recruiting songs of two wars with his own new composition, 'Twentieth Century Blues', which closed the evening and which took a bleak look at the thirties after the patriotic special pleading of the rest of the play. After Coward's last scene of 'dreary twentieth century din' his curtain speech redressed the loyal balance: '. . . it is still pretty exciting to be English.'

Another triumph, another cruise, another High Comedy. Sunning himself in Santiago, Chile, he was jolted by a telegram from the Lunts (OUR CONTRACT WITH THEATRE GUILD UP IN JUNE, WHAT ABOUT IT?) into writing *Design for Living*. There were no songs in *Design for Living*, but another revue for Cochran, *Words and Music*, was on the horizon. By this time Coward had got too big for Cochran's boots. He decided that he could dispense with stars, spectacles, and dance sensations. In spite of some of Coward's best songs and best notices, the revue ran for only five months. Weariness, ennui and saxophones were still much in evidence. Memories of Wall Street and the short Broadway run of *Bitter Sweet* add an extra sting to 'Children of the Ritz'. 'Mad Dogs and Englishmen' entered Coward's repertoire and became one of those songs which he would have to perform ever after when confronted by a Crowned Head, an Elder Statesman or a large audience. Another 'Mad' classic was 'Mad About the Boy' in which various women proclaimed their obsession for a current idol of the screen, and the 'sleepless nights they'd had about the boy . . .', the fact that 'Housman really wrote "The Shropshire Lad" about the boy . . .', one even '. . . 'ad a row with Dad about the boy . . .'. In setting his lyric Coward mixed a wistful quality with the efficiency which he always displayed in setting up his jokes. That wistful note is struck again with great assurance in 'Three White Feathers', a song for a working-class girl, played by Doris Hare, ennobled by marriage and stuck in the traffic in The Mall on her way to a Royal Garden Party. There were more frivolous songs too about rabbits having minds like sinks, about the way that sows behaved – 'delightfully quaint' – while the question was posed, 'Why should cows behave with *no* restraint?'. Apparently it was 'Something to do with Spring'. 'The Party's Over Now' sent the audience home in modish, sentimental fashion. Jule Styne and Comden and Green were to say the same thing with more assurance in *Bells are Ringing* a quarter of a century later; but in 1926 the party was over too for Coward's brother Erik. He died that summer.

Design for Living, designed for Broadway, was followed by *Conversation Piece*, a Regency musical, designed as a vehicle for the French star, Yvonne Printemps. Coward had his usual terrier-like chase for a big *valse* theme and having hurried it and worried it to no purpose decidedly gave up the whole project when,

> I poured myself a large whisky and soda, dined in grey solitude, poured myself another, even larger, whisky and soda and sat gloomily envisaging everybody's disappointment and facing the fact that my talent had withered and that I should never write any

more music until the day I died. The whisky did little to banish the
gloom, but there was no more work to be done and I didn't care if I
became fried as a coot, so I gave myself another drink and decided
to go to bed. I switched off the light at the door and noticed that
there was one lamp left on by the piano. I walked automatically to
turn it off, sat down and played 'I'll Follow My Secret Heart'
straight through in G flat, a key I had never played in before.

The rest of the score was lacklustre Coward, but Yvonne Printemps
scored a personal triumph and the show ran successfully. Two flashes of
pre-eminently Coward wit crept in. One wise 'and thoroughly worldly
wench, Knows there's always something fishy about the French . . .'.
And six lines summarily, if unfairly, dispose of the Pavilion at Brighton:

The Pavilion
Cost a million
As a monument to Art,
And the wits here
Say it sits here
Like an Oriental tart!

Tonight at 8.30 brought out a sturdier side of Coward's talent and was
his first venture under his own management. He had broken – amicably
– from Cochran whose farewell present was a Regency snuff box
inscribed 'For Noël, in memory of a not altogether unsuccessful
association.' For *Tonight at 8.30* Coward the playwright came up with
nine one-act plays. Coward the composer and lyric writer was required
to furnish ten songs. Eventually he and Gertrude Lawrence played three
programmes of three plays each, giving them both ample opportunity to
display their versatility. One playgoer saw six of the plays on a
marathon matinée day. 'I wonder', he enquired at the end, 'what he is
like on the tightrope?' The best songs came in the vaudeville routines for
the warring music hall pair in *Red Peppers*. A naval pastiche, 'Has
Anybody Seen Our Ship?', can be as funny and stageworthy today as
when it was first staged, or it can drag, limp and self-conscious,
depending on the candle-power of the performers.

Such was Coward's fame in the thirties, '. . . I was a highly publicised
and irritatingly successful figure, much in demand . . .', that he was
besieged by mothers almost as ambitious as his own, anxious to assist
their children's progress to the boards. In an attempt to get them to desist
he wrote an open letter, 'Regarding yours, dear Mrs Worthington, of
Wednesday the 23rd', advising her not to put her daughter on the stage.
But Coward's advice was not enough. It only served to encourage more
mothers to write to him, jocularly brushing aside his song as irrelevant

to their promise-crammed brats. Coward was philosophical. 'The road of the social reformer', he regretted, 'is paved with disillusion.' Another triumph in New York with *Tonight at 8.30* led promptly to another bout of nervous exhaustion, another recuperatory cruise and, inevitably, another show. Travel broadened his metre and inspired his mind. 'I travel alone,' he was to write in one autobiographical lyric. The show that sprang from this particular Odyssey was *Operette*, Coward's second attempt to recapture the success of *Bitter Sweet*. However, his dexterity with patter songs was rapidly outstripping his gift for romantic lyrics. The ragbag of backstage clichés which made up the plot was not strong enough to carry the evening. 'The Stately Homes of England', eminently detachable and, subsequently, detached for *Set to Music* (a 1939 Broadway revue), stood out.

Domesticity in Coward's own comfortable but less than stately home in Kent ran a troubled course. While the mercurial, talented, diverse genius, with his pickled Peter Pan side forever popping out, could escape to London or New York or Bollamazoo, taking his triumphs gracefully or indulging his tantrums shamelessly, his no less mercurial mother stayed at home and gave his ailing father hell. In particular, she suspected her husband's relationship with a neighbour, Miss de Pomeroy, who seems only to have been keen to show considerate kindness for the old gentleman where his wife showed none. Nothing could allay Mrs Coward's suspicions and indeed should something have come along to allay them she would have been furious. She elevated Miss de Pomeroy to the status of the Other Woman and after Mr Coward's death never forgave her for the gaffe of sending a larger wreath than her own. From then on there was only Coward on whom she could work off her bitter energy. Her letters pursued him around the globe and so, sometimes, did she. 'You neglected me for months because you had no time to write, and then found time to type pages of a pompous lecture at me. How dared you! Hitler is not governing us yet and I have as much right to my opinions as you have . . .'

In 1939 he revamped *Words and Music* for Broadway under the title *Set to Music*, a vehicle for Bea Lillie. The triumph was hers although Coward also incorporated a new song which he had written earlier, 'I've Been to a Marvellous Party'. With the advent of war in 1939, Coward wrote no more musicals until it was over. He produced plays in plenty, with no drop in standards in *Blithe Spirit* and *Present Laughter*; but much of his time was spent travelling the world even more restlessly than he had in peace-time, entertaining the troops, spurred on, or riled perhaps, by Winston Churchill's famous advice to 'go and sing to them when the guns are firing'. His programme, sometimes repeated four or five times a day, lasted an hour and a half and he kept his repertoire up to date. Ironically, he became so famous for his permitted parodies of Cole

Porter's 'Let's Do It' that half the world came to believe the whole song was Coward's. During this period he wrote patriotic songs like 'London Pride', or patriotic-satirical songs like 'Could You Please Oblige Us with a Bren-Gun?' or 'Don't Let's Be Beastly to the Germans'; or patriotic songs which now sound as though they were intended to be satirical though undoubtedly they were not:

> There have been songs in England
> Since our Island rose from the seas . . .

Some found their way into post-war revues like *Sigh No More*. There was the impossible 'Senorita Nina' from Argentina, and the 'Famous monumental men, the officers and gentlemen' of the Indian Army, in 'I Wonder What Happened to Him?'. One wartime song came to life again in *Pacific 1860* (which starred Mary Martin), his first, disastrous, post-war musical. It concerned 'Poor Uncle Harry' who 'wanted to be a missionary'. This was the show-stopping number; and stop the show it did after what Coward described as 'more a convulsive stagger than a run'. It deserved better but the odds were stacked against it. In cruel, cold weather the vast unheated Drury Lane Theatre was being re-opened for the first time after the war. Miscastings abounded – hopes were too high. Production problems proliferated; the last few weeks of preparation were Coward's unhappiest period in the theatre. Yet there are more pleasing touches among the lyrics than the audience could hear above the chattering of their teeth on that icy first night. Tropical images of 'bamboo shoots and tender roots – incredible! And fortunately edible!', and a lament from the person 'nobody understands', from 'the strange, irresolute glands of a big girl – like me!'. Once again, the romantic songs, 'Bright Was the Day' and 'I Never Knew', did not lift the show as they should have done, though there is great charm in 'This Changing World, My Dear'. It was a changing world above all for its author. He was to see his reputation plummet through the fifties, a decade of doubt and anxiety for him. Like so many people of his generation, he did not relish changes he did not understand and he lashed out wildly. He did not manage to write the new-style post-war musical which heartened so many of his American peers. He had not the comfort of knowing that ten years later the wheel would turn and that his earlier plays would gain classic status.

His mother died in 1954. In her last, enfeebled years they became reconciled and he wrote, 'without her I could only have achieved a quarter of what I have achieved . . . we have quarrelled, often violently, over the years, but she has never . . . tried to hold me too tightly, always let me go free . . .'

He was to write four more musicals, *Ace of Clubs* in 1950; *After the*

Ball, based on Oscar Wilde's *Lady Windermere's Fan*, in 1954; *Sail Away* in 1961; and *The Girl Who Came to Supper*, based on Rattigan's *The Sleeping Prince*, in 1963; but, like his later plays, these musicals did not add to his legendary stature. His spontaneous wit flourished with impeccable timing; his popular revivals and his personal appearances in cabaret took care of that. Imperturbably he delivered the old songs and the glittering exceptions with which his last four scores were studded. 'In the fifties, I emerged, to my own and everyone else's astonishment, as a highly successful cabaret entertainer,' he wrote, '. . . a captious journalist announced recklessly that I "massacred" my own songs. If I did I can only say it was the most triumphantly efficient massacre since Saint Bartholomew's Eve.'

Ace of Clubs has four amusing songs (and eight which wearily use the word 'gay' in its innocent sense as an easy, singable rhyme). 'Three Juvenile Delinquents' was one of Coward's most pointed point numbers – 'The Stately Homes of England' rewritten for adolescent, underprivileged malingerers. 'Mental doctors', they sang, 'try to civilise us, psycho-analyse us.' In the post-war period 'psycho-analysis' was to become as potent a word for Coward as 'syncopation' had been in the thirties. The song hit its target powerfully until a similar statement in *West Side Story*, 'Gee Officer Krupke!', said the same things with more sympathy and with more durable jokes.* 'Josephine', a cabaret song about Napoleon's consort, never established the place in cabaret repertoire which it should have commanded. One of Coward's most pleasant lyrical puns is tucked away in the second chorus:

> . . . She very soon married this short young man
> Who talked about soldiers all day;
> But who wasn't above
> Making passionate love
> In a coarse, rather Corsican way . . .

There is 'Chase Me, Charlie!', a cat-on-the-tiles mixture of vaudeville and Cole Porter, and 'I Like America', infinitely exportable though it failed to set the Thames on fire. It is a wonderfully adroit piece of geographical list-making:

> . . . All delegates
> From Southern States

---

* The authors have a vivid memory of the London first night of *West Side Story*. At the end of the play Coward leant across to Sir Harold Hobson, critic of the *Sunday Times*, and said, 'Careful, Harold.' A warning Sir Harold failed to heed, giving the show a bad notice.

> Are nervy and distraught,
> In New Orleans
> The wrought-iron screens
> Are dreadfully overwrought . . .

By now the forties of Broadway had happened to London. The American musical invasion had taken place with a vengeance and Coward had, unthinkably, to audition and accept managerial advice about his book. Whatever advice they gave did not afford the show a run. Coward's reaction was splendidly tetchy: 'I am furious about *Ace of Clubs* not being a real smash and I have come to the conclusion that if they don't care for first-rate music, lyrics, dialogue and performance, they can stuff it up their collective arses and go and see *King's Rhapsody*.' (*King's Rhapsody* was a traditional, period musical by Ivor Novello.)

Before his next full-scale musical, Coward sparred with several occasional songs, including one of his best, the saga of a widow, 'a mother and wife who, for most of her life, was famed for domestic virtue'. When her husband 'joined the feathered choir', she shot off to Capri where life called to her 'In a Bar on the Piccola Marina'. Then there was 'Alice', who had a similar but more youthful, bucolic, sexual drive. 'Alice' was always 'at it again'. To complete the trilogy of fifties ladies there was 'Louisa', a movie queen with quite a different Garboesque problem: she was terribly lonely.

After the Ball saw the final, inevitable marriage of Coward to Oscar Wilde. Few of the offspring were a credit to either parent. There were exceptions.

> What a Royal Academy
> Too Alma Tademy,
> Practical, mystical,
> Over-artistical,
> Highly pictorial,
> Albert Memorial
> Century this has been . . .

And an Australian sea-shanty for Mr Hopper, charmingly sung by Graham Payn. A song for Irene Browne, who had been in *No, No, Nanette* in its London première 40 years earlier, was an exhausted dowager's plea for 'A Little Eggy Something on a Tray'. On tour Miss Browne resented the good notices scored by the juvenile. Seeing her chance of revenge one evening when the unfortunate girl kept the stage waiting, she descended on her. The leading lady interceded, 'Don't hit her, Irene, she's as thin as a match.' Miss Browne was up to both Wilde and Coward in her come-back. 'Precisely,' she boomed. 'She should be struck and thrown away.'

There was a spirited celebration of 'London at Night':

Old men in lobbies
With dubious hobbies
Can still get the deuce of a fright
In London at night.

And a 'big' ballad:

Sweet day, remain for me
Clear in my memory . . .

Which led to the pillory in a revue of the actress who sang it and whose voice was no longer as flexible an instrument as she had assured Coward it would be. The parody version ran:

Sweet voice that used to be
Still cracking on Top C . . .

In later years Coward lost the gift for a big sweeping tune which invested his earlier scores with a romantic aura. His later shows lacked those swelling themes; on the other hand, he worked harder at upholding his reputation as a wit and his patter songs became more plentiful and more quotable. *Sail Away*, Coward's 1961 musical, revived 'Sail Away' from 1950's *Ace of Clubs* almost in its entirety. The verse was different but the chorus, ungrammatical though it was, survived: 'When you feel your song is orchestrated wrong . . .'. The trends of the sixties were appeased with an 'off-beat, on-beat Beatnik love affair . . .', and the expected Coward show-stopper was given to the leading lady, Elaine Stritch:

Why do the wrong people travel, travel, travel
When the right people stay back home?
What compulsion compels them
And who the hell tells them
To drag their cans to Zanzibar
Instead of staying quietly on Omaha?

The list of rhyming place names is relentless but irresistible; so was Miss Stritch.

The Girl Who Came to Supper took a thin play, carbonated into some sort of success by a sparkling cast (Laurence Olivier, Vivien Leigh, Martita Hunt and Richard Wattis) – and not only made it thinner, but flattened any surviving bubbles with a second-ranking cast who sat heavily on any lingering sign of effervescence. Roderick Cooke, who was later to make the definitive collection of Cowardiana, *Oh Coward*, was an exception, happily cast in the Richard Wattis role, and Tessie O'Shea stopped the show in an interminable anthology of indifferent Cockney music hall songs which represented Coward's last congé to a gutsy art form that he had always enjoyed and sometimes emulated. Naomi Jacob once pronounced him the perfect song writer for Marie Lloyd – a wild surmise, but this medley is the nearest he got to it.

In his introduction to his 'sixties' lyrics, Coward wrote, 'The compulsion to make rhymes was born in me,' and added, 'For those sated readers of my work who wish ardently that I would stop, the future looks dark indeed . . .' That last prophecy was not to prove true. He died in 1973, his last words to his special friends, 'Good night, my darlings, I'll see you tomorrow.'

Philip Hope Wallace has written, 'Never trust a man who decries the songs of Noël Coward'; if we have carped we have not forgotten that with Coward the whole exceeded the parts. We liked the man, we admired the artist, and we still revel in his wit. Coward had already written his own epitaph 40 years before he died; there are those lines most frequently quoted:

> . . . I believe that since my life began
> The most I've had is just
> A talent to amuse . . .

which he himself rejected as too limiting for his broad talent. But there are some other words from the same song which offer an even keener perception of his strengths, his limitations, and the tenacity with which he clung to success:

> Fate may often treat me meanly,
> But I keenly
> Pursue
> A little mirage in the blue.
> Determination helps me through.

JOHNNY MERCER

'My Momma Done Tol' Me'

Johnny Mercer is the standard-bearer of that vast regiment of song writers who turned out hit songs but who were not successful writers for the theatre. He carries the banner in these pages because of the special quality of his individual lyrics. There are a handful of people who write isolated popular songs as well as show scores – Irving Berlin and Frank Loesser are the two outstanding examples. There is Porter who wrote show songs which might as well have been conceived without context, but which habitually had one; and then there are Hart and Hammerstein, and Harnick and Lerner and Sondheim, who rarely start on a lyric unless it has a place in a show. Most of Mercer's enormous range of popular hits were aimed straight at Tin Pan Alley or created for films. Very few stem from the handful of shows on which he worked, only one successful. In 1971, in his lecture at the 92nd Street YMHA in Maurice Levine's *Lyrics and Lyricists* series, Mercer remarked that he never had a big song on the stocks when a big show 'came along' and that you can't let your big songs 'hang around' or 'some other fellow might write them'.

A casual glance at his repertoire leaves no doubt that he had a way with a phrase – 'Jeepers Creepers', 'You're Just Too Marvellous, too marvellous for words' and 'You Must Have Been a Beautiful Baby, 'cause baby look at you now'. E. Y. Harburg has called Mercer 'the greatest of Folk Poets' and argued that he owes this accolade to his Southern background. He was heir to a tradition which endowed him with the descriptive flair of Mark Twain, and which made the melodies of Stephen Foster a part of him.

He was born in 1909 in Savannah, Georgia and he refused, even before birth, to conform to the patterns of conception, arrival and upbringing which seem to be necessary qualifications for so many lyric writers of his generation. John Herndon Mercer was not the son of poor, Jewish, immigrant parents. The Episcopalian Mercers traced their roots in America back to before the Revolution. A Mercer ancestor, a Brigadier General, fought under Washington. Mercer's parents, Lilian and George A. Mercer, were living in comfortable circumstances when John Herndon was born. George Mercer was a lawyer who also dealt in real estate. Johnny Mercer remembered his home town with affection. 'Savannah's still like it used to be,' he said in the early seventies, 'hospitable, warm, friendly. Everybody goes around and sings songs, drinks and loves one another.' He fitted happily into this atmosphere. Family tradition has it that at six months his Aunt Hattie hummed him a tune which he proceeded to hum back to her. At three or four he began to listen to songs recorded on the old cylindrical Edison records and soon he was singing them. One day in 1916 he gave his mother the slip and disappeared for a whole day. 'I looked all over town for him,' she recalled. 'When he finally got home late in the evening, I found out that he had followed the town band, the Irish Jasper Greens, out to a picnic and stayed with them all day. He just couldn't resist the music.' After that his mother engaged a maid to monitor young John Herndon's movements, but she was soon dismayed to meet the girl in the street without her charge. Mrs Mercer asked why the seven-year-old had been abandoned. 'Nothing else I could do,' said the maid. 'Why?' 'He fired me!'

Gramophone records had now progressed to the sophistication of the early 78s and Mercer was listening and learning and becoming, in particular, an expert on obscure verses. Victor Herbert was for a long time his favourite composer; but he switched some allegiance to Jerome Kern when he heard 'They Didn't Believe Me'. By the time he was fifteen he had started to doodle his own lyrics, including one called 'Sister Susie, Strut Your Stuff'. His concentration on the routine school curriculum was casual; but his interest in words was genuine and intense, especially in the Southern dialect which he spoke himself and in the influence of Gullah speech and songs which he heard from the black people around him. He increased and enriched his vocabulary.

> Sue wants a barbecue, Sam wants to boil a ham,
> Grace votes for Bouillabaise stew,
> Jake wants a weeny-bake, steak and a layer cake,
> He'll get a tummy ache too . . .

At the same time he started to study the theatre – a trait which delighted Mrs Mercer who had modest ambitions to be a stage mother. In 1927, when Mercer was nearly eighteen, his father's business affairs fell into disarray and he narrowly avoided bankruptcy. The fight was desperate and involved an arrangement with the banks which required George Mercer to struggle over the years to pay off debts of almost a million

Johnny Mercer (*ASCAP*).

dollars. He died in 1940 before he had discharged his obligations. Mercer, who was by now a popular composer and lyric writer and also a well-known radio and recording personality, began to assume the responsibility. He completed the task in 1955; but not before he had mailed one cheque for $300,000 in full settlement and forgotten to sign it. A few days later, he sent another cheque to the trustee with a note which read, 'I made out that cheque and carried it a few days unsigned in case I lost it. When I got round to mailing it I suppose I forgot to sign it. But if by chance I did sign it, please tear up one or the other of them.'

In 1928 he stowed away on a ship to New York, was discovered and made to work his passage. He set out on the journey because the Savannah Drama Group to which he belonged had qualified to enter a one-act play competition in Manhattan. Unfortunately, the invitation did not include round-trip tickets. Once in New York, Mercer determined to stay and, when his colleagues went home, he moved into a one-room apartment in Greenwich Village. He tried to get a break as an actor – even, according to some sources, using a monocle as a trick to impress himself on directors and producers. The monocle was clear glass and one day a friend, not seeing it resting on a bar, crashed a mug of beer down on it. Conscience-stricken, he insisted on substituting a chic, square monocle. Mercer declined it. 'Anyone who would wear a square monocle is affected,' he explained. He went along to audition for the 1930 edition of the revue, *Garrick Gaieties*. Rodgers and Hart were no longer involved; this was the show which introduced Vernon Duke to American audiences; Ira Gershwin, E. Y. Harburg and Marc Blitzstein were other contributors. Mercer was told there were no roles for him – all that the production needed was 'girls and songs'. He supplied one of the songs and eventually married one of the 'girls', Elizabeth 'Ginger' Meehan; theirs was a long and happy partnership. The song, with music by Everett Miller, was 'Out of Breath and Scared to Death of You'. It did not stop the show but it admitted Mercer to a new world of song writers amongst whom he felt immediately at home. He and Harburg went on to contribute to J. P. McEvoy's 1932 revue *Americana*. Harburg's big hit was 'Brother, Can You Spare a Dime?', and the show introduced both men to the music of Harold Arlen with whom they were to collaborate so often. For *Americana*, Mercer, Harburg and Arlen wrote 'Satan's Little Lamb'.

However, the newly married Mercer was finding the insecurity of writing for Broadway shows dispiriting and tried to change his career – in his own words, 'misplacing stocks and bonds in a Wall Street brokerage office'. But he kept in touch with music – many of his friends worked with the big bands of the era as composers, arrangers, singers or instrumentalists. One of his principal influences was the highly idiosyncratic vocabulary of musicians:

Cigarette holder which wigs me,
Over her shoulder she digs me,
Out cattin' that Satin Doll . . .

The other, clearly discernible, source is the countryside from which
Mercer came. The feeling, the pace, and the rich imagery of the South
fill his songs. In 1932, with another musician friend, Hoagy Carmichael,
he wrote one of his most sundrenched rural lyrics, 'Lazy Bones'. It is a
perfect blending of the lessons he learnt from his roots.

Long as there is chicken gravy on your rice,
Ev'rything is nice.
Long as there is water melon on the vine
Ev'rything is fine . . .

How would he get his corn-meal made, sitting in the shade? When the
'taters' need sprayin', of course he keeps prayin' the slugs fall off of the
vine. And when he goes fishin' . . . he keeps wishin' the fish won't grab
at his line. 'How,' the song asks, 'loafin' thru' the day', does Lazy Bones
expect 'to make a dime that way'. Mercer provides a lovely pay-off:

He never heard a word I say!

Hoagy Carmichael has described its genesis. 'A song plugger introduced
me to Johnny Mercer. He was a young, bouncy, butterball of a man
from Georgia. He hadn't had a song hit, but I could tell that he could
write . . . we did a couple of things that weren't too important but then
one day he strolled into my apartment and said, "I'd like to write a song
called 'Lazy Bones'." "Sounds fine – let's start." Actually, in twenty
minutes we wrote the entire song . . .'
    Two weeks after it had been published and sung by Kate Smith,
Carmichael left for Europe in search of new influences. It was a barren
journey, all he heard from Lisbon to the Lido was American music; but
on his return he found that 'Lazy Bones' had become an overnight hit
and was selling 15,000 copies a day. It meant that Mercer could leave his
office job and concentrate on song writing. They wrote more songs
together, 'In the Cool, Cool, Cool of the Evening' and 'Skylark', for
example. However, by this time Mercer had committed himself to his
other interest – the bands. Sometimes he was writing, sometimes
singing, playing master of ceremonies or recording for Frankie
Trumbauer and his orchestra, for the Dorsey Brothers, and especially
for Paul Whiteman. It bred a fatal facility. He responded to the music
and fitted his words to it, enriching and enhancing it, and showing a
keen sense of what it was saying; his habit became casual and

conversational. There was no dramatic context to consider. Speed and felicity were what was admired. A demanding apprenticeship was served outside the discipline of the theatre. His instincts were conditioned by the microphone not the proscenium arch. He wrote a song a week for Whiteman for his Kraft Radio Show. Al Jolson and Jack Teagarden were regular performers and Mercer's lyrics had Whiteman's vocalists or his musicians in mind. For Benny Goodman he wrote 'Dixieland Band', Bernie Hanighen was the composer. With Ziggy Elman, who was the trumpeter in Goodman's band, Mercer wrote 'And the Angels Sing', the tune an adaptation of a traditional Jewish dance, the lyric pure Tin Pan Alley. More amusingly, at this time Mercer was indulging himself with novelty numbers like 'The Girl Friend of the Whirling Dervish', who 'gave him the run around'.

> Every night when he goes out to make an honest rupee
> She's making whoopee . . .!

Then there was 'The Yogi Who Lost His Willpower':

> A yogi is a man who sits and thinks
> And never has time for forty winks
> He seldom eats and he rarely drinks,
> And he's usually from Rangoon . . .

Mercer's regular appearances as singer or master of ceremonies focused attention on him. With Broadway in the doldrums Hollywood beckoned. He too went west – chiming at last with his peers in the lyric-writing profession by joining the exodus. At the same time his acting ambitions finally expired. He appeared in two films; indeed, he was featured in 1935 in *Old Man Rhythm*, singing his own lyric, 'I Never Saw a Better Night' to Lewis Gensler's tune in a camp-fire setting; but his first two film scores were flops and, with his wife, he set off for Georgia, driving across Texas. The mechanised cowboys of that state gave him an idea for a song for which he wrote both words and music, 'I'm an Old Cow Hand from the Rio Grande' – but this cowboy covers the Lone Star State in modern fashion: 'I ride the range in a Ford V Eight . . .'. Bing Crosby liked the song. It went into *Rhythm on the Range* in 1936; and Mercer felt that his career in movies was saved. The arbitrary disciplines of film musicals proved an ideal platform for him. It was appropriate that he should write 'Hooray for Hollywood' with Richard Whiting:

> That screwy bally-hooey Hollywood . . .
> Where you're terrific if you're even good.

He could always comment on a moment, serve a splendid tune, suit the style of a star, beguile an audience with a fresh turn of phrase, an original attitude, a congenial joke, tug their emotions or conjure up a nostalgic evocation of a universal memory.

His work with Jerome Kern, one of his boyhood idols, on the film *You Were Never Lovelier* introduced a new, more elegant note. 'I'm Old-Fashioned' was the first of Kern's melodies to which Mercer set words; he seems to have taken particular trouble over the verse, remembering, perhaps, the relish with which he used to memorise the verses to Kern's songs when he was a child.

> I am not such a clever one about the latest fads.
> I admit I was never one adored by local lads;
> Not that I ever try to be a saint,
> I'm the type they classify as quaint.

The film's title song has a smile about it which found its way into Astaire's voice. 'Dearly Beloved' ran through the whole picture as a unifying theme, but in this song Mercer's sense of humour is strictly under wraps.

Mercer admired the work of Dorothy Fields, another of Kern's great film collaborators, but one who discovered the secret of writing theatre songs as well. Like Mercer, Dorothy Fields wrote with a wide variety of composers and Mercer felt that they shared a 'feeling for tunes'. He compared her gift for lyrics to John O'Hara's ear for dialogue. Mercer made the point that when she wrote with Kern 'she rose right up to his melodies'. Kern had the same effect on Mercer; so did Harold Arlen.

'One For My Baby' captures a moment in many lives. It addresses an unrequited love song directly to an off-stage character – a barman, Joe, asked to set 'em up at a quarter to three:

> We're drinking my friend,
> To the end of a brief episode;
> Make it one for my baby and one more for the road . . .

Three other songs Mercer and Arlen wrote together do not have the same sense of time and place; but they are all classic lyrics in their fine, distinctive phrasing – 'That Old Black Magic', 'Hit the Road to Dreamland' and 'Accent-tchu-ate the Positive'. While he was writing songs for celluloid Mercer also found time to develop his business instincts – he was one of the founders of Capitol Records. He contributed largely to the early catalogue. One song was backed by a solid theatrical instinct, 'Arthur Murray Taught Me Dancing in a Hurry'. 'G.I. Jive' was a 1943 song for which Mercer wrote words and music. He was back to his band vocabulary mixed with military initials:

> . . . Out of your seat, into the street,
> Make with the feet!
> Reet!
> If you're a P.V.T. your duty
> Is to salute the L.I.E.U.T.
> But if you brush the L.I.E.U.T.
> The M.P. makes you K.P. on the Q.T.

In two of his film scores Mercer got nearer to the integration of theatre songs and had big commercial hits at the same time. On both films he was working with collaborators who had theatrical backgrounds and instincts. *The Harvey Girls* went into production in the wake of the stage success of *Oklahoma!* and Arthur Freed, the moving spirit behind the film, had skilfully reassured the suspicious Harvey family, sending them a wire drawing their attention to *Oklahoma!* and *Show Boat* and the 'gaiety and spiritual quality of the music'. This, he argued, gave shows a 'status in the theatrical literature of American folk lore . . .' which they 'could never have reached . . . as straight dramas . . .'. He promised to approach the story of the restaurant chain and its waitresses 'with a great deal of reverence . . . in an important dignified American work'. Guy Bolton and seven other writers were brought reverently to construct the screenplay. Roger Edens was in immediate charge of the project and presided over a distillation of the work of the eight authors. He had recently been to New Haven to see the opening of *Oklahoma!* and was keenly aware of the new significance of making the music help in the business of unravelling the plot. Mercer was reunited with a composer, Harry Warren, whose career stretched back to selling oranges at the Liberty Theatre in Brownsville when Jacob P. Adler ran a Jewish stock company there at the turn of the century. He continued his education as a stage hand at Loewe's Theatre on Liberty Avenue and as a pianist in silent movie houses. He graduated to writing songs for Broadway revues in the thirties including 'Cheerful Little Earful' with Ira Gershwin and, in 1931, 'I Found a Million Dollar Baby in a Five and Ten Cent Store'. In Hollywood Warren wrote *42nd Street, Gold Diggers of 1933* ('35, '37 and *Gold Diggers in Paris*) and a string of other film scores. George Sidney directed *The Harvey Girls*, Kay Thompson did the vocal arrangements with Ralph Blane, the cast included Judy Garland, John Hodiak, Ray Bolger, Angela Lansbury and Cyd Charisse. Edens and Kay Thompson worked closely with Mercer and Warren and even an Academy Award-winning block-buster like 'The Atchison, Topeka and the Santa Fe' was adapted to serve the identification of each of the Harvey girls as they arrived on the train.

The sequence took twenty days of rehearsal, covered acres of ground and, with Judy Garland's character already established by her daydreaming song on the train, 'In the Valley (Where the Evening Sun Goes Down)', 'The Atchison, Topeka and the Santa Fe' did its job of getting the picture off to a brash, believable start with superb vitality and humour.

In *Seven Brides for Seven Brothers*, Mercer was out in the open air again; Gene de Paul was his composer, Stanley Donen, an experienced hand at musicals, his director; and the choreographer was Michael Kidd who had already worked inventively with the composer and lyric writer on Mercer's one Broadway hit, *Li'l Abner*. The folk feeling combined with Mercer's native wit fill the score with brash Western argot. 'Bless Your Beautiful Hide' and 'Goin' Co'tin'' both speak for it. The vocabulary for the production number, 'Spring, Spring, Spring', is perhaps too sophisticated for the rural characters; but the ripple of humour which plays throughout the lyric catches with great charm the exuberant expectations of the young lovers.

> . . . Slow but surely the turtle
> Enormously fert'le
> Lays her eggs by the dozens,
> Maybe some are her cousins,
> Even the catamount is nonplussed by that amount
> It's Spring, Spring, Spring!

The main plot of the film, a Western retelling of the Rape of the Sabine Women, gives Mercer a marvellous opportunity to marry Roman myth with Western dialect.

Mercer's instinct for the occasional song attracted innumerable commissions for that isolated art form, the film title-song – usually a ballad like 'Laura', 'Charade' and (borrowing a title from Ernest Dowson and adding little more than a feeling for the music and some sunny country images) 'The Days of Wine and Roses'. Mercer won several Academy Awards for 'Best Song'; 'The Days of Wine and Roses' and 'Moon River' were two of them.

Sometimes Mercer provides not so much a title, more a signature for a film, as he did in writing 'Moon River' for *Breakfast at Tiffany's*. Again the tune was Henry Mancini's and the song's place in the final film was as perilous as that of 'Somewhere Over the Rainbow' in *The Wizard of Oz*. At a preview in San Francisco the movie was too long and the producers felt that the one thing that could easily go was 'that song'. It remained (to everyone's advantage) and stems again from Mercer's childhood recollections. Holly Golightly comes from his part of the world. In an interview with Max Wilk, trying to trace the memorable phrase 'Huckleberry friend', Mercer remembers growing up in the South, hunting for berries in the fields, and he ascribes the phrase to happy memories of those expeditions. He had toyed with 'Red River' as a title for the song – an image suggested by sleepy Southern mud – and then, thinking of Holly's predicament in New York and remembering the dark blue berries, he hit on 'Huckleberry' and knew that he had found an odd word but an attractive one – which is one glint on a lyric writer's Grail. The song proved a perfect marriage of folk poet and hired hand. A similar romantic union was achieved with 'Blues in the Night'. Harold Arlen wrote a steady repetitive blues theme; Mercer heard the train sound in it, which always attracted him. 'Trains are a marvellous symbol. Somebody's always coming in or leaving on one, so it's either sadness or happiness.'

> I took a trip on a train
> And thought about you . . .

Mercer covered several pages of notes and, as they worked on the song, Arlen came upon his opening phrases tucked away at the end of the jottings. They were quickly promoted, and one of popular music's most eloquent passages gained its proper place:

> My Momma done tol' me
> When I was in knee pants . . .

The train image is removed to the bridge of the song. Like so many American song writers, Mercer knew how to use evocative place names:

> From Natchez to Mobile from Memphis to St Joe
> Wherever the four winds blow . . .

Mercer had a preliminary skirmish with Broadway in 1940 in *Walk with Music*. His collaborators were Hoagy Carmichael and Guy Bolton. Carmichael remembered the show without affection, blaming the failure on two traditional villains, the book and the Shuberts. However, he liked his score, and ''Way Back in 1939 AD' sounds a promising premise for a Mercer lyric in AD 1940. His next Broadway sortie began in 1946. The show was *St Louis Woman*, the composer, Harold Arlen. It was to be Mercer's most interesting musical. It came three years after *Oklahoma!*, a year after *Carousel*. Lerner and Loewe had opened *The Day Before Spring*, their second show together, four months earlier; *Annie Get Your Gun* and Ira Gershwin's last Broadway show, *Park Avenue*, crowded in on its heels, all to very different receptions.

St Louis Woman was based on a novel, *God Sends Sunday*, by Arna

Bontemps. Her adaptation, with Countee Cullen, was a major flaw. However, in the euphoria of setting up the show, this went unobserved. The role of the fickle, black St Louis beauty, Della Green, was originally intended for Lena Horne. She attracted Arthur Freed to the project (according to Hugh Fordin in his book on the Freed era at MGM, *The World of Entertainment*). However, by the time the show went into rehearsal, Miss Horne had rejected the role and early performances in New Haven and Boston drew equivocal reviews. Freed persuaded Rouben Mamoulian to take over the direction from Lemuel Ayers and there was some rewriting. Antony Tudor was replaced as choreographer by Charles Walters. Mamoulian staged exciting climaxes to both acts, reminding audiences of his work in *Porgy and Bess*. The Nicholas brothers had a dancing success and Pearl Bailey, making her Broadway début, was given two show-stopping songs: 'It's a Woman's Prerogative to Change Her Mind' and 'Legalise My Name'.

> If you prize me, notarise me,
> Gimme an ol' piece of parchment I can frame,
> You gotta legalise my name.

But it is sad that the musical play for which Mercer wrote his best theatre songs (including 'Come Rain or Come Shine' and 'Any Place I Hang my Hat is Home') was flawed as musicals are wont to be. He tried again in 1949 with *Texas, Li'l Darlin'*. The score was by Robert Emmett Dolan. Only one song, a revival meeting number, 'The Big Movie Show in the Sky', had any great success. For *Top Banana*, a vehicle for Phil Silvers two years later, Mercer wrote both words and music. His songs hit a bright, bouncy, brassy note appropriate to a show which revolved around a leading comic and a series of vaudeville routines – Gerald Bordman's account of the plot, in his chronicle of *American Musical Theatre*, recalls a man carrying on a carton and saying, 'I'm taking this case to court,' and then coming back with a ladder and adding, 'I'm taking this case to a higher court.' *Top Banana* ran for nearly a year but did not repay its investment. Mercer waited four years for his longest Broadway run – *Li'l Abner*. This time his composer was Gene de Paul, and the caricature countryside of 'Dogpatch' provided him with a vivid exaggeration of his favourite folk background. A ballad for Li'l Abner and his sweetheart, Daisy Mae, 'Namely You', became popular; and 'Jubilation T. Cornpone' is a fine Gilbertian celebration of a local equivalent of the Duke of Plaza-Toro.

Saratoga, a second theatrical liaison with Harold Arlen, was a second disappointment. Morton da Costa, the director and book writer, failed to extract the same splendours from Edna Ferber's novel that Oscar Hammerstein had derived from her *Show Boat*. The songs never soared over the complicated strains of the plot or Cecil Beaton's exquisite but unwieldy picture of New Orleans and Saratoga in the 1880s.

Mercer's last Broadway musical was *Foxy*, which was lost amidst a crowded mixed bag of musicals during the 1963–4 season. The others included Meredith Wilson's *Here's Love*; Jones and Schmidt's *110 in the Shade*; Noël Coward's *The Girl Who Came to Supper*; the Coward-derived *High Spirits*; Jerry Herman's *Hello Dolly*; Sondheim's *Anyone Can Whistle*; the Merrill-Styne *Funny Girl*; and Jule Styne's other collaboration with Comden and Green, *Fade Out, Fade In*. *Foxy* was Bert Lahr's last Broadway show. Two great clowns who had shared several triumphs were making their farewells in the same year – Lahr in Mercer's show, and Beatrice Lillie in *High Spirits*. Lahr had been with *Foxy* since its try-out production in Dawson City, Yukon Territory, in 1962. Ring Lardner Jnr and Ian McLellan Hunter based the show on Ben Jonson's *Volpone*, setting it in a Gold Rush background. The music was by Robert Emmett Dolan. Lahr's son summarises the show as 'a mediocre book, fair songs and choreography that rarely kicked an original leg . . .'. His (Lahr's) laughter and his improvisations gave it a chance; and yet the authors burdened him with language that was not funny and scenes that did not build to a comic climax. After the abortive Dawson City try-out, Lahr was tempted to give the musical another chance when David Merrick came in as producer. 'His hopes having won out over his experience . . . Johnny Mercer, the lyricist, was in his estimation a pro, and could be counted on continually for good songs.' Mercer found one fine vehicle for Lahr, 'Bon Vivant', vividly characterising a strolling player.

Gerald Bordman calls it 'a good show'. The rousing score included one ballad, 'Talk to Me, Baby', whose popularity survived the production. Merrick had nine other shows on Broadway at the time and two on the road. Although *Foxy* got reasonable notices – 'The whole show is as cheerful as any show ought to be which rejoices in the presence of the funniest man left alive' (*Time*) – it closed after 72 performances and Lahr laid the blame squarely at Merrick's door – 'It's a wonder we played as long as we did with the treatment Merrick gave us.' *Hello Dolly* was the bright pink apple of Merrick's eye that season, which perhaps accounts for a comment of Mercer's in an interview with Max Wilk some years later: 'I want to do a show that's really good, a show that's a credit to myself and the composer . . . and I – well, this may sound conceited to you, but I just don't want to write *Hello Dolly*. I think it's a dreary show.'

He tried once more. This time the place was not Broadway, but the West End of London. With André Previn's music and a book by Ronald Harwood, he attempted J. B. Priestley's picaresque story of early twentieth-century English vaudevillians, *The Good Companions*. Once

again, he failed to find the secret of the theatre song – even though he
included a re-vamped version of 'Bon Vivant':

> . . . Manchester and Dorchester and Chichester and Perth
> Sailing on the Firth of Forth, or is it Forth of Firth? . . .

He still had his fine feeling for place names, but somehow English towns
do not have the eloquence of Natchez or Mobile or Atcheson, Topeka
and Sante Fe. Ronald Harwood who worked closely with him and
enjoyed his company has written retrospectively, '. . . Mercer had little
insight into the theatre. His fancy was for vaudeville. He thought of a
lyric as complete in itself – telling a story or expressing the emotion, the
sentiment of the moment. He found it difficult to immerse his
imagination in the dramatic action which might lead to a song so that
often the song did not really grow out of a scene. During rehearsals of
The Good Companions he came in one morning and said he had seen a
wonderful brass band on *Opportunity Knocks* (a TV talent show) the
night before. He thought we should try to get them into Act Two. He
said, "They were cute little fellers." He was rather disappointed when
we did not respond with equal enthusiasm.'

Johnny Mercer was crammed with talent. He died on 25 June, 1976.
Twelve years earlier, he had written both words and music for
'Something's Gotta Give' for the film *Daddy Long Legs*:

> When an irresistible force such as you,
> Meets an old immovable object like me
> You can bet as sure as you live,
> Something's gotta give.

What gave in Mercer's case was his awareness of how to deploy his
songs in the proper construction of a play; nothing gave in the easy,
graceful way he could put a song together, as long as he had been
provided with a country theme to play with or a sympathetic musician
to set him off.

FRANK LOESSER

'My Time of Day is the Dark Time'

It is a sad irony that the man who was to inherit the mantle of Irving Berlin died three years before the master was ready to hand down so much as a stitch. Born in 1910, 22 years after Berlin, Frank Loesser died of lung cancer in 1969. Berlin presented his upright piano to the Smithsonian Institute in Washington, DC in 1972. Like Berlin, Loesser was weaned on Tin Pan Alley, but like Berlin he discovered that he could write songs which sat sunnily on the stage. Indeed, in his handful of shows he was ambitious to stretch and challenge the form with an instinct for innovation that outstripped his master. He came from a family of musicians; his father was a piano teacher and his older brother, Arthur Loesser, an accomplished pianist and a music critic. His first song was written at the age of six; the lyric, 'The May Party', celebrated the children's processions he watched in Central Park. At seven he listened to the clinking railroad rhythms of the Elevated running through his neighbourhood and put words to them. He ignored his family's encouragement towards a formal musical education and trained himself, improvising on the piano, composing on the harmonica, and winning third prize in a harmonica contest. His father disapproved of popular songs.

Loesser followed one ritual path on the lyric writer's highway by going to Townsend Harris High School; but, like Ira Gershwin, he dropped out of City College after one year. He explained his rejection of a formal musical education by saying, 'I didn't have the patience to concentrate'; he explained his departure from City College by saying, 'I wasn't in the mood to learn.' However, Cynthia Lindsay, in her introduction to the *Frank Loesser Song Book*, points out his extraordinary versatility and his insatiable curiosity:

Having by-passed formal musical and academic education, Loesser ... had an overwhelming fund of knowledge of art, literature,

Frank Loesser (*ASCAP*).

philosophy, the mortise-and-tenon construction of sixteenth-century cabinetry and the mating habits of the redwing blackbird ... he once constructed ... with great craftsmanship, the corner (just the corner) of a Regency desk, inlaid and perfectly finished. He then sent it to his friend, John Steinbeck, a piece of notepaper attached, with the printed words FROM THE DESK OF FRANK LOESSER.*

His first job was working with words. At eighteen he was briefly employed in New Rochelle, New York, as city editor on the local newspaper. However, his brother Arthur remembers that when he was sent out to cover a local Lions Club dinner, he 'obliged an officer by supplying couplets celebrating the exploits of the club members'. Arthur Loesser quotes the first recorded Loesser couplet, 'Secretary, Albert Vincent, Read the minutes, right this instant.'

Born ten years too late to follow the classic lyricist's treadmill of writing Broadway shows in the twenties preparatory to thirties exile in Hollywood, Loesser did not get to California until 1937 when his older colleagues were beginning to come home; however, he had packed a crash course into the early years of the thirties by using his days off to write acts for vaudevillians, touring on the Keith variety circuit. Later he left an account of this period. 'Somehow you had to find a way of getting a job ... the Depression was here and I even got one job checking the food and service in a string of restaurants. I was paid 75 cents each to eat eight or ten meals a day. At least I was eating, which a lot of people weren't. You had to keep alert all the time. I suppose that's where this tremendous energy of mine originated.' Energy he had, explosive energy. He needed it to cover the range of other jobs he tried in the early thirties, working as a process server, a jewellery salesman, a waiter in a Catskill's hotel, and a press agent; and then finally getting a contract to write lyrics for the Leo Fiest Music Company.

'In Love With a Memory of You' was Loesser's first published song, written in 1931 in collaboration with William Schuman. Neither composer nor lyricist was deterred by its lack of success. Schuman went on to teach at Julliard and Loesser got a job playing and singing at The Back Drop, a night club on 52nd Street. Finally, he placed five songs in a Broadway revue, albeit a fiasco. *The Illustrators' Show*, at the 48th Street Theatre, had been presented earlier in 1936 by The Society of Illustrators. The ambition of the stage-struck cartoonists was to focus attention on themselves rather than to delight their audiences. On the

---

* Shades of Noël Coward's reply to a similar message, unaccompanied by woodwork: 'Dear desk of ...'.

whole they succeeded. Many well-known illustrators made personal appearances and scandal soon centred around Otto Soglow who played 'The Little King', a cartoon character he had created for *The New Yorker*; a dubious sketch involving the chubby monarch attracted the police to the revue in its uptown incarnation. They raided and closed it. When the show graduated to Broadway the public failed to match the alacrity of the police in rushing to the theatre. *The Illustrators' Show* closed after five nights, this time with no assistance from the Law. However, one of the Frank Loesser lyrics, 'Bang, the Bell Rang' (he was writing with Irving Actman) already displayed his interest in intriguing and unusual verbal rhythms. The revue also featured a tune by Frederick Loewe, who seems to have been similarly true to a tradition he was to follow – his contribution was called 'A Waltz Was Born in Vienna'. The lyric was by Earle Crooker. After the show closed Loesser and Actman set off for California and a brief contract with Universal Pictures. It is here that history begins to record Mr Loesser's eruptions. It is improbable that this ebullient and combative man did not explode before but, without access to the first Mrs Loesser's promised biography, the history of her husband's embattled progress for us starts here.

Burton Lane has recorded his impression of Loesser's arrival on the Hollywood scene at a time when musicals were fashionable and, in Hoagy Carmichael's words, 'Everybody was eatin' high on the hog.' Lane was at Paramount, in another of Carmichael's phrases, 'a boiling, roaring madhouse during the late thirties; but I don't think they needed quite all the song writers they had under contract.' Lane was immediately impressed by Loesser's lyrics and arranged for Lewis Gensler, the head of the Paramount music department and a former song writer (he had written some songs with Oscar Hammerstein in the twenties), to hear them. Gensler was equally impressed and recommended that Paramount give Loesser a contract. In an interview with Max Wilk, Lane vividly evokes the suspense. 'While they were making up their corporate mind whether to sign him on, I had a call from Frank . . . could I come over, he wanted to show me some of his work that I hadn't heard. He lived on Sunset Boulevard, I had to walk about two hundred steps down from the street to get to his apartment. I'd been there about five or ten minutes when Lynn, his first wife, asked if I'd like to have dinner with them. I said no, I'd already eaten. She opened a can of beans – one can for both of them – and an apple which she sliced for their dessert. They were absolutely broke . . . Paramount came through with the contract. A ten-week deal for starters. So I told Frank he could use my office any time. I came in the day after he signed, and I'll never forget this – there was one guy measuring him for shirts and shorts, another guy measuring him for suits – the works! The day after he'd signed that contract, everything was going to be made to order.'

Loesser and Lane worked together on a number of pictures for Paramount (Loesser also had a song hit with Alfred Newman in 1937; 'Moon of Manakoora' was sung in a movie called *The Hurricane* by Dorothy Lamour). With Lane he wrote B picture scores for Bob Hope and Shirley Ross beginning with 'The Lady's in Love With You'. More amusing was 'Dancing on a Dime', a witty literal investigation of the romantic possibilities of a tiny dance floor. Perhaps their most charming romantic song was 'Says My Heart', which Lane set in five minutes one afternoon when a B picture producer picked Loesser's lyric out of a pile and decided it was just what he needed.

Burton Lane early recognised Loesser's difficult, secretive nature. 'He'd sit across the room from me . . . and then I'd see him smile . . . and suddenly he'd jump up and he had it all written out, a complete lyric. I'd put it on my piano and he'd want me to sing it right away. Hell, I hadn't even seen the lyric yet! And if I'd stumble, he'd yell, "God damn it, can't you *read?*" '

Hoagy Carmichael remembers his arrival. 'Out of nowhere came a young hopeful named Frank Loesser. He had written a few songs with tunesmiths that weren't too well known. Eventually the studio more or less teamed me with him.' Carmichael had earlier been intrigued by Loesser − an assured 'little character swinging his coat-tails and whistling', glimpsed through the window of an office at Paramount. 'I never saw anybody so self-assured.' Loesser was on one of his dozen or so safaris to the commissary for the constant cups of coffee with which he moistened his dogged, lonely, tormented search for appropriate words. 'At first the kid shook me up − his exuberance and zany talk were too much for me.' Carmichael felt that Loesser was insufficiently serious about his craft. He soon found that this indifference was a front. 'He'd only been joking with me to keep me happy and alive.' Their first song was 'Heart and Soul' which was first used in a picture. Then '. . . Frank said he wanted to write a song called "Small Fry". I said, "Sure", and we did.'

'Frank Loesser interested me,' Carmichael writes. '. . . Frank was gifted and most energetic; but he was very flighty at first in his choice of lyrics. It was a good thing that he worked with me for a while; I had a sobering Indiana effect on him . . .' How else in those pre-valium days would he have calmed Loesser down sufficiently to write 'Two Sleepy People'? 'He had a tendency to want to write things "way out". This may be because he was so packed full of ideas then that he was overloaded.' Meanwhile, Loesser was unloading his ideas on a regiment of composers.

At Republic Pictures, a considerably less fashionable outfit than

Paramount, the music department was run by Cy Feuer, who was later, with Ernest Martin, to produce Loesser's biggest successes. In 1941 he engaged an all-round musician, vocal coach, rehearsal pianist, choral director and utility conductor, Jule Styne, to do whatever chores were required. They ranged from making sure that Gene Autry sang in 'sync' to recorded soundtracks to writing original songs. Styne's unsubtle first attempt was 'I Love Watermelon' – 'The man is eating watermelon,' explained the director; 'that's what the song has to be about. When a man is sewing a boot and singing, I want him to sing about sewing a boot.' Some months later Republic Pictures grew more ambitious. They were considering investing the, for them, huge sum of half a million dollars in a musical called *Sis Hopkins*. It was to star the comedienne Judy Canova, Bing Crosby and Jerry Colonna – Styne was required to write seven songs. He asked for a good lyric writer – specifically he wanted Frank Loesser who was being paid $250 a week at Paramount. However, his loan-out rate was $500. A compromise, which involved trading John Wayne, a Republic star, to Universal for a film was reached, and everyone was happy except the explosive Loesser. First he windmilled into Cy Feuer's office, yelling, according to Jule Styne's biographer, 'You son of a bitch, I'm writing for Hoagy Carmichael now. I'm not coming to work with some half-ass piano player who is really a vocal coach.' After two hours of persuasion Frank Loesser agreed at least to talk to Styne; he had not yet agreed to work with him. Feuer recalls that when Loesser was really angry both feet had a tendency to leave the ground. Certainly neither touched the floor when he arrived at Styne's bungalow. Again the account comes from Theodore Taylor's biography of Styne: 'You have demeaned me by asking for me,' he shouted; 'you have no respect for my talent, not that I can't understand why you'd want me. But Jesus Christ, every big picture at Paramount they've been giving to Johnny Mercer. Now goddamit, who writes the hits? Me!' Apart from 'Small Fry' and 'Two Sleepy People', they already included '(I've Got Spurs That) Jingle, Jangle, Jingle' and 'Snug as a Bug in a Rug', with music by Joseph Lilley and Matt Malneck respectively, then there were 'Sand in my Shoes' and 'Kiss the Boys Goodbye', written with Victor Schertzinger. Uncharacteristically, Jule Styne sat silent through Loesser's verbal lashing. His explanation that he could not get a word in edgeways carries more conviction. Loesser slugged on. 'Now this pile of shit, Republic,' he continued, 'you've destroyed me forever.' The fists pounded Styne's desk. 'I'm going to write these f.... songs in four days; but you're not going to hand them in for three weeks. I'm going to Palm Springs and sit on my butt. You understand that?' Abruptly Loesser asked Styne to play him something. Styne, at last able to get a word in, explained that he had requested Loesser because he wanted to write something good. He began to put his heart on his sleeve. 'I've watched horses whinny in sync. I've written arrangements for coyotes, I've written songs about watermelon and guts and gravy . . .' Loesser's characteristic menacing pace around the confined space persisted and he silenced Styne savagely, 'I don't want your history. I hate your guts.' Styne started to play a tune and Loesser's immediate response was to stop pacing, rush to the door and slam it shut. 'Never play that song here again,' he shouted, and then, modulating to a conspiratorial whisper, 'don't ever play that song for anyone else. We'll write that song at Paramount.' 'He was that kind of schemer,' Styne commented in another interview.

Hating the ambience of Republic, Loesser nevertheless worked out his time there, covering the bungalow office in which they worked with signs reading 'No Cowboys Allowed, No Horses Allowed, No Gunshots'. He did not go to Palm Springs or sit on his butt. He continued to fight with Feuer and even more fiercely with the director of the film. Styne got used to his highly individual working methods: the tiny figure pacing and pacing the little bungalow, listening and listening to a tune over and over again, never confiding a lyrical idea until it was fully formed in his mind. As soon as *Sis Hopkins* was finished, Loesser arranged for Styne to be loaned to Universal for *Sweater Girl* and Styne crossed the border without declaring the tune that had so appealed to Loesser a few months earlier. Loesser took five weeks of anxious perambulation, smiling mysteriously to himself, drinking from his bottomless well of coffee and smoking endless cigarettes while Styne played the song again and again. At last, with no warning, Loesser arrived one morning and said that he was ready to reveal the lyric — simple, direct, with hardly a rhyme to commend it; but sitting on the music with an assurance that kept it in the hit parade for twenty weeks.

I don't want to walk without that sunshine —
Why did you have to take away that sunshine?
Oh, baby, please come back or you'll break my heart for me,
I don't want to walk without you, baby,
No, siree.

During his first stay in Hollywood, Loesser was also to write with Arthur Schwartz, Jimmy McHugh and Frederick Hollander. With Schwartz he wrote 'They're Either Too Young or Too Old' for Bette Davis in Warner Brothers' *Thank Your Lucky Stars*. With McHugh the pick of the pack were written for *Happy Go Lucky* — 'Let's Get Lost, Lost in Each Other's Arms', and, working towards his later mastery of the colloquial, Loesser wrote:

Finally found a fellow
He says 'Murder!' – he says!
Every time we kiss he says 'Murder!' – he says!
Is that the language of love?

With Frederick Hollander, Loesser wrote the score for *Destry Rides Again* including Dietrich's 'See What the Boys in the Back Room Will Have'.

Loesser left Hollywood for the army with a characteristic gesture. When Jule Styne asked him with whom he should now collaborate, Loesser had no hesitation in saying, 'You've been spoiled. There's no one like me . . . I'll tell you what. If you want someone like me, don't get a clever rhymer, because there is a thing called a rhyming dictionary. Anybody can rhyme, you can find a rhyme for anything. But get a guy who can say something clever and warm because you need warm lyrics for your music.' 'Warm and clever' is an apt summing-up of Loesser's distinctive skill – twice as hard a recipe to achieve as warm *or* clever, which rarely satisfied him.

Yes, time heals all things,
So I needn't cling to this fear,
It's merely that Spring will be a little late this year . . .

In the forties, like the prototype we have imposed on him – Irving Berlin – Loesser wrote a series of army songs. He also attempted, without much success, to annex the one anniversary Berlin had left unassailed, with 'What Are You Doing New Year's Eve?'. The army does not seem to have done much to change Loesser's character. Abe Burrows has recorded his new military image. '. . . He insisted on having his private's uniform tailored. He was the sharpest buck private you ever saw – he had a uniform that a general would have given his four stars for!' One of Loesser's army songs was prompted by a friend, E. J. Kahn Jnr, who was a public relations officer for the infantry. That branch of the service was smarting under feelings of neglect. While Irving Berlin was looking after the army in general and while the navy, the air force and especially the marines had their marching songs, there was nothing which applied specifically to the infantry. In 1942 Loesser himself had written 'Praise the Lord and Pass the Ammunition'. The next year, in his more amused vein, he had written 'What Do You Do in the Infantry?' However, neither this nor 'The Road to Victory' was doing quite what Mr Kahn wanted for his branch of the service. Looking for inspiration, Loesser asked for a list of infantry heroes. Unfortunately, all the heroes Kahn could think of had unpronounceable six-syllable names, except 'Rodger Young'. Rodger Young's story was enough to set Loesser off and the song was introduced by the Combat Infantry Band at Young's birthplace in Ohio.

> . . . In ev'ry soldier's heart in all the infantry
> Shines the name, shines the name of Rodger Young . . .

The song gladdened Mr Kahn's heart too, and those of listeners to every radio station in America, as well as the tardily celebrated infantry. Casting envious eyes on this successful piece of image-making the Women's Army Corps called on Loesser to perform a similar service for them and sure enough he complied with 'First Class Private Mary Brown'. The war, in one of its more useful side-effects, had subtly pushed Loesser further along the song writer's road. For a long time the abrasive little man had been more ambitious to write his own music. Some of his collaborators had encouraged him on this path. It would be unworthy to suggest that they were trying to distance themselves from his explosions; they had noticed that, in Stanley Green's words, 'The very construction of his lyrics almost dictated the melodies that would carry them.' 'Praise the Lord and Pass the Ammunition' was the first song for which he wrote words and music and it gave him confidence to experiment further.

There is no doubt that Loesser's war songs represent the Tin Pan Alley side of his talent; but now it was time for him to start to show his Broadway paces. His first attempt was modest, but fresh and engaging. Feuer and Martin were trying to make their own Broadway début as producers. Their project was a musical version of the old English farce, *Charley's Aunt*; the new title was *Where's Charley?*. Feuer's first instinct was to team Loesser with Harold Arlen; but, when Arlen proved unavailable, he and his partner decided to risk Loesser alone. There were a number of other people who had to be convinced. First there was the star, Ray Bolger; but Loesser charmed him. Then there were backers to be impressed. Rodgers and Hammerstein, who were familiar with Loesser's music, invested in the show. In 1948 there was no more potent lure to persuade speculators to throw their money away than to give them the chance to follow Rodgers and Hammerstein up any garden path. George Abbott directed and made a charming leisurely adaptation of the play; Georges Balanchine did the choreography; but it is the range and freshness of Loesser's work which still stand out. He contributed love songs like 'Once in Love with Amy'. Both words and tune have a lovely, amused, mildly intoxicated excitement which perfectly captures the feeling of hopeful summer love in Oxford quadrangles. Equally, Loesser explored the diffident side of young love in 'My Darling, My Darling'; and he brings a silky grace to a nostalgic duet for older lovers equally alien to his own embattled temperament,

'Spring Time, You're Looking Lovelier than Ever'. Perhaps the song that points most directly to the innovative qualities for which Loesser's scores were to become famous is the march, 'The New Ashmolean Marching Society and Students' Conservatory Band'; it embodies all his relish for setting an amusingly convoluted phrase happily on an irresistible tune, as he was later to do with 'some irresponsible dress manufacturer' in *How to Succeed* and 'The Oldest Established, Permanent, Floating Crap Game in New York' in *Guys and Dolls*.

Strangely the show was slow to catch on, despite congratulatory telegrams from Rodgers and Hammerstein, Cole Porter and countless other composers. Finally, Arthur Schwartz wrote an unsolicited article in the *New York Times* stating quite simply that Frank Loesser was 'the greatest undiscovered composer in America'. It tipped the balance at the box office.

Loesser's next show with Feuer and Martin was *Guys and Dolls*. This time he was teamed with Abe Burrows (after an abortive book by Jo Swerling) and, as director, George S. Kauffman. He had found the perfect subject, the Broadway world of Damon Runyon and in particular *The Idyll of Miss Sarah Brown*. Loesser's essence was urban. Max Wilk cites Ernest Martin, 'strictly a city boy. Loved to quote Nunnally Johnson, who said that if he had a place with green grass he'd pave it.' Martin has also described Loesser's working habits at this period. 'They were eccentric to say the least. He rose at around four-thirty or five and made himself a martini. He was not a lush, it simply got him going. He would write from five to eight and then go back to sleep. The stint of sleep would be followed by another three or four-hour burst of work and another nap.' Friends whom he knew were early risers were liable to get six o'clock telephone calls to be treated to his latest work – to paraphrase his lyric, his time of day was the dark time, a couple of bars before dawn. He never agreed formally to write *Guys and Dolls*; the day he handed Feuer and Martin the first four songs was the day they knew they had a show. His eccentricities were Runyonesque. He had a phobia about sitting in public places unless his back was to the wall, and teaming with Runyon made a perfect marriage. It was Loesser who threw out Swerling's original book; but perversely he still wrote his score around it. However, his sure theatrical instinct developed so rapidly that Burrows found it possible to construct his new story line writing from song to song. 'I had those songs of Frank's to go by,' Burrows told Max Wilk, 'but then we'd sit and we'd look hard for song-spots.' An exception was 'The Fugue for Tin Horns', which seemed to have no place in the plot and so was placed at the opening of the show, wonderfully setting the mood for the play and the exotic world and picturesque vocabulary of the Runyon characters who inhabited it.

'The Oldest Established, Permanent, Floating Crap Game in New York' is another perfect example of Loesser chiming with Runyon, a song title which sprang directly from a line in Burrows' book. *Guys and Dolls* confirmed Loesser's reputation not only as a song writer, but also as a volatile colleague. One of his most towering displays of temper came during the first stage rehearsal of the crap game number, which was interpolated into the show in Philadelphia. Michael Kidd, the choreographer, was starting to set it when Loesser launched himself at the stage from the back of the orchestra in a flurry of four-letter words. He wanted to hear the song loud and perfect every time. In his book 'loud was good'. Kidd's plea for patience was ignored; Martin's intervention simply increased the fury. 'You're Hitler! . . . I'm the author and you're working for me!' The rehearsal came to a standstill. The cast came to attention. Motionless at the tops of their voices they bellowed the song; Feuer and Martin saw Loesser backing away up the aisle and followed him out of the theatre, where they watched him buy an ice cream and lick it contentedly all the way to his hotel. He had drawn attention to the music and was happy. He had heard it loud and good. On another occasion, he was rehearsing Isobel Bigley in a romantic song of considerable range, 'I'll Know'. So infuriated was Loesser by Miss Bigley's performance of the song with a break somewhere in the middle of her range that he leapt on stage and punched her on the nose. Her flood of tears brought him to an awareness of what he had done and from that moment she had the upper hand – and an extremely expensive apologetic bracelet to decorate its wrist. The sharp, funny songs came quickly to Loesser, drawing on the idiom and lifestyle of the crooked but basically soft characters he had met in the thirties while playing piano at The Back Drop: 'A Bushel and a Peck', 'Take Back Your Mink' and 'Adelaide's Lament' – '. . . A person can develop a cold . . .'. Loesser originally wrote the lyric for a stripper who catches cold; then later he decided to make her cold psychosomatic, an example of his guiding rule of using songs 'to examine character not events'; though he was happy to turn his rule upside down and use an event brilliantly to trigger a song – as in 'Sit Down You're Rockin' the Boat'. The score is particularly fine in the way it contrives to be varied and at the same time to preserve an overall unity. The romantic songs are not as vivid as the comic numbers, dear though they were to Loesser's heart; but they all comply cleverly with his dictum, character not event. In 'If I Were a Bell' he daringly gets his leading lady slightly drunk to underwrite her exuberance. The most sentimental song, 'More I Cannot Wish You', is awarded to the oldest and most endearing character in the play, and the one sore-thumb song, 'A Woman in Love', was written not for the play but for the movie version. A sizeable song hit was required for the film and the Tin Pan Alley side of Loesser supplied it.

'I'm in the romance business,' Loesser used to yell at Feuer and Martin during the out-of-town try-outs of *Guys and Dolls*. The argument centred around his wish to reprise ballads in the second act. Finally George S. Kauffman, director, and in this case arbitrator, quietened the composer, who was yelling, 'When are they going to hear my songs? What the hell do you think I'm in this for?', by agreeing to reprise Loesser's ballads in the second act if Loesser would allow Kauffman to reprise some of the first-act jokes alongside. Now that Loesser was winning awards, his characteristic response was an unvarnished 'I thought I should have had it three years ago.'

His next project was a musical based on Sydney Howard's 1924 play, *They Knew What They Wanted*. This time there were to be no collaborators – he knew what he wanted – to go it alone. There were only fifteen minutes of spoken dialogue. Loesser was working towards an almost operatic form, but he was careful not to say so. On one occasion he called the show 'an extended musical comedy'. On another he said, 'I may give the impression this show has operatic tendencies. If people feel that way – fine. Actually all it has is a great frequency of songs.' The arranger, Don Walker, phrased it most succinctly. 'This is a musical comedy expanded. Not an opera cut down.' Cynthia Lindsay recalls Loesser quoting George S. Kauffman: 'Of course be corny – just don't let them catch you at it.' So Loesser sneaked what was virtually an opera on to the stage and they failed to catch him at it. 'The programme simply called it a musical.' Loesser was attracted by the simple, central story of an elderly grape-grower in California who falls in love at first sight with a mail-order bride – the most happy fella in the whole Napa Valley. Loesser's approach to Howard's material was direct and uncompromising. 'I figured take out this political talk, the labor talk and the religious talk. Get rid of all that stuff and you have a love story.' It took Loesser four years to write *The Most Happy Fella*. Violent depressions would be followed by bursts of enthusiasm and abundant creativity. He packed his score with more than 30 separate musical numbers: choral passages, recitatives, arias, duets, trios, quartets; but this time the enormous range from vaudeville turns to floridly arioso operatic passages was not bound together by the same consistent style and tone – how could it be? – that he had found for *Guys and Dolls*.

Loesser was on home ground in the city. The green grass of the Napa Valley needed to be paved over with Broadway concrete before he could tread the turf with assurance. Perhaps the subject was too close to him and its central situation too sentimental. Cynthia Lindsay points out that Loesser, 'although a deeply sentimental person himself, detested oversentimentality on stage'; he took as his working slogan 'the heart must bleed, not slobber.' The degree to which his work matched that motto is the degree to which *The Most Happy Fella* succeeds. Whatever the verdict, it was a work of prodigal richness. The conductor, Herbert Green, affectionately described by Loesser as 'a fat sylph', paints a vivid picture of Loesser in the vortex of production. 'If you knew Frank Loesser you were involved. You had no choice, because the man was a genius. Working with him was a mixture of wanting to kiss him or kill him. He was such a mixture of personality opposites. Professionally he was unreasonable, irascible, unfair and infuriating; socially he was gracious, thoughtful, gentle and totally enchanting – the kind of person who would find the most miserable-looking person at a party and go talk to him.' 'Standing on the Corner' quickly became a hit; 'Big "D"', an anthem to Dallas, is also a joyous song of recognition. The romantic songs are graceful and reach imaginatively for appropriate rural images. In 'Joey, Joey, Joey', a song for Joey, the itinerant labourer who fathers the heroine's child, and hears the call to move on, Loesser mingles his open-air poetry with a harder philosophy which is a striking mixture of sweet and sour:

> . . . The wind blows in the bunk-house
> Like the smell of a perfumed woman,
> Smellin' of where she's been
> Smellin' of oregon cherries
> Or maybe Arizona sugar beet.
> The wind blows in and she sings to me,
> Cause I'm one of her ramblin' kin.

The Most Happy Fella ran for a year and a half; perhaps its flaws can best be summed up in one of its chorus numbers, 'Abbondanza! . . . Che Stravaganza'; Loesser was offering an abundance of abundance. Stories of his tough business deals were always contrasted with 'funny stories, outrageous stories, stories of his enormous generosity . . . there were the friends who couldn't talk about him without crying, because he was so many things to so many people and special to each.' In *The Most Happy Fella* he was too generous to his audience.

In one of Frank Loesser's blocked periods during his work on *The Most Happy Fella*, Samuel Goldwyn offered him *Hans Christian Andersen*, starring Danny Kaye. Loesser had done other Hollywood work since his pre-war period there – notably *The Perils of Pauline* for Betty Hutton in 1947, and *Red, Hot and Blue* in 1949 for which he synopsised *Hamlet*. He adopted a colloquial approach. Hamlet was a prince of a 'spot called Denmark'. He 'bumped off his uncle and he mickey-finned his mother'; and he drove his girlfriend to suicide. And 'he stabbed her big, big brother, ''cause he didn't want nobody else but himself should live – he was what you might call unco-operative. . . . Murder', he points out, '. . . was one thing Hamlet sure did enjoy . . . he was, how shall I say . . .

quite a mischievious boy . . . and the moral of this story . . . was . . . very, very plain; you'd better get a mussle if you've got a great Dane!' However, *Hans Christian Andersen* was Loesser's only major score for the movies once he acquired the taste for Broadway. It was essentially a film for children, but it provided an alternative National Anthem for the Danes, 'Wonderful Copenhagen', and the simple philosophy of 'Inchworm, Inchworm, measuring the marigolds, seems to me you'd stop and see how beautiful they are'. In 'Thumbelina' and 'The Ugly Duckling' he deals directly with two of Andersen's themes with patient skill, and 'No Two People' is one of the most charming of his characteristic, happy, overlapping duets. If jaunty self-confidence was what Hoagy Carmichael had seen in Frank Loesser in his first glimpse of him on the Paramount lot, it was a quality which was always erupting in his music. It is interesting that when a leaden stage version of *Hans Christian Andersen* was presented at the London Palladium, the difference between Loesser's musical imagination and dramatic instinct when writing directly for the theatre and when writing individual songs designed simply to decorate a picaresque film plot was stunningly revealed. Had he intended *Hans Andersen* to be a theatre score he would have written it differently. The man who could take on Tin Pan Alley and the theatre certainly understood the distinction between the two.

However, in *Greenwillow*, 1960, his next Broadway show, his theatrical instincts were not strong enough to breathe drama into the delicate, fragile story of pastoral life in an imaginary community living on the banks of the imaginary Meander River. It was always Loesser's way to come at his audience from an unexpected angle and he had been fascinated by J. B. Chute's novel. The musical was a mood piece, a labour of love, and it was held together by a collection of quaint customs, like baptising a cow, rather than by a plot. In this bucolic atmosphere Loesser's score acquires a folkish character; but, as Walter Kerr's review said, 'Folklore may be one dish that can't be cooked to order.' The greensward sounds in need of another coat of concrete. Simplest and best was:

Never, never will I marry
Never, never will I wed,
Born to wander solitary
Wide my world – narrow my bed.

A contrapuntal sermon for two parsons; one enthusing on the God of Love, the other threatening a God of Wrath, got nearer to the wit one always looks for in Loesser; but not it, nor the presence of Anthony Perkins in the cast, nor a substantial advance, could prolong the show's run beyond three months. Loesser was in London on the closing night;

his telegram which replaced the usual formal notice to the cast ran, OOPS – SORRY.

Next time his feet were firmly back on the asphalt. *How to Succeed in Business Without Really Trying* is a satire on big corporations which provided him with an urban environment almost as mannered as and much more immediate than the Runyonesque fantasy of *Guys and Dolls*. Willy Gilbert and Jack Weinstock had adapted Shepherd Meade's non-fiction guidebook as a comedy with no music. Feuer and Martin took it to Loesser and Abe Burrows. Along with Bob Fosse they hammered at the right approach for songs that would epitomise the world of big business they were evoking. At the end of these sessions Loesser wrote the score in four weeks. Fosse could hear the sound of an office full of typewriters in a soft shoe number. Loesser wrote 'A Secretary is Not a Toy': '. . . her pad is to write in not to spend the night in . . .' Rudy Vallee, making his first Broadway appearance since *George White's Scandals of 1936*, inspired one of Loesser's epic rages. He did not want to perform one of his songs the way Loesser had written it. 'I am an interpreter of songs,' was his point of view. Correctly the producers stuck to the principle that the creator's instinct must be served and Loesser got his way; but not before he had fired off a telegram two pages long arguing that Feuer and Martin had betrayed him by not punching Vallee firmly on the nose. Shades of Isobel Bigley! Burrows provided the suggestion that the show's main love song, 'I Believe in You', should be kept firmly in context by having the leading man sing it to himself:

> You have the cool, clear eyes of a seeker of wisdom and truth,
> Yet there's that up-turned chin and the grin of impetuous youth,
> Oh, I believe in you . . .

'I Play it the Company Way' is every time-serving company servant's credo; 'Happy to Keep his Dinner Warm' pinpoints just as wittily the predicament of the company wife, wearing the wifely uniform, while he goes onward and upward:

> Oh! to be loved by a man I respect,
> To bask in the glow of his perfectly understandable neglect.

The stage picture accompanying the song showed the hero's progress onward and upward from mail room to boardroom. Throughout the show, Loesser was rigorously following his dictum: 'Remember a song is like a freight train moving across a stage. Every boxcar has a word on it. Those people have to hear everything and understand it – fast, because in a minute the car will be gone and they'll never see it again. Make them listen and then lay it in their laps.' They listened to *How to*

Succeed for 1416 performances; and it joined the select band of American musicals to be awarded a Pulitzer Prize.

Loesser worked on one more musical, *Pleasure and Palaces*, which closed out of town, sunk, it would appear, by its book. He died at the age of 59 on 26 July, 1969, a breathing machine on one side of him, a packet of cigarettes on the other.

He was a genuine original, and an innovator, not in the sense that he came to the musical theatre with a considered statement of what he felt it should achieve; but with a pragmatic assurance about what he could make it do for him. He was married twice. His first wife was Lynn Loesser, who is writing a biography, *Two Sleepy People*. His second was Jo Sullivan Loesser, leading lady of *The Most Happy Fella*. His business enterprises were as time-consuming as his creative work. His music-publishing company developed and encouraged young writers, notably Adler and Ross who wrote *Pyjama Game* and *Damn Yankees*; Meredith Wilson who wrote *The Music Man*; and, in England, Peter Greenwell, the composer of *Twenty Minutes South*, *The Crooked Mile* and *The Mitford Girls*.

A strange, contentious, ebullient, ambitious, gifted man; a street boy, always with a deal in his mind, a felicitous phrase on his lips and his eye on the stars; a genius entitled to his own assessment that he had it.

ALAN JAY LERNER

'Almost Like Being in Love'

The literacy rate among the great lyric writers of musical plays is high – not an average shared by many of their Tin Pan Alley song-writing colleagues. Alan Jay Lerner puts a premium on literacy and has a natural clarity, especially when writing about himself. 'When Fritz (Frederick Loewe) and I began our collaboration I had a precise goal in view. Larry Hart, brilliant as he was, was not a dramatic writer. The wit was the lyric writer's, never the character's. Oscar Hammerstein, on the other hand, was very much a dramatic lyric writer and with *Oklahoma!* the musical comedy became a musical play. With all the fears and confidence of youth I set out to combine the dramatic lyrics of Hammerstein with the wit and tenderness of Larry.' Lerner was also setting out to inform the broad tradition of operetta with the dramatic sophistication which the theatre had acquired over the last 50 years and to satisfy his instinct for the colourful, the theatrical and the romantic – the last quality perhaps the one with which he identifies most readily in real life. In his lyrics, Alan Lerner is constantly animadverting, wittily, romantically or ruefully, on the incompatibility of men and women. He himself has been married seven times and has written, 'There is no greater fan of the opposite sex than me, and I have the bills to prove it.'

He is of the next generation of lyric writers after Hart, Hammerstein, Harburg, Berlin, Gershwin, Mercer, Fields, Dietz, Porter, Coward – more nearly a contemporary of Frank Loesser (he is nine years younger), and a generation earlier than Harnick and Sondheim. Is the species dying out? Perhaps not. For many of today's song writers the gramophone record demands less discipline of its lyricist. Lerner was born in New York in 1918 and, unlike many of his earlier colleagues, born into an affluent family. However, like many of them he had a Character for a father (in Hammerstein's case, read 'grandfather'). In his book, *On the Street Where I Live*, an elegant and definitive study of a lyric writer's role seen through close scrutiny of his most famous shows,

Alan Jay Lerner (*Hulton Picture Library*).

Alan Lerner paints an irresistible picture of his father – a rich man who renounced dentistry to found Lerner's stores. He explains that his father was rich and his mother good lookin', 'but by the time I came along my father no longer thought so.' His father's four passions were literacy, the theatre, ladies and boxing. Lerner inherited the first three enthusiasms for keeps, but lost the sight of one eye practising the fourth. The Character, his father, suffered a less painful, but still dramatic, fate when he followed an evening with a lady by using boxing as an alibi to his wife. When she stirred earlier than usual in the morning, she asked who had won the big fight. Lerner Senior tossed a mental coin, mentioned a name and went into the next room as his wife went back to sleep. Opening the *New York Times*, he found that he had guessed the wrong fighter. As soon as he reached his office he called home and ordered that everything should be packed by 'the one maid specifically assigned to looking after his clothes'. (The odds are that this phrase cannot be used about the domestic staff of any other lyricist's family in this book.) Lerner Senior was installed in the Waldorf before his wife could read the paper. The Character's practical legacy pervades Alan Jay Lerner's life. From the age of five his father took him to Broadway shows. He saw them all. By the time he was twelve he knew that he wanted to spend his life in the musical theatre. His father was determined that he should be literate and sent him to Bedales, an English public school, to foster his respect for the English language. Some 300 years earlier another lyric writer, John Gay, described learning at English public schools as being 'lashed with Latin by a tingling rod'; but Lerner appears to have enjoyed it and not to have suffered at the hands of the sort of housemaster who dials the speaking clock for the thrill of hearing the voice say '. . . at the third stroke . . .'. A dozen years later he spent a weekend with his father hard upon winning an award for *Brigadoon*. The Character told him that on the evidence of that weekend he had an active vocabulary of 297 words – Father had counted. 'I don't see how you can make a career as a writer with an active vocabulary of 297 words,' he said; 'however, I believe you have talent and if you would like to return to school and study, I would be more than happy to subsidise you.' On this occasion Lerner did not take his advice.

The Character was eloquent also on the subject of women. It was his opinion that it is always the woman's fault. 'The proof of it is that you will go to bed with one woman on Monday and it will be a failure and another on Tuesday and it will be successful. You are the same person. Only the woman has changed. Therefore, whose fault is it? Hers.' Lerner's seven marriages suggest perhaps a desire to out-do his father. Many lyricists are driven by poverty to write their way into affluence, scribbling themselves from the wrong side of the tracks to the right. Lerner, always affluent, was driven by his father's urging and by his example to aspire to excellence. Some of his collaborators have accused him of periods of idleness, but in the main the cushion of money and education seems to have strengthened his will to succeed.

He studied music at Julliard and he went to Harvard. His father had intended to prepare him for the diplomatic service. However, when he was expelled for smoking from the Choate School in Connecticut, the Character cancelled diplomacy in a fit of pique. At Harvard he wrote music and lyrics for two Hasty Pudding revues. The 1938 show was called *So Proudly We Hail* and one song, 'Chance to Dream', was actually published. In 1939 the show was *Fair Enough* and that year the canonisation of publication fell upon a song called 'From Me to You'. Little has been heard of either since. It was at this time that Lerner lost his eye in a boxing match. Unable to enlist, he became a radio script writer for two years, turning out hundreds of scripts. He moved to the Lambs' Club on West 44th Street – a theatrical club where he met and became friendly with Lorenz Hart. He tells a sad story of switching on the radio one night during a power failure, while sitting in the dark with Hart. The first station was playing a song from *Oklahoma!*. Hammerstein had just stepped into Hart's shoes for this play. Lerner saw Hart's cigar glowing brighter in the darkness. He changed to another station – another tune from *Oklahoma!*. The puffing on the cigar grew more nervous. He found a third station, but they heard the same score. Mercifully the lights came back and the twisting knife of melody was never mentioned by its victim.

Lerner learned from his meetings with Hart, but another encounter at the Lambs' Club transformed his life. He had written some sketches and lyrics for a revue performed by members of the club – *The Lambs' Gambols*. Soon afterwards Frederick Loewe presented himself at Lerner's luncheon table and said, 'You are Lerner, aren't you? You write lyrics, don't you? Would you like to write with me, my partner just joined the navy?' Lerner said yes to the Viennese-born composer, who was eighteen years his senior and who had come to New York in 1923 as part of the baggage of his father, Edmund Loewe, a distinguished singing-actor imported by Belsaco for a Broadway show. Loewe Senior died during rehearsals and the son, who had already won the Amsterdam medal for the best young pianist in Europe at the age of sixteen, was left to support his widowed mother. Concert piano engagements being hard to come by, he became a bus-boy, a boxer, a riding instructor, a cowboy, a gold prospector, and a horseback mail deliverer. During Prohibition he played piano on ships which plied between Miami and Havana, catering exclusively to the thirsty. After Prohibition he played for rehearsals, in Greenwich Village nightclubs and in New York's German beer cellars. He had written several shows with little success before he introduced himself to Lerner. At that moment Loewe was required to rewrite some songs for a show in Detroit – *Life of the Party*; their collaboration made it the first Lerner and Loewe musical. *Life of the Party* did not move past Detroit, but Lerner and Loewe wrote first *What's Up?*, directed by Georges Balanchine, without success, and then *The Day Before Spring*, which gained some critical support. With *Brigadoon* they achieved critical approval and a long run.

This romantic idea of an idyllic land now lost is a recurring theme in Lerner's work. Whether time is playing tricks in *On a Clear Day*, or whether the threatened ideal is the chivalry of *Camelot* (and the determination that it should be preserved as a place of happy memories like Peter Pan's Never Never Land or the youth of Gatsby or Le Grand Meaulnes) the theme exerts a powerful fascination for him. It is part of his romantic nature and elsewhere he has written, 'As a rule it is not sadness that brings tears to my eyes, but a longing fulfilled.' The Character, Lerner's father, had a characteristic reaction to the good notices for *Brigadoon*. Cancer had forced the doctors to remove his tongue. On a beach in Florida a neighbour approached him. 'I just read the reviews of *Brigadoon*,' he said; 'your son is certainly a lucky boy.' The Character always carried a pad and pencil with him. On it he wrote his reply, 'Yes, it's a funny thing about Alan. The harder he works the luckier he gets.'

Cheryl Crawford – having presented Lerner's *Brigadoon* and Kurt Weill's *One Touch of Venus* – then produced their joint venture, *Love Life*, in 1948. *Love Life* employs characters who travel across America through two centuries without ever growing older – a device not unlike that which Lerner was to use with Leonard Bernstein in *1600 Pennsylvania Avenue* in 1976, a play which followed various inhabitants of the White House, upstairs and down, through the centuries, all portrayed by the same actors. In the case of *Love Life*, Lerner's purpose was allegorical. His family was a Mr and Mrs Everyman embodying the decaying values of American life, moving from happy small-town scenes to work in soulless industrial towns – and ending as victims of a 'materialistic society', abandoning their ideals and helpless to avoid the breakdown of their marriage. It sounds more like Weill than Lerner, with the implied shadow of Brecht looming over Lerner's shoulder. 'My own taste has always run towards the romantic (meaning larger than life, not operetta). I have no gift for satire and I look for humour in the antics of personality . . .'

However, chameleon-like, Lerner absorbed a strong colour from Weill's music which overwhelmed his romantic instinct. The device of alternating the scenes of family life with vaudeville sequences, offering a harsh satiric commentary, also smacks more of Brecht's dramaturgy than Lerner's. *Love Life* divided the critics and puzzled a lot of the people who saw its 252 performances. Lerner endorses Moss Hart's verdict: 'the first act was a satire and in the second act the satire was abandoned and the play was solved realistically.' Hence the audience confusion.

In 1949 Lerner went to Hollywood at the bidding of Arthur Freed, the great producer of musicals at MGM. To him Lerner ascribes the advice, 'Why try to be different? To be good is different enough.' Harry Warren suggests in Max Wilk's book, *They're Playing Our Song*, that Lerner and Loewe had been there before — also on an invitation from Freed. 'I remember years ago he called me up . . . "I got a couple of young kids coming in from New York." (Loewe must have been 45.) "They've done some shows and they're going to play me some stuff." . . . In walk these two guys from New York, with their little raincoats on, with horn-rimmed glasses. They looked like two little comics. They played a lot of tunes, and when they left, somebody asked Freed what he thought of them, and he said. "I think they stink" . . . but . . . right after that he was bright enough to see that he'd made a big mistake and he reversed himself and hired Alan Lerner, who's a great big talent . . .' Warren also suggests that at one point later Lerner tried to enlist him as an alternative composer for the musical of *Pygmalion*, then let the subject drop, enabling Warren to say, when they met ten years later, 'Now, aren't you glad you *didn't* get me?' But the time Lerner spent in Hollywood cemented a bond with Arthur Freed which eventually led to *Gigi*; and it started a partnership with Burton Lane which painted another set of colours on his chameleon hide in the score of *Royal Wedding*. For the same film, in a song called 'I Left My Hat in Haiti', Lerner took so long to convert his dummy lyrics for the middle eight bars into a lyric he considered acceptable that the song was shot and included in the film with the gibberish dummy lyric. No one seemed to mind. Even Lerner appears philosophical about it these days. With Lane he also wrote six songs for a version of *Huckleberry Finn*. It was due to star Danny Kaye and Gene Kelly, but soon after shooting started Kelly asked to be released, permission was given by the producers and the film was abandoned.

Lerner dismisses the film version of *Brigadoon*, for which he also wrote the screenplay, summarily. 'I have always believed that only genuinely talented people can create something that is genuinely bad. As Jean Giraudoux once said, "Only the mediocre are always at their best." '

Lerner's romantic instinct continued to attract him to colourful foreign subjects: the Paris of *Gigi*, the Scotland of *Brigadoon*, the Italy of *Carmelina!*. Returning from Hollywood and sated with the earnest Germanic America of *Love Life*, he looked for once for a fully romantic approach to his own country, 'a musical that would embrace all the robustness and vitality and cockeyed courage that is so much a part of our American heritage'.

Where'm I goin'?
I don't know.
Where am I headin'?
I ain't certain.
What will I get? I ain't equipped to say,
But who gives a damn, I'm on my way.

Lerner and Loewe (the former gold prospector) decided to write about the Californian gold rush.

Wheels are made for rollin'
Mules are made to pack.
I never seen a sight that didn't look
Better lookin' back.
I was born under a wandrin' star.
Mind can make you pris'ner
And the plains can make you dry.
Snow can burn your eyes but only
People make you cry.
Home is made for comin' from,
For dreams of goin' to
Which, with any luck, will never come true.
I was born under a wandrin' star . . .

Lerner calls the show, *Paint Your Wagon*, 'a success but not a hit. By that I mean the reviews were mixed and the bankers eventually made a small profit . . . after sixteen years.'

During his period in Hollywood Lerner had started to think about *Pygmalion*. So far all his shows had been based on original premises. He was beginning to wonder if adaptation might not have advantages, when he was approached by Gabriel Pascal, the extraordinary, self-styled Hungarian, but actually Rumanian, producer, who had persuaded Shaw to give him the film rights in several of his most attractive plays. Pascal's unique approach appealed to Shaw who asked him how much money he had. Running through his pockets, Pascal said, 'twelve shillings'. Shaw welcomed him as the first 'honest' film producer he had ever met.

The producer's approach to Lerner was not unique. Indeed, before or after approaching him he also approached Rodgers and Hammerstein, who could not solve the problem of writing it; Noël Coward, Cole Porter, Dietz and Schwartz and E. Y. Harburg, who felt the play was perfect and should not be tampered with. Harburg seems nearest to Shaw who, having suffered *The Chocolate Soldier* (born of *Arms and the Man*), had always refused to allow a musical based on *Pygmalion*. 'I absolutely forbid such outrage. If *Pygmalion* is not good enough for your friends with its own verbal music . . . let them try Mozart's *Cosi Fan Tutti*, or at least Offenbach's *Grand Duchess*.' After Shaw's death in 1950, Pascal's 'honesty' persuaded the administrators of the Shaw estate. His initial approach to Lerner was direct. 'I want to make a musical of *Pygmalion*. I want you to write music.' Unaware of Loewe, he had assumed that Lerner was the composer – a change from most people who, according to Lerner, think that someone called Lerner 'n' Loewe writes the music to which the words attach themselves as if by magic. Interspersing his blandishments with Rabelaisian tales of Shaw's sex-life and Gandhi's sex-life, Pascal convinced both Lerner and Loewe that they should go to work. 'We began, as we always did, meeting regularly, either in town or country and talking, talking, talking.' They found the neatness, the completeness, of Shaw's play inhibiting. When they saw a production, specially staged for them, it became even harder to see how it could be opened up and made to sing and dance. Finally they gave up the challenge for two years. During that time both chased other projects – Lerner working at *Li'l Abner*, first with Burton Lane and then Arthur Schwartz, and Loewe attempting Paul Vincent Carroll's *Saints and Sinners*. Neither project reached the stage with these writers. Then in 1954 Lerner read that Pascal had died. His immediate reaction was to remember *Pygmalion*. He talked to Loewe and suddenly they found that changes in theatrical taste had solved some of their problems for them, and that distance lent a perspective to the others. They realised that it was no longer important to add a diversionary sub-plot, or two large and inappropriate ballets. They could justify an ensemble; and they could write songs for a leading character who was determined not to fall in love, or if he did, not to show it. Most reassuring, they saw how to open up the show, not by damaging Shaw's beautifully constructed mechanism inside his scenes, but simply by filling with musical ensembles the moments between them – incidents in many cases suggested by the screenplay of the film which Pascal had produced with Leslie Howard and Wendy Hiller in the thirties.

A month before Lerner began to write *My Fair Lady*, the Character died. The end of his life had been a relentless, cheerful battle against illness. When he signed the official form giving permission for one operation, Lerner saw on it 'number of operations: 49'. His father had written underneath, 'When it gets to 50 sell.' He came through that ordeal to hear that Lerner had won an Oscar for the screenplay of *An American in Paris*. It was a sad irony that he missed his son's involvement in the show that was not only his most successful work, but the one which dealt faithfully with the literacy his father so prized.

Lerner and Loewe's plans proceeded smoothly, but for two incidents. One was more a prolonged guerilla war with executors, banks and copyright lawyers over the rights – a battle eventually won. The other was a short, sharp shock. Mary Martin, who was then Peter-Panning her way across the Broadway sky, having been told of the show, asked to hear the songs Lerner and Loewe had written so far. Although they did not think her suitable they played her five numbers, following Lorenz Hart's dictum, 'if a star seems interested, do not say "no" for at least 24 hours'; and if she could get away with Barrie's fey boy, why not Shaw's Cockney girl? Mary Martin's verdict, delivered over lunch by her husband some days later, was shattering. 'How could it have happened? ... those dear boys have lost their talent.' Loewe was philosophical: 'Well, I guess she didn't like it'; but the effect on Lerner was more serious. In his book he describes the mental block which it produced out of which he had to be expensively analysed into activity. The first fruits of the cure were 'Wouldn't It Be Loverly?', conceived after an early-hours tour round Covent Garden Market in the nights when Covent Garden Market was in Covent Garden. Looking back, we see that three of the numbers Mary Martin had heard were later dropped. Of the two survivors, 'Just You Wait' should have been all right, but the other, the 'Ascot Gavotte', must have seemed pretty small beer at a piano audition without the benefit of a black and white stage-full of Cecil Beaton's most effective costumes. However, Lerner was not annoyed with Miss Martin for being right; and her candour was at least Julie Andrews' opportunity. She seized it with both arms, high notes and some extraordinary vowel sounds that convinced American ears that she was speaking 'Cockney' when in fact her dialect coach was teaching her a quite new *My Fair Lady* language unknown to living man. If Shaw was interested in Galatea as embodied by Mrs Patrick Campbell, Lerner was happier with *Pygmalion* – especially in the formidable person of Rex Harrison. Lerner affectionately describes Harrison's difficult reputation as stemming from 'a unique approach to human relations'. However, he supplies innumerable stories of the way Harrison's personality and his actor's instinct helped shape the librettist's approach to the whole play and to specific lyrics. Item: when they played him the first two songs – later lost – he hated them. 'We knew it because he immediately said, "I hate them," ' and they realised that they were professional song-writing exercises, not helpful to the character and offering nothing to the actor. Item: Harrison's apparent vocal limitations forced Lerner and Loewe into writing the closest possible approximation of natural speech. Item: Harrison's unhappiness with the intricate rhyming of 'Why Can't the English?'. 'It makes me sound like an inferior Noël Coward!'* He made Lerner look again at his rhyme scheme.

---

* Noël Coward, mistaken on one occasion for Rex Harrison, is quoted as having said, 'Do I look like a secondhand car salesman from the Euston Road?'

Why can't the English teach their children how to speak?
In Norway there are legions
Of literate Norwegians . . .

Lerner changed it to the more natural:

Why can't the English teach their children how to speak?
This verbal class distinction by now should be antique.

Debit item: Harrison was not infallible. His favourite song – everyone's favourite song, Higgins persuading Eliza to 'Come to the Ball', disappeared after one performance in New Haven. Item: at the first read-through Harrison was, not surprisingly, the first man to worry that he was getting lost in Act Two. In the circumstances, the creators wisely agreed and Lerner recalled a conversation he had had with Harrison on their mutual much-marriedness. Halfway down Fifth Avenue, Harrison stopped and said loudly, 'Alan! Wouldn't it be marvellous if we were homosexuals?' It was not the answer for either man; but it did provide Lerner with an idea, 'A Hymn to Him' ('Why Can't a Woman be More Like a Man?').

Item: when Lerner began to think that turning *Pygmalion* into a musical was possible, it was his fascination with Higgins and then with Harrison as Higgins which dictated his artistic choices. That and his idea 'that Higgins was Shaw', whose 'love affairs existed on paper only'. Lerner chose to reveal his feeling only in 'I've Grown Accustomed to her Face'. As answers came to the central questions posed by Professor Higgins, Lerner found a simple, direct language for Eliza: unfussy statements like 'I Could Have Danced All Night' and 'Without You'. Perhaps the most successful musical number theatrically is 'The Rain in Spain', in which Higgins, Eliza and Pickering celebrate Eliza's breakthrough in elocution. It was the one song which was substantially written in the traditional ten minutes. For Stanley Holloway, as Doolittle, Lerner and Loewe produced two English music-hall songs with all the vitality of 'Any Old Iron' or 'Boiled Beef and Carrots'.

Lerner believes that 'A musical play is a popular art form. I do not believe there is such a thing as an avant-garde musical; it is a contradiction in terms.' *My Fair Lady* is the quintessence of that popular art form; an adaptation of a comedy only some 40 years old but already a classic, treated with love and respect and afforded every available sophistication in its conversion to the musical stage. It is not necessary to take issue with Mr Lerner's second point to realise that *My Fair Lady* is definitively popular.

The progress of Lerner and Loewe from project to project was a regular high-comedy routine. In the euphoria of a success Lerner would go away and play and perhaps start or end a marriage. (On reflection, it seems extraordinary that a man who went to a decent English public school and who had such a feeling for impeccable grammatical usage should not have realised that when you are talking to a woman the last thing you should do is end the sentence with a proposition.) Loewe, long and permanently unmarried, though rarely unattached, would depart for the gaming tables, usually at the Palm Beach Casino, Cannes, latterly in Palm Springs. After a decent interval Lerner's creative fingers would begin to itch. He would get an idea or he would be offered a commission or would read a book review. A telegram would go off to Loewe ... or a phone call would be made ... The first reply was invariably 'no'. Perhaps Lerner would toy with book or screenplay ... and then another call would be made to Loewe. If he liked what he read the answer would eventually be 'yes'. And so in 1957 Loewe and Lerner, prompted by Arthur Freed, to whom Lerner owed a picture, started work on the last in the great tradition of MGM musicals, Gigi. It was not made without drama; but they were the characteristic dramas of film-making.

Lerner and Loewe stuck to the style they had evolved in *My Fair Lady*, adding a Gallic bounce. One song, 'Say a Prayer For Me Tonight', having been dropped from *My Fair Lady*, in which it summed up Eliza's moment of trepidation before going to the ball, became Gigi's moment of trepidation before going on the town. Lerner had two objectives while writing *Gigi*: not only to tell his story through his songs, but also, most artfully, to suit his songs to the star performers he and Freed had assembled – Chevalier, Caron, Jourdan, Gingold, Eva Gabor, and most elegant, Isabel Jeans (no song for Miss Jeans, unfortunately). Maurice Chevalier's role – Honoré Lachailles – is a sketchy character in Colette's novella who does not make an appearance in the stage version of *Gigi*. For Lerner, Chevalier was not only a favourite, but a key performer. He feels that it is reassuring for an audience to see an actor whom they associate with singing at the start of a musical film. It helps them to accept the artificial convention and carries them towards the necessary suspension of disbelief. Moreover, Chevalier gave Lerner the idea for 'I'm Glad I'm not Young Anymore'. At 72, he told Lerner and Loewe, 'I am too old for women, too old for that extra glass of wine, too old for sports. All I have left is the audience but I have found it is quite enough.' 'Thank Heaven for Little Girls' enabled Chevalier and the director, Vincente Minnelli, to introduce the audience to Honoré, to Paris, to the period and to the leading lady. The use of Louis Jourdan to play the bored Gaston presented the writers with the age-old problem of preventing a bored character from becoming boring to the audience. They were not sure that they could get the same sparkle from Jourdan that they felt would have been assured had Dirk Bogarde, their original choice, been available to play the part. So they wrote Jourdan's songs wittily pointing Gaston's boredom at being in Paris. Again, in 'She's Not Thinking of Me', an interior monologue sung from within Gaston's head as he sits in Maxim's, his concealed irritation gives energy and excitement to the song; and in the climactic song, *Gigi*, Lerner continues to explore Gaston's puzzlement and frustration. Finally, in the same song he allows Gaston to slide into realising that he is in love:

Oh Gigi, have I been standing up too close
Or back too far? . . .

One of Lerner's Chevalier stories echoes an incident in the careers of Rodgers and Hart. Lerner and Loewe were to play the great man his songs. He arrived exactly on time. He listened to the songs thoughtfully. He thanked them and left. Panic struck. Perhaps he had not liked the material. The next day he called for another appointment. Was he coming to tell them just that? Only when he arrived did they learn that he liked the songs so much he had come back to make sure that he had the right phrasing on the middle eight bars of 'Thank Heaven'. 25 years earlier, Rodgers and Hart had gathered in an office at Paramount to play Chevalier their songs for *Love Me Tonight*. Rodgers tells the story in his *Musical Stages*. 'With Chevalier practically sitting on my lap in our cramped quarters I played the music and Larry and I took turns in singing the words. Chevalier sat silent throughout, his usually expressive face without a trace of either approval or disapproval, and when we'd finished he simply rose and left without saying a word. We were stunned . . . the next morning we didn't do any work. We simply stared at each other and at the walls like prisoners in Death Row . . . after a couple of hours the door burst open . . . "Boys," Chevalier said, "I just had to come back to tell you. I couldn't sleep a wink last night because I was so excited about your wonderful songs!" ' They might have warned Lerner and Loewe.

From the triumphant London opening of *My Fair Lady*, the present authors only remember one discordant note. As the curtain went up on Oliver Smith's rideau, a stylised map of London around the winding Thames, the distinguished designer, the late Oliver Messel, sitting alongside, breathed the acid phrase, 'Greetings telegram!'

Dodging from London to Paris for *Gigi*, Lerner and Loewe bought themselves a Rolls Royce — each. It is not true that, Lerner having bought lunch, Loewe said, 'Okay. I'll pay for the cars.' Lerner took his straight to Paris. Chaperoning the car was a formidable Scottish chauffeur, MacIntosh, provided by the thoughtful Messrs Rolls. Arriving in the Champs Elysées, Lerner met Art Buchwald, the columnist, who wanted to examine the engine. MacIntosh refused. 'If I raise the hood', he explained, 'people might think there was something wrong with the car.' Finally Buchwald was allowed a peep, but in a discreet back street. 'In your opinion,' he asked the chauffeur, 'is Mr Lerner worthy of a Rolls?' 'Oh yes, sir,' said MacIntosh. 'Why?' asked Buchwald. 'Because he's so careless with it.' Lerner was to grow less careless as familiarity bred concern. He records a telephone conversation with Moss Hart when he was staying at the Waldorf Towers looking out of the window. ' "God damn it," I began one day. "What's the trouble?" he asked. "The Duchess of Windsor's air conditioning is dripping on my Rolls." '

Gigi won ten Oscars – a record number at that time – and had the distinction of having its winning lyric interpreted by an absent-minded Tony Martin as follows:

Gigi, la-la-la-la- do-do-do
La-la-la-la do-do-do,
La-la-la-la,
Oh Gigi, la-la-la etc.

If Lerner's life had gone on from rich boy to richer man, the social standing of his characters was escalating simultaneously. From the solid upper middle class London society of *My Fair Lady* he had progressed to the 'poules de luxe' of turn-of-the-century Paris and their protectors. The natural next step was royalty and Lerner found it at the Court of King Arthur.

Camelot has become his favourite subject for two reasons. After President Kennedy's assassination, the show gained an aura by its association with his brief term in office; moreover, on the road and in the early months of its Broadway run it was always in trouble and Lerner grew to love it like the parent of a delicate child. Based on T. H. White's *The Once and Future King*, *Camelot* recounts Arthur's betrayal by Guinevere and Lancelot. For Loewe it was simply the story of a cuckold, a figure of fun – a Viennese attitude far removed from the tender, sympathetic, romantic point of view of the book. However, after his usual hesitation, Loewe agreed to try. He and Lerner decided to produce the show themselves and embarked on the ritual of clearing the rights, assembling the director, Moss Hart, and the cast, Richard Burton, Julie Andrews, Robert Coote, Robert Goulet and Roddy McDowall, the designers, Oliver Smith and Adrian, and the choreographer, Hanya Holm. At roughly the same time, but slightly in arrears, the process of actually writing the play proceeded. Lerner again suffered a mental block from which he had to be analysed. This time it could not be laid at Mary Martin's door; the answer was nearer home. 'All I can say is that if I had no flare for marriage, I also had no flare for bachelorhood.' This

particular traumatic marital upset happened through June, July and
August. The first verse to materialise on his recovery was:

If ever I would leave you
It wouldn't be in summer . . .

The fascination which the original novel exercised for Lerner lay not
so much in its love story – King meets Queen, King loses Queen, King
fails to regain Queen – as in the dénouement of the play. 'Arthur has
lost his love, his friend and his Round Table and believes his life has been
a failure. Then a small boy appears from behind a tent who doesn't
know the Round Table is dead, and wishes to become a knight. Arthur
realises that as long as his vision is alive in one small heart he has not
failed. Men die but an idea does not.' 'Once there was a fleeting wisp of
glory called Camelot . . .'

Unfortunately, this clarifying vision of what really interested him in
the play did not reveal itself to Lerner until the show had reached
Boston. *Camelot* on tour was a disaster area. Adrian, the costume
designer, died halfway through his preparatory work; the show opened
a vast new theatre in Toronto, the O'Keefe, with all the inadequacies
and especially the inaudibilities seemingly inevitable in opening a new
theatre; half an hour had been cut from the running time before the
show left New York, but on its first night in Toronto it still ran for four
and a half hours. Three days later, an ulcer exploded inside Lerner and,
as he recovered, a coronary felled Moss Hart. As Lerner left his hospital
bed he saw Hart being wheeled in to fill it. Then Lerner and Loewe
differed on the idea and on the choice of a replacement director. Lerner
directed any changes that could be made himself, without Loewe's
approval. To take four hours and twenty minutes to get around to
delivering the message of chivalry being handed on was still too long.
There were lovely songs on the way, but despite the richness of the
music, despite the cutting and tightening that Lerner attempted, the
show obstinately refused to find its right theatrical shape. A huge
advance and high hopes translated themselves into a half-cock first
night, a half-hearted press and halting attendance figures. Lerner pays
generous tribute to the salvage work done by Moss Hart when some
months later he was eventually fit enough to come back to the theatre.
His changes, and an extraordinarily successful excerpt on the Ed
Sullivan show (which coincided with Hart's return), gave *Camelot* a
two-year run; but it raised a barrier between Lerner and Loewe which
has not been fully demolished. They have prepared a stage version of
Gigi which had some success; and they actually collaborated on a film of
Saint-Exupéry's *The Little Prince* – a failure which, in his book, Lerner
lays fairly and squarely at the door of its director, Stanley Donen, whom

he accuses of betraying Loewe's music – indeed of kidnapping and ransacking the very notes.

The memory of *Camelot* which stays most vividly in Lerner's mind is of the days which followed Kennedy's assassination. Lerner, John F. Kennedy and Theodore White were classmates at Harvard. After the President's death, Jacqueline Kennedy gave an interview to White for *Life* magazine. She said: 'When Jack quoted something it was usually classical; but all I keep thinking about is this line from a musical comedy – at night, before we'd go to sleep, Jack liked to play some records and the song he loved most came at the very end of this record. You must think of him as this little boy, sick so much of the time, reading in bed, reading history, reading the Knights of the Round Table. For Jack, history was full of heroes and if it made him this way, if it made him see the heroes – maybe other little boys will see . . . the lines he loved to hear were:

> . . . Don't let it be forgot
> That once there was a spot,
> For one, brief, shining moment
> That was known as Camelot!

His widow felt that it would never be like that again. History and optimism may challenge her verdict; but Lerner remembers that suddenly Camelot 'became the symbol of those thousand days when people the world over saw a bright new light of hope shining from the White House'. The first act of *Camelot* had always been stronger than the second; but from that moment the balance changed. 'The first act became the weak act and the second act the strong one.' Presumably what the early audiences had found an unfamiliar story began to assume the power and inevitability of a modern folk-myth, superseding the ancient unfamiliar one on which it was based. Lerner adds, 'God knows I would have preferred that history had not become my collaborator.'

With Loewe in Palm Springs, the first new collaborator Lerner sought out – or was it the other way around? – was Richard Rodgers. From the evidence of their two books it would seem that the overtures came from Rodgers and the idea for the show from Lerner. Lerner has been fascinated by the supernatural ever since missing the chance to hear Conan Doyle lecture on the existence of God while he was still at Bedales. Death cancelled Conan Doyle's appearance. Now, Lerner had an idea for a show based on parapsychology and reincarnation – its plot having echoes of *Berkeley Square*. He and Rodgers called it *I Picked a Daisy*. In Rodgers' exasperated account in *Musical Stages* he writes: 'I couldn't understand why, once having made an appointment, he would often fail to show up or even offer an explanation – or if he did arrive, why the material that was supposed to be completed was only half finished.' Lerner might almost have been Hart. The last straw came on Labour Day weekend, 1962, when the two men were due for a solid three days' work over the holiday. Lerner turned out to be on Capri. (If our dates are right he was probably acquiring the idea for *Carmelina*, finally produced on Broadway in 1979.) Rodgers and he agreed to part and Lerner took his idea to Burton Lane. They called the show *On a Clear Day You Can See for Ever*.

As well as having the theme of extra-sensory perception, the musical contrasted the life styles of Georgian England and contemporary Manhattan; but in spite of excellent individual songs the book seemed to break its back as it leapt to and fro between the centuries. *On a Clear Day* has a charmingly whimsical verse exactly germane to the subject of the play:

And who would have the sense to change his views?
And start to mind his ESP's and Q's?

There is the same bubble of fun in 'Hey! Buds Below', and also in a comedy song, 'The SS Bernard Cohn', a round-the-Isle-of-Manhattan cruise ship. The most moving song is the climactic 'What Did I Have That I Don't Have?'.

Since *On a Clear Day*, Alan Lerner has worked with four other composers as well as once again with Burton Lane. With André Previn in 1969 he produced a romanticised biography of Coco Chanel – a vehicle for Katharine Hepburn, who scored what success was going. *Lolita, My Love*, Lerner wrote with John Barry. On one of his rare explorations of modern America it is interesting that he looked for a source to Nabokov, wisest and wittiest of European commentators on the American scene since Fanny Trollope. Again there is a chameleon change in Lerner's lyrical style under the influence of Barry's music:

Love is going, going, gone,
Prices ev'ry day increase.
Better grab ev'ry piece
You can lay your hands upon.

And a lyric, 'How Far Is It to the Next Town?', bleakly charts Humbert's progress across America:

How long, how long will the road be winding,
The dark, too dark and the pain too blinding . . .
. . . How far is it to the next town?
Too far.

However, *Lolita, My Love* closed out of town.

Then, in 1976, Lerner and Leonard Bernstein combined for *1600 Pennsylvania Avenue*, a bicentennial below-stairs view of the White House. Presidents and their ladies from Washington to Theodore Roosevelt were seen through the eyes of an eternal Black Butler. Again, it was a bold, original device which failed spectacularly. Lerner's verdict on it is, 'Well, you remember the Titanic.'

In 1979 Lerner reunited with Burton Lane. The result, *Carmelina*, had a charming, frivolous and tuneful score, and a plot set in reasonably modern, rural Italy, submerged under antediluvian sets, lighting, sound, acting and direction. Georgia Brown, a shining exception to the general rule, had a rueful comedy song, 'Why Him?', which finds Lerner expressing a woman's point of view as sharply as ever. The play was not well received. Nor was his 1983 collaboration with Charles Strouse, *Dance a Little Closer*, which starred his beautiful and clever wife, Liz Robertson.

In a recorded lecture in Maurice Levine's *Lyrics and Lyricists* series at the 92nd Street YMHA, Lerner defines lyric writing as a 'minor art form – somewhere above photography and woodcarving'. But his heart does not sound as if it is in the definition. Alan Lerner is not an easy lyric writer to sum up. His work is elegant, both witty and funny; stylish, but rarely bland – he can also catch your throat with a simple emotional coup. The urbanity in his work ill accords with the evidence of turbulence in his professional and private life. However, a problem often offers its own solution and perhaps the polish we observe in Lerner's professional output is achieved through the pain we do not see.

13

SHELDON HARNICK

'If I Were a Rich Man'

Sheldon Harnick is a modern lyricist as charming and diverse and skilful as any on show. The range of subjects on which he has written attractive and popular songs includes family and tradition, religion, money, politics, graft, greed and vice, peace and war – together with the inevitable love. Invariably, he makes his unusual themes wisely and wittily singable.

He was born in Chicago on 30 April, 1924 – grew up in that town at the height of the Al Capone era; he was a violin pupil at the Carl Schurz High School and probably the only kid on the block whose violin case actually contained a violin. Having mastered that instrument he began to write songs and sketches at school, while in the army and after the war at North Western University. College over, he began to play the violin professionally for dance bands in the Chicago area. One moment of triumph came when he was engaged to play with Xavier Cugat's orchestra. Disaster followed hard on its heels when he was sacked the next day. By 1950 he had decided to move to New York and to work there as a composer and lyricist. His formative influences had been a love of classical music, with which he grew up during his early musical education, and then his discovery of Gilbert and Sullivan when his violin-playing at school won him a place in an orchestra accompanying an amateur Gilbert and Sullivan production at the Goodman Theatre in Chicago. One university lyric which makes a deep obeisance to Gilbert has survived – 'The Suave Young Man ... in the military-style American trench coat . . .':

Take an ordinary guy from any street
And give him a trench coat;
He glows with satisfaction.
Behold! The transformation is complete.
He's now an imperturbable, undisturbable
Man of Action!

At the same time Harnick was finding especial sympathy for the humour of Robert Benchley and James Thurber, and for the social awareness of Upton Sinclair: all were to colour his later work. His decision to make theatrical song writing a career was finally triggered not only by being fired by Cugat but also by hearing a friend's record of *Finian's Rainbow* when he was still at North Western. 'If ever there was an actual turning point in my life, I think that was it. I was dazzled. To be able to say such pertinent things; and to say them in such entertaining ways – that was a career worth pursuing.' Harburg's influence could soon be detected, whimsical rhyme by rhyme. It is unmistakable in one lyric of this period:

So visible your charms
I'm mis'able when I'm not in your arms . . .

As Harnick has pointed out, 'It may not be good, but you have to admit it's derivative!' Harburg was to provoke another turning point in Harnick's life, but not until later. Meanwhile, the tyro arrived in New York with $800 and with all the confidence of one whose experience of the musical theatre outside Gilbert and Sullivan was limited to Chicago touring productions of *Finian's Rainbow*, *Call Me Mister*, *On the Town*, *Allegro* and *Carmen Jones*. He made up for lost time by seeing everything on offer in New York. Above his desk he hung as a reminder the quotation 'Inspiration is the act of drawing up a chair to the writing desk.' He gained some experience as an entertainer at Green Mansions, a summer resort in upstate New York which had been provided as an opportunity for another composer-lyricist, Harold Rome, nearly twenty years earlier. From New York and from Green Mansions Harnick worked primarily at revue numbers, for which he wrote both words and music, in his attempt to break into the charmed circle of On or Off-Broadway. Revue did not now have the vogue it had enjoyed in the thirties, the days of the expansive Ziegfeld, Earl Carroll and George White *Follies*, *Vanities* and *Scandals*, and of the smaller-scale, more thoughtful shows like *Garrick Gaieties* and the Dietz and Schwartz revues; but Ben Bagley's *Shoe String Revue*, Leonard Sillman's *New Faces* and John Murray Anderson's *Almanac* were all fair game for an ambitious young writer prepared to sit at home without a commission and then to take the result of his labours along and perform it at innumerable pianos.

'The Boston Beguine' for Alice Ghostley in *New Faces of 1952* was the first number by Harnick to attract much attention. He had just paid a visit to Boston, a town he particularly disliked, and specially at that moment when it was in the grip of a vicious attempt at book suppression. Returning on a bus he found himself sitting next to a man

Sheldon Harnick (*R*) with Jerry Bock (*Hulton Picture Library*).

whose radio was blaring a song of no distinction, sung by Tony Martin, praising the exotic delights of Johannesburg. Harnick's attempt to do the same for Boston was sung in *New Faces* by a gauche and schoolmarmish spinster recalling:

> . . . I met him in Boston
> In the native quarter.
> He was from Harvard
> Just across the border . . .

Encouraged by his revue success, Harnick started doing the rounds of the music publishers. To a man they turned him down. In each case the verdict was the same, 'Mr Harnick, you put too many ideas into your songs.' In each case, Harnick modestly asked for guidance and on one glorious occasion received the unvarnished answer, 'Listen to the crap that's around. That's what we want.' Two parodies stem from this period. 'At the Basilica of St Anne' was also inspired by its composer's revulsion at appalling quasi-religious pop songs of the period.

> I kissed you under the nave
> At the Basilica of St Anne . . .
> . . . There in a scene celestial
> You acted clean and I acted bestial . . .

No performer was bold enough to perform such blasphemy in the fifties. 'Garbage' was another parody — this time of a tempestuous, passionate, Italianate sort of love song then in vogue. Again this song was never published, though had it been it would, presumably, have been the first instance in the history of pop music when a music publisher would have had to admit that he was actually selling 'Garbage'.

It was during the fifties that Harnick met his idol Harburg, who listened to his songs and, adding advice to example, counselled him that composing music as well as writing words was inhibiting him as a lyricist. Harnick, although an educated and skilful musical craftsman, realised that his most successful songs so far had been parodies and that if he was to allow his increasingly authentic and distinctive lyrical voice to be heard he must find a composer with whom he could work. During rehearsals of *Two's Company*, he had been impressed by David Baker's ballet music. According to Harnick, not only Harburg, but 'many of my friends and well-wishers had persuaded me that my music would be better if it were written by somebody else.' In 1953, with Ira Wallack, Harnick and Baker collaborated on a musical based on Wallack's treatment of the Horatio Alger books, 'legends of poor but honest youths who became successful through perseverance, hard work and a score of similar virtues . . .' – at least '. . . the Alger heroes did indeed pursue success with dogged nobility, but, when success was achieved, hard work and clean living had nothing to do with it . . . it was the result of coincidence or sheer fluke.' Their show started out in Texas as *Horatio*; it was a smash there and they began an annual ritual of auditions for a Broadway production. By now it was called *Waldo* and by the second audition in 1956 it had gained the name *Fair-Haired Boy*. Finally, after Harnick's Broadway successes, it arrived off-Broadway at the Cherry Lane Theatre for 22 performances under the title *Smiling, the Boy Fell Dead*, and it shows the especially gentle Harnick relishing for the first time the lyric writer's truth that the devil gets the best jokes. One song cheerfully denies the influence of environment in forming character, throwing in some very Harburgian rhymes for good measure:

My father's so meek that it's criminal,
Incredibly gentle and mild.
To hear him sing hymns from a hyminal
You'd never believe I'm his child . . .

(Harnick once worked as an amanuensis for Ogden Nash whose idiosyncratic head also seems to be raising itself in this verse.)

During the years that Harnick was waiting for the production of *Smiling, the Boy Fell Dead*, he continued to work on revue songs and on industrial shows given during sales meetings, according to Harnick, 'to keep salesmen awake between speeches . . . an exercise in craft and staying alive . . .'. Occasionally he was asked to minister to ailing Broadway shows. One such was *Shangri-la* which had a run of two and a half weeks in June 1956. He made some last-minute, uncredited interpolations (the score was Harry Warren's) and after the opening dropped into a bar which held more promise of happiness than had *Shangri-la* on stage. Inside, Jack Cassidy, who was in the cast of *Shangri-la*, introduced Harnick to Jerry Bock, whose Broadway record until that time consisted of three songs for a revue, *Catch a Star*, written with Larry Holofcener, and of *Mr Wonderful*, a successful Sammy Davis show with two durable songs, the title number and 'Too Close for Comfort'. The lyrics were again by Holofcener. Bock, like Harnick, had started by writing words and music as a student; but he had moved the other way towards full-time composing.

Harnick is thoughtful and introspective about his own work and about the part his personal life has played in his development as a lyricist. In his lecture in Maurice Levine's *Lyrics and Lyricists* series at the YMHA, recorded on 14 February, 1970, he charts his development as lyric writer and relates it to the pace at which he matured as a person. He made the disconcerting discovery that he had not written a straightforward love song since college days. 'No emotional content', he points out ruefully, 'can be a fault in a love song.' The nearest he got to it was in a title like 'Afraid of Love', a phrase which lacks that confident zing, and in his parodies. By the time he started to work with Bock, he was beginning to come to terms with this concern. Their first shows were *Man in the Moon*, a musical for the Bill Baird puppets produced in 1963, and *The Body Beautiful*, their first Broadway show, conceived at the time that Harnick was being divorced. Although it was ostensibly about prize fighters, titles like 'Leave Well Enough Alone', 'Just My Luck' and 'The Honeymoon is Over', suggest that, however unconsciously, the lyric writer was at last drawing more on his own predicament than on his research into prize fighting. One song, 'Summer Is', survives as an especial favourite with singers when auditioning.

The Body Beautiful ran for only 60 performances and its first night was less than triumphant; however, before drowning their sorrows at a party at Sardi's afterwards, Bock and Harnick were introduced to Hal Prince by the designers of the show, William and Jean Eckert. With Robert Griffith, Prince was about to produce a musical based on the life of Fiorello la Guardia. The director, Arthur Penn, had had the idea in the first place and he and Prince brought in Jerome Weidman to write the book. By the time Weidman had completed two rich scenes – a discussion of politics in the course of a poker game and another for the same political figures, some years later at the height of Jimmy Walker's power – Penn disapproved of the way in which the book was developing. According to Prince, 'he wanted it deeper, psychologically deeper.' George Abbott came in to direct instead and Bock and Harnick were asked to write three songs which would suggest both a sharp satirical attitude to the politics of the period and also a feeling for its nostalgic appeal. Such was the cloak of secrecy that the identity of the central character was not revealed to them. One song had to resemble a popular song of pre-1914; remembering the old tune, 'Just a Song at Twilight', Harnick took the word 'twilight' as his first nostalgic image. He was looking for what he calls 'a laced valentine sound' and he got it from 'Twilight'. For another exercise, Harnick and Bock attacked Weidman's poker game in which, Prince says, 'Weidman . . . captured the tone, the peculiar vitality of the era, the style of our show.' Big-city politics seem to exert some particular fascination for Harnick – or perhaps his lyric in this case sprang from Weidman's original draft; whatever the explanation, 'Politics and Poker' is a remarkable example of making a funny, intricate conversational song do the work of a scene:

Dealer: How about Dave Zimmerman?
Ben: Davie's too bright.

2:	What about Walt Gustafson?
Ben:	Walt died last night.
3:	How about Frank Monohan?
4:	What about George Gale?
Ben:	Frank ain't a citizen
	And George is in jail.
5:	We could run Al Wallenstein.
Ben:	He's only twenty three.
Dealer:	How about Ed Peterson?
2:	You idiot, that's me!
All:	Politics and Poker . . .

Bock and Harnick got the job and as soon as they were told about whom they were writing, they dashed off 'On the Side of the Angels,' a song which immediately set the keynote for the evening. They also found a stirring march, 'The Name's La Guardia', and a Charleston, 'Gentleman Jimmy', to work for his opponent, the stylish incumbent mayor; and they were able to top 'Politics and Poker' with an even more ingenious song for the same group of corrupt politicians. The number had to be added at the last moment in Philadelphia. Sentiment was bogging down the second half of the play and Harnick and Bock had, at about eleven o'clock in the evening, to lift it up. In their song various low-paid city officials improvise excuses to explain to a judge how they have come into suspiciously large sums of money. They gave up smoking, they took empty bottles back to the grocer or, in the last chorus:

I can see Your Honour doesn't pull his punches
And it looks a trifle fishy I'll admit;
But for one whole week I went without my lunches
And it mounted up Your Honour bit by bit.
(Up Your Honour bit by bit)
Into a little tin box . . .

Harnick was helped in writing the lyric under pressure by using a tune of Bock's which had been discarded early on. That had been a song of service rivalry, and having the form of most of the song at hand helped Harnick complete it, literally overnight. Prince has the final word. 'I remember hearing about eleven o'clock numbers all my life. Though I don't care much for formulas, I would settle for an eleven o'clock showstopper every time. Those don't even hurt operas.'

George S. Kauffman and Ira Gershwin had had to wait years for their Pulitzer Prize, for *Of Thee I Sing*. Rodgers and Hammerstein, who got one for *South Pacific*, and Frank Loesser, who collected his for *How to*

Succeed in Business Without Really Trying, could hardly be said to be tyros. However, Bock and Harnick received the fourth Pulitzer Prize ever awarded for a musical for their second show, within two years of starting to work together. According to Hal Prince, 'We had such a good time doing *Fiorello* that we could not bear splitting up after it opened – so we did *Tenderloin*.' He makes the point that the story seemed the perfect material for a musical – reforming minister tangles with the thieves, pimps and whores of the red-light district, determined to close down the colourful saloons and brothels and gambling halls in which they hang out. It seemed so rich a subject that they hardly took time to find an attitude which would lend a unifying character to the material. Although the book and the production failed to set a tone, Bock and Harnick's work is even better than in *Fiorello*. The opening song, 'Little Old New York is Plenty Good Enough For Me', is raucous and rowdy and wonderfully winning and perfectly prepares the audience for the show which failed to follow. Prince calls it 'as good an opening number as I have ever seen – as good as *Forum*, or the train scene in *Music Man* or for that matter "Wilkommen" in *Cabaret*.' Harnick gets at graft again in 'How the Money Changes Hands', and tugs hearts strings in 'My Gentle Young Johnny', a prostitute's wistful fantasy in which all her 'Johns' become one Johnny. He ebulliently pastiches a music-hall song telling of the virtues of vice in 'A Picture of Happiness'. Perhaps, most memorably, he pastiches a sentimental ballad of the period, wickedly tipping the wink to the audience as the unfortunate girl's story emerges.

> With paper and shears, with wire and wax,
> She laboured and never complained,
> 'Til cutting and folding, her health slipped away
> And wiring and waxing, she waned.
> Making
> Artificial flowers . . .

Lehman Engel makes the point that 'occasionally a creative artist possesses a character and nature that is truly guileless and ingenuous. Sheldon Harnick is one of these. His simple honesty and sweetness are to be discerned everywhere in his work. Never is he vituperative. Though he is invariably gentle, he is never dull or innocuous in his lyrics. The humour they contain is not achieved at the expense of others. The pity and sadness and sweetness are never cloying.' In fact, Harnick is always at his best when the material presents a challenge – not only to his technique but also to his temperament. Ruthless, crooked, criminal characters bring out a sharpness and wit by their very contrast to his own instincts. His shows after *Tenderloin*, for all their virtues, rarely present the abrasive opportunities on which he had thrived. His biggest success lay ahead; but he has never quite matched the vitality of the early shows and his choice of gentler or more sentimental material and of less full-blooded protagonists is partly to blame.

She Loves Me was the next Harnick, Bock, Prince collaboration. This time Prince was directing a charming slender story based on Miklos Lazlo's play, *Parfumerie*, and the film, *The Shop on the Corner* (Judy Garland had appeared in another film version of the same story, *In the Good Old Summertime*). Even though he was not so much stretched by the subject-matter, which is gently romantic, Harnick is still never less than elegant, observant, amused and precisely detailed. The show is full of music. 40 minutes had to be cut arbitrarily before opening and what remains still crams two LP records. However, the only song to have a life outside the play is the exuberant title song – a lyric in which Harnick feels he found his own lyrical voice for the first time in a love song.

> . . . My teeth ache
> From the urge to touch her.
> I'm speechless
> For I mustn't tell her.
> It's wrong now
> But it won't be long now
> Before my love discovers
> That she and I are lovers.
> Imagine how surprised she's bound to be.
> She loves me!

The whole scene is a triumph for the 'integrated' musical. Songs further the plot, explore character, pass the seasons, see people in and out of a shop. It is a textbook for the use of music in a musical by nice people about nice people. Nice sentiment is piled upon nice response. Somewhere in the sea of niceness lurk off-stage adultery and an attempted suicide; yet the two most striking musical moments come from the one character in the piece who is not to be trusted. Hal Prince in his *Contradictions* ponders the reason for the show's lack of commercial success. '*She Loves Me* is one of the best things this office has done . . . if you want to analyse carefully why it only ran nine and one half months on Broadway . . . I have given it more thought than I like to give projects after the fact. It was a style piece, an unsentimental love story. It had irony and an edge to it. It was funny, but not hilarious. It was melodic but not soaring . . . it was a soft-sell.' He suggests that it came at the wrong time; that a larger theatre would have helped to balance the books on the good nights; perhaps Julie Andrews, had the time been apt, would have made a profound difference at the box office. The London production, directed with similar assurance and sympathy by Prince, had a similar track record, and a staged reading off-Broadway, charmingly played, failed to draw the town in 1977. Part of the answer surely lies in Sheldon Harnick's need to confront a generous dose of wickedness when he settles down to write; a salt and pepper stimulus to spice his considerable qualities into full flavour.

He and Bock next tackled a subject which gave them, if not wickedness, certainly drama on a larger scale and a central character of enormous strength, *Fiddler on the Roof*. They had brought *Tevye and His Daughters* to Prince before *She Loves Me* in 1962; but he had suggested that they put it away unless Jerome Robbins was available to direct it. He wasn't and they did. After *Fiorello* Harnick was taken by Howard da Silva, who sang 'A Little Tin Box', to see his production of some of the Sholem Aleichem stories. Bock and Harnick went to work with Joseph Stein, who had written the book of *The Body Beautiful*. Harnick's secondary source was a book called *Life is with People*, a sociological examination of communal life created by the Jews forced to live separately in 'shtetls'. Prince's instinct to involve Jerome Robbins had been prompted by a wish to take the subject out of its narrow Yiddish parochialism, to give it size and substance, to make more integral the story of parents striving to uphold their traditions in the face of the pressures of change. Robbins rearranged the opening scenes beginning not, as in Bock and Harnick's draft, with Tevye and his family at prayer but setting them in the midst of their whole community, introducing the key idea of 'tradition'. Harnick has said, 'Professionally, by this time, I had both experience and a reasonable amount of self-confidence. Personally, I was finding it much easier to deal with emotional situations, both in my lyrics and my life. There was also the fact that there was no question of identity. I knew who I was. I knew who Sholem Aleichem's people were. I knew where our lives touched . . . I was so filled with ideas and thoughts and feelings that I frequently had the lovely experience of being given a melody and then having the words crystallise on it.' Bock and Harnick did not originally conceive their Tevye for Zero Mostel. They had seen him as a thin, small man. Jerome Robbins saw him as Tom Bosley who had scored a success as Fiorello. When Mostel was signed it became necessary to write songs specifically for him. 'If I Were a Rich Man' has passed into the language of popular song, but despite its universal quality it is still marvellously particular in its original form, both as a piece of Tevye, and a piece of material for Mostel, who was given a free hand in inventing his musical language for the refrain:

If I were a rich man
Iaidle deedle daidle

Digguh digguh deedle daidle dum.
All day long I'd biddy, biddy bum,
If I were a wealthy man.

Almost more compelling is 'When Messiah Comes', a song which
was also especially written after Mostel had been cast, and which was
dropped in Philadelphia. For this song Harnick had the idea that Tevye
should be heard speculating on the possibility of a Messiah who might
eventually arrive on earth with a guilty conscience because he has taken
so long to get here:

When Messiah comes,
He will say to us
'I apologise that I took so long,
But I had a little trouble finding you.
Over here a few and over there a few –
You were hard to reunite,
But everything is going to be all right.
Up in heaven there
How I wrang my hands
When they exiled you from the Promised Land.
Into Babylon you went like castaways
On the first of many, many moving days.
What a day and what a blow,
How terrible I felt you'll never know!'

Fiddler was a staggering success and seemed to place them in an
impregnable position.

In 1965 Bock and Harnick attempted an evening of three one-act
musicals. They took their time in narrowing the field. They were to
work again with Jerome Robbins and the theme that would unify the
three stories would be Man, Woman and the Devil. First they toyed
with stories by de Maupassant, Malamud and Aymé. Further
consideration replaced them with a trio by Bruce Jay Friedman (*Show
Biz Connections*); Hawthorne (*Young Goodman-Brown*) and Mark Twain
(*The Diary of Adam and Eve*). The three stories spanned a range from
modern permissiveness, back through early American puritanism, to the
innocence of the Garden of Eden. Until Robbins left the production it
was called *Come Back! Go Away! I Love You!*. Mike Nichols, who came
in to replace Robbins, also replaced two of the stories. Twain survived;
but Jules Feiffer's *Passionella* replaced the Friedman and Frank Stockton's
The Lady and the Tiger came in for the Hawthorne. Bock and Harnick
took over the book themselves from the original writer Jerome
Coopersmith, they reversed the order of the stories so that life started in

Eden instead of finishing there and *The Apple Tree* became the title. Lovely songs thread their way through an evening which lacks a unifying element.

If *The Apple Tree* suffered from narrative undernourishment, *The Rothschilds*, the story of a dynasty, was on the scale of a banquet, a repast so rich and various that it resisted digestion. The book followed the Rothschild family from their German origins to the Congress of Vienna. Harnick and Bock seem for once to have been too ambitious in their efforts to make music from politics, family history, diplomacy, religion and economics.

The Rothschilds has been Sheldon Harnick's last show with Jerry Bock so far. Harnick has been represented on Broadway with *Rex*, a musical about Henry VIII, written with Richard Rodgers in 1976; but it was unsuccessful and the score is prodigal with love songs and calls for little wit. One wag dismissed it as '35 ballads and a prayer'. Harnick, meanwhile, is not silent, busy with opera libretti, a musical for children, translating and adapting *The Umbrellas of Cherbourg*; but it is a long time since he and Bock have worked together. Every artist is entitled to his fallow periods; but Sheldon Harnick is too considerable, too special a dramatic song writer for his public not to wish him back at work, with the composer with whom he has written his best songs, on a subject that will extend them – preferably containing at least five thoroughly disreputable characters.

14

STEPHEN SONDHEIM

'Everything's Coming up Roses'

Not perhaps the obvious philosophical statement from the furrowed brow and questioning mind of Stephen Sondheim, a song writer dedicated to investigating the darker side of life, marriage and disenchantment. Other writers write their plays in words. Sondheim makes music play at least an equal part and more wherever he can; but then he is blessed among song writers, for he has both words and music at his fingertips to an extent unequalled by his peers – with the possible exception of Frank Loesser, whose dramatic experiments had a breadth and bravura sometimes coarsened by the crash and clang of Tin Pan Alley. Sondheim's hair shirt is pulled firmly on and his vigorous, puritan attitude excludes the obvious effect. In evading it he invariably finds an alternative which is infinitely haunting.

He has said, 'I like writing songs that take place in dramatic situations within the proscenium arch. I'm not particularly interested in art songs and pop songs that stand on their own.' Sondheim is not only the best lyric writer of his time; he is also the most adventurous composer of musicals, and the most considerable musical dramatist.

It is this role of dramatist which the reader must remember in listening to his songs, for from it stem his very origins as a lyric writer. At the age of fifteen he had written a school musical which he risked showing to Oscar Hammerstein II, who was a friend of his family.

> I had visions of being the youngest ever to have a show on Broadway, and I asked him to treat it as if it were a professional work and he did not know me. Next day, when I went back for the verdict, he said, 'It's the worst thing I ever read,' and as my lower lip trembled a bit he added, 'I didn't say it was untalented, I just said it was terrible, and if you want to know why I'll tell you.' We started with the opening stage direction and went through, and by the afternoon I had a complete and very concise course in

writing for the musical theatre. We spoke about everything –
characters, plays, scenes, songs, how to structure each. So I daresay
I knew more about song writing at the end of that afternoon than
most people know in a lifetime, because I got the distillation of his
experience. I was just at the right age and I soaked it all up. He then
outlined a course for me which, in fact, I followed quite precisely.

Seven years for Rachel were diminished to four years for Stephen.
Under his mentor's eye he turned a comedy which he admired – *Beggar on
Horseback* by Kauffman and Connelly – into a college musical; he
attacked a play by Maxwell Anderson, *High Tor*, which he found
fascinating but flawed; he struggled unavailingly to dramatise the short
stories entitled *Mary Poppins*; but who said the struggle naught availeth?
He learned some of the problems of dramatic structure, if not all the
answers. For his last task, Hammerstein required a completely original
work. However, when over 160 pages of originality had flowed from
his eager pupil's pen, Hammerstein pencilled a 'Wow!' on page 99 –
which they both knew to be the length of the complete libretto of *South
Pacific*.

Sondheim took a music degree at Williams College and with a
scholarship studied composition under Milton Babbitt for three years.
For a time he wrote scripts for the television series, *Topper*. His abortive
professional début – aborted because of the death of his producer,
Lemuel Ayers – was the result of sharing the duties of usher at a
wedding with Mr Ayers, who had acquired the rights in a play by Julius
J. and Philip S. Epstein, *Front Porch in Flatbush*. The musical was to be
called *Saturday Night*. George Kauffman's time-honoured epigram,
'Satire is what closes on Saturday night', was outsmarted by *Saturday
Night*, which never opened at all. However, in its money-raising
auditions lay the seeds of Sondheim's first Broadway success, *West Side
Story*. Arthur Laurents, who was writing the book, had heard
Sondheim's songs and when he and the director, Jerome Robbins, and
the composer, Leonard Bernstein, were looking for someone to
collaborate on the lyrics with Bernstein, Laurents suggested Sondheim.

These days, Sondheim is apt to be the sternest critic of his own lyrics
for *West Side Story*. Even when the invitation came he found it hard to
think of himself only as a lyricist. However, Oscar Hammerstein said, 'I
think it will be very valuable for you to work with professionals of this
calibre. The project sounds very exciting so I think you ought to do it.'

That advice taken, lyrics like 'Something's Coming', 'America', and
'Gee, Officer Krupke' followed. With Jule Styne, Sondheim wrote the
admirable songs for *Gypsy*. Again, he needed shoe-horning into the
limiting role of mere lyric writer, again on Hammerstein's advice; but
both musicals have been considered critical in their influence on other

Stephen Sondheim (*Hulton Picture Library*).

writers. As well as 'Everything's Coming up Roses', 'Little Lamb', 'If Momma Was Married', 'Small World', 'You'll Never Get Away from Me', 'You Gotta Get a Gimmick', and 'Have an Egg Roll, Mr Goldstone', all the lyrics bear eloquent testimony to his increasing accomplishment.

In order to write the songs for *Gypsy*, Sondheim had had to interrupt work on the first Broadway success for which he was to be both composer and lyricist – *A Funny Thing Happened on the Way to the Forum*. The book was by Burt Shevelove and Larry Gelbart from an idea Shevelove had been nurturing since his Yale days – that there was one musical to be gleaned out of all the plays of Plautus. Here Sondheim had to stand back and consider the function of his songs. In this fast-moving farce they hardly held the stage as dramatic advances on the plot or revelations of character. They are charming interludes, opportunities for the audience to get its breath back in the midst of broad and break-neck comic incident. The song which provided most problems was the opening number. A beguiling light tune, 'Love Is in the Air', failed to set the right tone for the evening. A formal invocation to the Gods of the Theatre was rejected too. The final version, 'A Comedy Tonight', prepares the audience perfectly for the antics which are to follow.

Sondheim was now in a position to attack an ambitious original musical, once again with Arthur Laurents. They called it *Anyone Can Whistle*, though in the event not enough people did. It was the most controversial musical of the sixties, angry, disturbing, non-conforming. Some audiences left angry, some disturbed, most refused to conform by coming in at all. However, among those who saw the show and those who have regularly revived it since, it has become a cult and is considered well ahead of its time. Its individual songs like 'Anyone Can Whistle' and 'There Won't be Trumpets', are among Sondheim's most challenging and eloquent. Sadly it was at this time that Sondheim was to receive his last counsel from Oscar Hammerstein who felt that his protégé would never be a fully-fledged Broadway craftsman until he had been blooded by a full-scale flop. *Anyone Can Whistle* provided the last lesson.

Do I Hear a Waltz?, written with Richard Rodgers and Arthur Laurents, based on Laurents' fine play, *The Time of the Cuckoo*, was a half-hearted affair. The chemistry between Sondheim and Rodgers did not work and the experience was unhappy for them both.

The authentic Sondheim voice began to emerge in his own words and music for *Company*, derived with George Furth from Furth's one-act plays. It was a brittle picture of couples in Manhattan happily making each other unhappy. 'Another Hundred People' pouring out of the subways into an unfriendly 'City of Strangers'. A married pair bitterly analysing 'The Little Things We Do Together'. A lunching lady toasting 'The Ladies Who Lunch'. An air hostess on a one-night stand, reluctant to give up bed for 'Barcelona' and staying over to the annoyance of her host. A torn bride shying away from the altar and trying to convince herself at the last minute that she's 'Not Getting Married Today'. A sort of hero trying earnestly to convince himself of the importance of 'Being Alive'.

In *Company*, and in his next show, *Follies*, the developing Sondheim still supported his innovative talents heavily on the crutches of pastiche. *Follies* is a wonderfully ambitious show, owing a lot of daring to the imagination of Hal Prince who co-directed and produced it. It is built around James Goldman's idea of a reunion of old Ziegfeld Follies girls in the rubble of their old theatre, some decades after their heyday. Pushing back the barriers of song writing and coming up with quite new ideas, Sondheim knows very well the traditions he is leaving behind. Indeed, he often comments affectionately on earlier song forms, whether the source of his inspiration is the Broadway bounce of De Sylva, Brown and Henderson for 'Broadway Baby'; the Big Passing Parade tunes of Irving Berlin for 'Bring on Those Beautiful Girls'; or a vaudeville blues number like 'The God-Why-Don't-You-Love-Me Blues'. Even in pastiche he can still wring powerful emotion from dramatic situations in 'Too Many Mornings', the Gershwin-coloured 'Losing My Mind', and 'I'm Still Here' – a hymn to show business survival. In 'Could I Leave You?' his savagery on the subject of marriage remains undiluted. The show was a triumph and lost $665,000.

In their next venture, the charming *A Little Night Music*, Sondheim and his faithful Hal Prince decided that, if they were to sell their new bonbon, the pill must be sugar-coated, but they made sure that there was still an acid drop at the centre. The sugar coating comprised the elegant aspect of upper-middle-class turn-of-the-century Scandinavia and the valse time in which Sondheim set himself to write this entire score. The acid drop was the witty dissection of marital infidelity behind Bergman's smiles on a summer night. Bygone 'Liaisons', 'A Glamorous Life', and an adulterous 'Weekend in the Country' had a cutting edge which was concealed by their surface appeal, their wit and their attractive melodies; and almost against his better judgment Sondheim, in fitting a sensitive song to a particular actress at a specific moment, found himself with his biggest popular hit, 'Send in the Clowns'.

Much emboldened by balancing his books, Hal Prince looked west to the east, and persuaded Sondheim to write *Pacific Overtures* – a musical which deals not with love nor with human relationships nor with nostalgia (nor, as one wit suggested, with foreplay in a Malibu beach house) but with the commercial colonisation of Japan in the nineteenth century. The piece was played in the Kabuki manner mixed with Japanese ideas of how a western musical ought to look and sound. The strange elusive haunting songs provided Sondheim's nearest approach to the operatic convention until *Sweeney Todd*. Alas, Broadway audiences were not made of stern enough stuff to enjoy them; and having embarked on a didactic musical, Sondheim's collaborators carried, perhaps, too few intellectual guns to win their argument in the theatre. Had a Shaw, a Tom Stoppard or a Peter Nichols set to work on the book, it might have been a different story.

Sondheim turned next to a left-wing retelling of the Sweeney Todd legend. Here your authors find themselves in disagreement – not for the first time. Caryl Brahms considers the story and its treatment compelling; but the score derivative. Ned Sherrin, though puzzled by some of the strains that Marx and Broadway have put upon the old Penny Plain and Twopence Coloured melodrama, relishes the ironic, intricate lyrics; and finds the lovely music which decorates some of the most gruesome moments (as the Demon Barber warms to his task of despatching human victims to Mrs Lovell, the pie-maker, down below) as effective and as ravishing as the more conventional love duets for the pallid juveniles. Cutting the young hero down by a social class or two robs him of character rather than giving him proletarian vigour.

Your authors agree, however, in applauding the fact that such a dangerous and daring subject should find a place in huge Broadway and West End musical houses and sweep the board in the annual award ceremonies. They mourn the fact that in neither case was the run profit-making. The play will probably find its place in the repertoires of the more adventurous opera houses. In 1983 it played with great success in a production from the Liverpool Playhouse. A more simple and direct staging allowed the power and the humour of the play to have a much greater effect on audiences.

Another show, *Merrily We Roll Along*, which seemed to represent another attempt to blandish Broadway audiences, failed in that endeavour but was successfully produced in England in 1983 by students of the Guildhall School of Music and Drama. Once again the complicated conceit of the story was better served by the more simple student treatment. The show was well received critically but, at the time of writing, no professional transfer to the West End has been authorised.

There are incidental Sondheim songs to relish too. The atmospheric 'The Girls of Summer' which started life as an orchestral theme for a Broadway straight play – the words came later. 'I Never Do Anything Twice' – the ribald memoirs of a courtesan (written for a film). 'I Remember' – a nostalgic reverie for a girl in a mystical night society written for the television musical, *Evening Primrose*. And a rare excursion into revue writing with 'The Boy From', to Mary Rodgers' music for *The Mad Show*.

Compared to the work of say, George Gershwin, who died more than ten years younger than Sondheim is now, his output has been niggardly, but the brightest hope for the musical theatre is the prospect of more songs from Sondheim put Song by Song, Side by Side in their turn.

APPENDIX

Compiled by REX BUNNETT

The dates of production and the numbers of performances given are for Broadway unless otherwise stated.

Music and lyrics are by the subject unless otherwise stated.

The songs listed have been chosen for their standard rating or out of interest in context with the text of the book and are not intended to be a complete listing of songs written by the lyricist in question.

p = performances

Irving Berlin

Born 11 May 1888, Temun, Russia.

Shows

The Boys and Betty 1908 112p	She Was a Dear Little Girl
The Jolly Bachelors 1910 84p	Stop That Rag
	If the Manager Only Thought the Same as Mother
	Sweet Marie
	Make a Rag-a-Time Dance With Me
Up and Down Broadway 1910 72p	Oh That Beautiful Rag (lyrics: Ted Snyder)
	Sweet Italian Love (lyrics: Ted Snyder)
Ziegfeld Follies of 1910 1910 88p	Goodbye Becky Cohen
	Dance of the Grizzly Bear
Temptations 1911 92p	Answer Me
	I Beg Your Pardon
	Dear Old Broadway
	Spanish Love
	Keep a Taxi Waiting Dear
Ziegfeld Follies of 1911 1911 80p	Woodman, Woodman Spare That Tree
	Epraham
Hanky-Panky 1912 104p	Million Dollar Ball
Hokey-Pokey 1912 108p	Alexander's Bagpipe Band
The Whirl of Society 1912 136p	That Society Bear
	I Want To Be in Dixie
My Best Girl 1912 68p	Follow Me Around
The Passing Show of 1912 1912 136p	Ragtime Jockey Man
Ziegfeld Follies of 1912 1912 88p	Little Bit of Everything

Watch Your Step 1914 171p	Play a Simple Melody
London 1915 275p	I Love To Have the Boys Around Me
	Syncopated Walk
	Minstrel Parade
	When I Discovered You
	Settle Down in a One-Horse Town
	Lock Me in Your Harem and Throw away the Key
Queen of the Movies 1914 106p	Follow the Crowd
Stop! Look! Listen! 1916 105p	I Love a Piano
	That Hula Hula
	When I Get Back to the USA
	The Girl on the Magazine Cover
	Everything in America is Ragtime Crazy
The Century Girl 1916 200p	The Broadway Chicken Walk
	You've Got Me Doing it Too
	Alice in Wonderland
Jack O'Lantern 1917 265p	I'll Take You Back to Italy
Dance and Grow Thin 1917	Way Down South
– a midnight revue	Cinderella Lost her Slipper
	Dance and Grow Thin
The Cohan Revue of 1918 1918 96p	King of Broadway
	Down Where the Jack o' Lanterns Grow
The Canary 1918 152p	It's the Little Bit of Irish
Everything 1918 461p	The Circus is Coming to Town
	Come Along to Toyland
Ziegfeld Follies of 1918 1918 151p	Blue Devils of France
	I'm Gonna Pin a Medal on the Girl I Left Behind
Yip, Yip, Yaphank 1918 32p	Mandy
	Oh, How I Hate to Get Up in the Morning
	We're on Our Way to France
	Soldier Boy
	Ding Dong
	What a Difference a Uniform Will Make
	The YMCA
Ziegfeld Follies of 1919 1919 171p	A Pretty Girl is Like a Melody
	You'd Be Surprised
	Mandy (from *Yip, Yip, Yaphank*)
	I Want to See a Minstrel Show
	The Guy Who Guards the Harem
	You Cannot Make Your Shimmy Shake on Tea
Ziegfeld Follies of 1920 1920 123p	The Girls of My Dreams
	Tell Me, Little Gypsy
	The Leg of Nations
	The Syncopated Vamp
Ziegfeld Girls of 1920 1920 78p	Metropolitan Ladies
Ziegfeld Midnight Frolic 1920 123p	I'll See You in C.U.B.A.
Broadway Brevities of 1920 1920 105p	Beautiful Faces Need Beautiful Clothes.

Music Box Revue 1921 313p	Say it with Music
	Everybody Step
	They Call it Dancing
	The Schoolhouse Blues
Zeigfeld's 9 o'Clock Frolic 1921 35p	I Like It (lyric: Harry Akst)
Music Box Revue 1922 273p	Lady of the Evening
	Pack up Your Sins and Go to the Devil
	Crinoline Days
	My Diamond Horseshoe of Girls
	Porcelain Maid
Music Box Revue – 1923 1923 273p	Waltz of Long Ago
	Tell Me a Bedtime Story
	Learn to do the Strut
	An Orange Grove in California
Music Box Revue – 1924 1924 184p	The Call of the South
	Tokio Blues
	Tell Her in the Springtime
	Rock-a-Bye Baby
	In the Shade of a Sheltered Tree
The Cocoanuts 1925 377p	Lucky Boy
	A Little Bungalow
	Why Do You Want to Know Why?
	We Should Care
	Monkey Doodle Doo
Betsy 1926 39p	Blue Skies
Ziegfeld Follies of 1927 1927 167p	Shaking the Blues Away
	My New York
	Ooh, Maybe It's You
	It All Belongs to Me
	It's Up to the Band
	Jimmy
Shoot the Works 1931 87p	Begging for Love
Face the Music 1932 165p	Let's Have Another Cup of Coffee
	Soft Lights and Sweet Music
	On a Roof in Manhattan
	Manhattan Madness
As Thousands Cheer 1933 400p	Easter Parade
	Lonely Heart
	To Be or Not To Be
	Not for All the Rice in China
	Supper-time
	Majestic Sails at Midnight
	The Funnies
	I've got Harlem on My Mind
	Heat Wave
	Our Wedding Day
	How's Chances
Louisiana Purchase 1940 444p	It's a Lovely Day Tomorrow
	Fools Fall in Love
	What Chance Have I With Love?
	Dance With Me
	Lord Done Fixed up My Soul
This is the Army 1942 113p	This is the Army, Mr Jones
London 1943 24p	I Left My Heart at the Stage Door

Canteen
 The Army's Made a Man out of Me
 Oh How I Hate to Get Up in the
   Morning
 What the Well-dressed Man in
   Harlem Will Wear
 I'm Getting Tired So I Can Sleep
 My British Buddy (added for the
   London production)

Annie Get Your Gun 1946 1147p
  London 1947 1304p

 Doin' What Comes Natur'lly
 The Girl that I Marry
 You Can't Get a Man With a Gun
 There's No Business Like Show
   Business
 Moonshine Lullaby
 My Defences Are Down
 I Got Lost in his Arms
 I Got the Sun in the Mornin'
 Anything You Can Do
 They Say It's Wonderful
 An Old-fashioned Wedding (added
   to the 1966 revival)

Miss Liberty 1949 308p

 A Little Fish in a Big Pond
 Let's Take an Old-fashioned Walk
 Only for Americans
 You Can Have Him
 Give Me Your Tired, Your Poor

Call Me Madam 1950 644p
  London 1952 485p

 The Hostess With the Mostes' on the
   Ball
 Washington Square Dance
 Can You Use any Money Today?
 It's a Lovely Day Today
 You're Just in Love

Mr President 1962 265p

 Meat and Potatoes
 The Secret Service
 It Gets Lonely in the White House
 Glad to be Home
 This is a Great Country

Films

The Cocoanuts 1929

 Stage score
 When My Dreams Come True

Hallelujah 1929

 Waiting at the End of the Road
 Swanee Shuffle

Lady of the Pavements 1929

 Theme
 Where is the Song of Songs For me?

Mammy 1930

 Let Me Sing and I'm Happy
 Across the Breakfast Table, Looking
   at You
 To My Mammy
 In the Morning
 Knights of the Road

Puttin' on the Ritz 1930

 Title song
 With You

Reaching for the Moon 1931	Reaching for the Moon
Top Hat 1935	Cheek to Cheek
	Isn't This a Lovely Day
	Top Hat, White Tie and Tails
	No Strings
	The Piccolino
Follow the Fleet 1936	I'm Putting all My Eggs in One Basket
	But Where Are You?
	We Saw the Sea
	Let's Face the Music and Dance
	Let Yourself Go
	I'd Rather Lead the Band
On the Avenue 1937	This Year's Kisses
	He Ain't Got Rhythm
	I've Got My Love to Keep Me Warm
	The Girl on the Police Gazette
	Slumming on Park Avenue
Carefree 1938	Change Partners
	I Used to be Color Blind
	The Night is Filled With Music
	The Yam
Alexander's Ragtime Band 1938	Now It Can Be Told
	My Walking Stick
	(rest of score made up of old numbers)
Second Fiddle 1939	I Poured My Heart into a Song
	Back to Back
	I'm Sorry for Myself
	When Winter Comes
	An Old-fashioned Tune Always is New
Louisiana Purchase 1941	Stage score
Holiday Inn 1942	White Christmas
	Happy Holiday
	Let's Start the New Year Right
	I've Got Plenty to be Thankful For
	Abraham
	Song of Freedom
	Be Careful, It's My Heart
	You're Easy to Dance With
	I Can't Tell a Lie
	Lazy
This is The Army 1943	Stage score
Blue Skies 1946	You Keep Coming Back Like a Song
	Getting Nowhere
	A Couple of Song and Dance Men
	A Serenade to an Old-fashioned Girl
Easter Parade 1948	Steppin' Out with My Baby
	Better Luck Next Time
	A Fella with an Umbrella
	It Only Happens When I Dance with You
	Drum Crazy
	Happy Easter

	A Couple of Swells
Annie Get Your Gun 1950	Stage score
Call Me Madam 1953	Stage score
White Christmas 1954	Count Your Blessings Instead of Sheep
	Sisters
	The Best Things Happen While You're Dancing
	Love, You Didn't Do Right by Me
	Choreography
	Snow
	What Can You Do With a General?
There's No Business Like Show Business 1954	Old songs
	A Sailor's not a Sailor 'til a Sailor's Been Tattooed
Sayonara 1957	Title song

Other songs not originally written for either stage or film scores

Alexander's Ragtime Band
Everybody's Doing It
Do It Again
When the Midnight Choo-Choo Leaves for Alabam
Snookey Ookums
That International Rag
Araby
I've Got my Captain Working for Me Now
After You Get What You Want You Don't Want It

All by Myself
Lazy
All Alone
What'll I Do?
Always
Remember
Russian Lullaby
How Deep is the Ocean
God Bless America
The Song is Ended
Putting on the Ritz
Say It Isn't So

Cole Porter

Born 9 June 1891, Peru, Indiana.
Died 15 October 1964, Santa Monica, California.

Shows

Hands Up 1915 52p	Esmeralda (interpolated into a Sigmund Romberg score)
Miss Information 1915 47p	Two Big Eyes (lyric: John L. Golden)
See America First 1916 15p	See America First
	I've a Shooting-Box in Scotland
	Buy Her a Box at the Opera
Very Good Eddie London 1918 46p	Alone With You (Music: Melville Gideon) (interpolated into the score)
Telling the Tale London 1918 80p	Altogether Too Fond of You (written by Cole Porter, James Heard and Melville Gideon)
The Eclipse London 1919 117p	I Never Realised (Music: Melville Gideon; used in *Buddies*)
	Chelsea (Music: Melville Gideon)
Hitchy-Koo of 1919 1919 56p	My Cosy Little Corner in the Ritz
	Another Sentimental Song
	When I Had a Uniform On
	Old-fashioned Garden
	The Sea is Calling
Buddies 1919 249p	I Never Realised (Music: Melville Gideon)
As You Were 1920 143p	Washington Square (same tune as 'Chelsea'. Lyric: E. Ray Goetz and Cole Porter)
A Night Out London 1920 309p	Look Around (Lyric: Clifford Grey)
	Our Hotel (Lyric: Clifford Grey)
	Why Didn't We Meet Before? (Lyric: Clifford Grey)
Mayfair and Montmartre London 1922 77p	The Blue Boy Blues
	Cocktail Time
	Olga
Phi Phi London 1922 132p	The Ragtime Pipes of Pan
Hitchy-Koo of 1922 1922, closed out-of-town	The American Punch
Within the Quota Paris 1923	A Jazz Ballet produced later that year in New York
Greenwich Village Follies of 1924 1924 127p	I'm in Love Again
	Two Little Babes in the Wood
	Make Everyday a Holiday
La Revue des Ambassadeurs Paris 1928	Lost Liberty Blues
	Omnibus
Paris 1928 195p	Let's Do It
	Let's Misbehave
Fifty Million Frenchmen 1929 254p	You Do Something to Me
	You've Got that Thing

Wake Up and Dream 1929 136p
   first produced in London
   earlier that year, 263p
The New Yorkers 1930 168p

Find Me a Primitive Man
What is this Thing Called
   Love?
also used 'Let's Do It'
Love for Sale
Where Have You Been?
I Happen to Like New York
Let's Fly Away
I'm Getting Myself Ready for You
Take Me Back to Manhattan

The Vanderbilt Revue 1930 13p
Gay Divorce 1932 248p
   London 1933 180p

What's My Man Gonna be Like?
Night and Day
I've Got You on My Mind
I Still Love the Red, White and Blue
How's Your Romance?

Nymph Errant London 1933 154p

Experiment
It's Bad for Me
How Could We Be Wrong?
Nymph Errant
The Physician
Solomon

Anything Goes 1934 420p

I Get a Kick Out of You
All Through the Night
You're the Top
Anything Goes
Public Enemy Number One
Blow, Gabriel, Blow

Hi Diddle Diddle London 1934 198p
Jubilee 1935 169p

Miss Otis Regrets
Begin the Beguine
Just One of Those Things
When Love Comes Your Way
The Kling-Kling Bird in the Divi
   Divi Tree
A Picture of Me Without You
Why Shouldn't I!

Red, Hot and Blue 1936 183p

Down in the Depths
De-lovely
You've Got Something
Ridin' High
Red, Hot and Blue!
Ours

Leave It to Me 1938 291p

Get Out of Town
From Now On
My Heart Belongs to Daddy
Most Gentlemen Don't Like Love

You Never Know 1938 78p

You Never Know
At Long Last Love
For No Rhyme or Reason
Don't Let it Get You Down
From Alpha to Omega

The Sun Never Sets London 1938 32p
Dubarry was a Lady 1939 408p

River God
It Ain't Etiquette
Come On In
But in the Morning, No
Do I Love You?

Give Him the Oo-La-La
Well, Did You Evah?
Friendship

The Man Who Came to Dinner
1939 739p
London 1942 178p

A Play with one song: What Am I To Do?

Panama Hattie 1940 501p
London 1943 308p

I've Still Got my Health
Let's be Buddies
Make it Another Old-Fashioned, Please
My Mother Would Love You

Let's Face It 1941 547p
London 1942 308p

Farming
Ace in the Hole
A Lady Needs a Rest
Ev'rything I Love
Let's Not Talk about Love

Something for the Boys 1943 422p

The Leader of a Big-Time Band
When My Baby Goes to Town

Mexican Hayride 1944 481p

Count Your Blessings
Sing to Me, Guitar
I Love You

Seven Lively Arts 1944 183p

Ev'ry Time We Say Goodbye
Big Town
Only Another Boy and Girl

Around the World in Eighty Days 1946 74p

Look What I Found
Should I Tell You I Love You?
If You Smile at Me

Kiss Me Kate 1948 1077p
London 1951 501p

Another Op'nin', Another Show
Why Can't You Behave
Wunderbar
So in Love
I Hate Men
Too Darn Hot
Where is the Life That Late I Led?
Always True to You in My Fashion
Brush Up Your Shakespeare
I Sing of Love
We Open in Venice
Tom, Dick or Harry
I Am Ashamed that Women are so Simple

Out of this World 1950 157p

Use Your Imagination
I Got Beauty
Where, Oh Where
I Am Loved
I Sleep Easier Now
Cherry Pies Ought to be You
Nobody's Chasing Me

Can Can 1953 892p
London 1954 394p

Maidens Typical of France
Never Give Anything Away
C'est Magnifique
Come Along with Me
Live and Let Live
I Am in Love
It's All Right with Me
I Love Paris

Silk Stockings 1955 478p

Satin and Silk
Paris Loves Lovers
Stereophonic Sound
All of You

Aladdin television 1958
   Staged as a musical, London 1959
   and ran for 145p with
   other Cole Porter songs added.

Come to the Supermarket in Old
   Peking
Wouldn't it be Fun!

Films

The Battle of Paris 1929

They All Fall in Love
Here Comes the Bandwagon

Fifty Million Frenchmen 1930
Paris 1930
The Gay Divorcee 1934

Stage score used as background music
Part of stage score
Only 'Night and Day' was used out
   of the stage show *Gay Divorce*

Born to Dance 1936

Easy to Love
I've Got You Under My Skin
Rap-Tap on Wood
Love Me, Love My Pekinese

Anything Goes 1936
Break the News 1937
Rosalie 1937

Stage score
It All Belongs to You
Rosalie
In the Still of the Night
Who Knows?
Close
Why Should I Care?
I've a Strange New Rhythm in My
   Heart

Broadway Melody of 1940

I've Got My Eyes on You
I Concentrate on You
Between You and Me
Please Don't Monkey with
   Broadway

You'll Never Get Rich 1941

So Near and Yet So Far
Dream Dancing
The Wedding Cake-Walk

Panama Hattie 1942
Dubarry was a Lady 1943
Let's Face It 1943

Stage score
Stage score
Stage score
Who Did? I Did, Yes I Did

Something to Shout About 1943

You'd be so Nice to Come Home to
Something to Shout About

Hollywood Canteen 1944
Something for the Boys 1944
Night and Day 1946
The Pirate 1948

Don't Fence Me In
Stage score
Old songs
Be a Clown
Love of My Life
You Can Do No Wrong

Adam's Rib 1949
Kiss Me, Kate 1953

Farewell Amanda
Stage score
From This Moment On

High Society 1956

You're Sensational

True Love
Well, Did You Evah?
I Love You, Samantha
Who Wants to be a Millionaire?
Now You Has Jazz
Mind If I Make Love to You?

Anything Goes 1956	Stage score
Les Girls 1957	Ladies in Waiting
	Ça C'est l'Amour
	You're Just Too Too
	Les Girls
Silk Stockings 1957	Stage score
	Fated to be Mated
	Ritz Roll and Rock
Can Can 1960	Stage score
	Other old songs

Other songs not originally written for either stage or film scores

The Oyster
Thank You So Much, Mrs
    Lowsborough-Goodby

The Laziest Gal in Town

Ira Gershwin

Born 6 December 1896, New York.
Died 17 August 1983, Hollywood.
Songs marked with an asterisk have music by George Gershwin.

Shows

Ladies First 1918 164p
    The Real American Folk Song*

Piccadilly to Broadway
  closed out-of-town

Two Little Girls in Blue 1921 135p
  Music: Vincent Youmans and Paul
  Lannin
    Two Little Girls in Blue (written
      under the pseudonym 'Arthur
      Francis')
    Oh Me, Oh My, Oh You (written
      under the pseudonym 'Arthur
      Francis')

George White's Scandals of 1922 1922
88p
    I'll Build a Staircase to Paradise*
      (lyric: Ira Gershwin and B. G.
      de Sylva)

Little Miss Bluebeard 1923 175p
    I Won't Say I Will, I Won't Say I
      Won't

Lady Be Good 1924 330p
  London 1926 326p
    Hang On To Me*
    So Am I*
    Fascinating Rhythm*
    Oh, Lady Be Good*
    The Half of it Dearie Blues*
    Little Jazz Bird*

Be Yourself 1924 93p
    I Came Here (music: Lewis Gensler;
      lyric: Marc Connelly, George S.
      Kauffman and I.G.)
    Uh-Uh! (music: Milton
      Schwarzwald; lyric: as above)
    The Wrong Thing at the Right Time
      (as above)

Captain Jinks 1925 167p
    You Must Come Over Blues (music:
      Lewis E. Gensler; lyric B. G.
      de Sylva and I.G.)

Tell Me More 1925 100p
  Lyrics: B. G. de Sylva and I.G.
  London 1925 263p
    Tell Me More*
    Kickin' the Clouds Away*
    Why Do I Love You So?*
    My Fair Lady*

Tip-Toes 1925 192p
  London 1926 182p
    Tip-Toes*
    That Certain Feeling*
    Sweet and Low Down*
    Looking for a Boy*
    Lady Luck*

Oh, Kay! 1926 256p
  London 1927 214p
    Dear Little Girl*
    Maybe*
    Clap Yo' Hands*
    Someone to Watch Over Me*
    Fidgety Feet*
    Do, Do, Do*

Americana 1926 224p	Blowing the Blues Away (music: Philip Charig)
	The Lost Barber Shop Chord*
	Sunny Disposish (music: Philip Charig)
Funny Face 1927 244p	Funny Face*
London 1928 263p	High Hat*
	He Loves and She Loves*
	Let's Kiss and Make Up*
	'S Wonderful*
	Tell the Doc*
	My One and Only*
	The Babbitt and the Bromide*
Rosalie 1928 335p	How Long Has This Been Going On?*
	Beautiful Gypsy*
	Let Me Be a Friend to You*
	Oh Gee, Oh Joy* (lyric: P. G. Wodehouse and I.G.)
	Say So* (as above)
	New York Serenade* (as above)
	Everybody Knows I Love Somebody*
Treasure Girl 1928 68p	I've Got a Crush on You*
	Feeling I'm Falling*
	K-ra-zy for You*
	Got a Rainbow*
	I Don't Think I'll Fall in Love Today*
Show Girl 1929 111p	Liza*
Lyrics: Gus Kahn and I.G.	Do What You Do*
	So Are You*
	American in Paris (background music)*
Strike Up the Band 1930 191p	Strike Up the Band*
	Soon*
	I've Got a Crush on You*
Girl Crazy 1930 272p	I Got Rhythm*
	Bidin' My Time*
	But Not for Me*
	Embraceable You*
	Could You Use Me?*
	Treat Me Rough*
	Sam and Delilah*
	Boy, What Love has Done to Me*
Nine Fifteen Revue 1930 7p	Toddlin' Along*
Garrick Gaieties of 1930 1930 158p	I'm Only Human after All (music: Vernon Duke; lyric: E. Y. Harburg and I.G.)
Sweet and Low 1930 184p	Cheerful Little Earful (music: Harry Warren; lyric: Billy Rose and I.G.)
	You Sweet So and So (music: Philip Charig and Joseph Meyer; lyric: I.G.)
Crazy Quilt (Billy Rose's) 1931 79p	In the Merry Month of Maybe (music: Harry Warren; lyric: Billy Rose and I.G.)

The Social Register 1931 97p	A Play with one song: The Key to My Heart (music: Lou Alter)
Of Thee I Sing 1932 441p	Wintergreen for President*
	Because, Because*
	Love is Sweeping the Country*
	Of Thee I Sing*
	Who Cares?*
Let 'em Eat Cake 1933 90p	Mine*
	Climb up the Social Ladder*
	Let 'em Eat Cake*
	Why Speak of Money?*
Pardon My English 1933 46p	My Cousin in Milwaukee*
	Lorelei*
	Isn't It a Pity?*
Life Begins at 8.40 1934 237p	You're a Builder Upper
Music: Harold Arlen	Let's Take a Walk Around the Block
Lyrics: E. Y. Harburg and I.G.	Fun to be Fooled
	What Can You Say in a Love Song?
	Shoein' the Mare
Porgy and Bess 1935 124p	Summertime*
Lyrics: DuBose Heyward and I.G.	A Woman is a Sometime Thing*
	I Got Plenty of Nuttin'*
	Bess, You is My Woman Now*
	It Ain't Necessarily So*
	I Loves You, Porgy*
	There's a Boat Dat's Leavin' Soon for New York*
	My Man's Gone Now*
	Buzzard Song*
	It Takes a Long Pull to Get There*
Ziegfeld Follies of 1936 1936 227p	I Can't Get Started
Music: Vernon Duke	That Moment of Moments
	An Island in the West Indies
	Words Without Music
	He Hasn't a Thing Except Me
The Show is On 1936 237p	By Strauss*
Lady in the Dark 1941 467p	Girl of the Moment
Music: Kurt Weill	Tschaikowsky
	Jenny
	My Ship
The Firebrand of Florence 1945 43p	A Rhyme for Angela
Music: Kurt Weill	You're Far Too Near Me
	Love is My Enemy
	Sing Me not a Ballad*
	I Know Where There is a Cosy Nook*
Park Avenue 1946 72p	Tomorrow is the Time
Music: Arthur Schwartz	For the Life of Me
	There's no Holding Me
	Stay as We Are
	Don't Be a Woman if You Can
	There's Nothing Like Marriage for People

Films

Delicious 1931	Delishious*

Somebody from Somewhere*
You Started It*
New York Rhapsody*

Girl Crazy 1932   Stage score*
A Damsel in Distress 1937   A Foggy Day*
                                      Nice Work if You Can Get it*
                                      Things are Looking Up*

Shall We Dance? 1937   Shall We Dance?*
                                      Let's Call the Whole Thing Off*
                                      They All Laughed*
                                      They Can't Take that Away from
                                         Me*
                                      Beginner's Luck*
                                      Slap That Bass*

Goldwyn Follies 1938   Love is Here to Stay*
                                      Love Walked In*
                                      I Was Doing All Right*
                                      I Love to Rhyme*
                                      Just Another Rhumba*

Girl Crazy 1943   Stage score*
                                      You've Got What It Takes*

Cover Girl 1944   Long Ago and Far Away
   Music: Jerome Kern   Sure Thing
                                      Put Me to the Test
                                      Cover Girl
                                      The Show Must Go On
                                      Who's Complaining
                                      Make Way for Tomorrow

Lady in the Dark 1944   Stage score
Where Do We Go from Here? 1945   All at Once
   Music: Kurt Weill   If Love Remains
                                      Song of the Rhineland
                                      Morale
                                      Columbus

The Shocking Miss Pilgrim 1947   For You, For Me, For Everyone*
                                      Aren't You Kind of Glad We Did?*
                                      Changing my Tune*
                                      The Back Bay Polka*
                                      Waltzing is Better Sitting Down*

The Barkleys of Broadway 1949   My One and Only Highland Fling
   Music: Harry Warren   You'd Be Hard to Replace
                                      Shoes with Wings On
                                      Manhattan Downbeat
                                      Weekend in the Country

An American in Paris 1951   Reused Gershwin songs*
Give a Girl a Break 1953   Applause, Applause! (music: Burton
                                         Lane)

A Star is Born 1954   Gotta Have Me Go with You
   Music: Harold Arlen   The Man that Got Away
                                      Here's What I'm Here For
                                      It's a New World
                                      Someone at Last
                                      Lose that Long Face

The Country Girl 1954   Commercial
   Music: Harold Arlen   It's Mine, It's Yours

Love and Learn
The Land around Us
The Search is Through

Funny Face 1957

Stage score plus added Gershwin
   numbers*

Porgy and Bess 1959

Stage score*

Lorenz Hart

Born 2 May 1895, New York.
Died 22 November 1943, New York.
All music is by Richard Rodgers unless otherwise stated.

Shows

A Lonely Romeo 1919 87p	Any Old Place with You
Poor Little Ritz Girl 1920 119p	You Can't Fool Your Dreams
	What Happened Nobody Knows
	Mary Queen of Scots
The Melody Man 1924 56p	A Play with two songs: Moonlight Mamma
	I'd Like to Poison Ivy
Garrick Gaieties 1925 211p	Manhattan
	Sentimental Me
	Do You Love Me?
	On With the Dance
Dearest Enemy 1925 286p	Here in My Arms
American TV production	Cheerio
shown in 1955	Here's a Kiss
	Old Enough to Love
	Bye and Bye
The Fifth Avenue Follies 1926	Lilie, Lawrence and Jack
a Night Club presentation	Where's that Little Girl
	Maybe it's Me
June Days 1925 85p	Anytime, Anywhere, Anyhow
The Girl Friend 1926 301p	The Blue Room
	The Girl Friend
	Why Do I?
Garrick Gaieties 1926 174p	Mountain Greenery
	Sleepyhead
	Where's That Rainbow
Betsy 1926 39p	Sing
	If I Were You
Lido Lady 1926 London 259p	A Cup of Tea
	Here in my Arms
	Try Again Tomorrow
Peggy Ann 1926 333p	Where's that Rainbow
London 1927 130p	A Tree in the Park
	A Little Birdie Told Me So
	Havana
	Maybe it's Me
A Connecticut Yankee 1927 418p	Thou Swell
London 1929 43p – retitled	My Heart Stood Still
A Yankee at the	On a Desert Island With Thee
Court of King Arthur	I Feel at Home With You
One Dam Thing After Another	My Heart Stood Still
1927 London 237p	My Lucky Star
	I Need Some Cooling Off
Present Arms 1928 155p	You Took Advantage of Me
	A Kiss for Cinderella
	Down by the Sea
	Tell It to the Marines
She's My Baby 1928 71p	My Lucky Star

You're What I Need
A Little House in Soho
Try Again Tomorrow
Chee Chee 1928 31p   I Must Love You
Dear, Oh Dear
Moon of My Delight
Better Be Good to Me
Spring is Here 1929 104p   Spring is Here
Yours Sincerely
With a Song in My Heart
Why Can't I?
Heads Up 1929 144p   Why Do You Suppose?
    London 1930 19p   My Man is on the Make
It Must be Heaven
Lady Fingers 1929 132p   Sing
I Love You More than Yesterday
Simple Simon 1930 135p   I Still Believe in You
Ten Cents a Dance
Send For Me
Ever Green London 1930 254p   Dancing on the Ceiling
No Place but Home
In the Cool of the Evening
America's Sweetheart 1931 135p   I've Got Five Dollars
In Califor-n-i-a
How About It?
Crazy Quilt (Billy Rose's) 1931 79p   Rest Room Rose
Jumbo 1935 233p   Over and Over Again
The Most Beautiful Girl in the World
My Little Girl Blue
My Romance
Something Gay 1935 72p   A play with one song: You Are So
        Lovely and I'm So Lonely
On Your Toes 1936 315p   The Heart is Quicker than the Eye
    London 1937 123p   There's a Small Hotel
It's Got to be Love
Too Good for the Average Man
Babes in Arms 1937 289p   Where or When
I Wish I Were in Love Again
My Funny Valentine
Johnny One-Note
The Lady is a Tramp
The Show is On 1936 237p   Rhythm
I've Got Five Dollars
I'd Rather be Right 1937 290p   Have You Met Miss Jones?
Off the Record
I'd Rather be Right
I Married an Angel 1938 338p   At the Roxy Music Hall
Angels without Wings
I Married an Angel
The Boys from Syracuse 1938 235p   Dear Old Syracuse
    London 1963 100p   What Can You Do with a Man?
Falling in Love with Love
This Can't be Love
Sing for Your Supper
Too Many Girls 1939 249p   I Like to Recognise the Tune

	I Didn't Know What Time it Was
	Too Many Girls
	Give it Back to the Indians
Higher and Higher 1940 108p	Nothing but You
	It Never Entered My Mind
	Blue Monday
Pal Joey 1940 374p	I Could Write a Book
London 1954 245p	That Terrific Rainbow
New York revival 1952 542p	What is a Man?
	Bewitched, Bothered and Bewildered
	The Flower Garden of My Heart
	Zip
	Take Him
By Jupiter 1942 427p	Nobody's Heart
	Here's a Hand
	Life with Father
A Connecticut Yankee 1943 135p	This revival had six new songs written for it, including:
	To Keep My Love Alive
	The Camelot Samba
	Can't You Do a Friend a Favor?

Films

Leathernecking 1930	Screen version of *Present Arms* with the stage score
Heads Up 1930	Stage score
Spring is Here 1930	Some of the stage score
The Hot Heiress 1931	Nobody Loves a Riveter
	You're the Cats
	Like Ordinary People Do
Love Me Tonight 1932	Love Me Tonight
	Isn't it Romantic
	Mimi
	Lover
	The Song of Paree
	How Are You?
	A Woman Needs Something Like That
	Poor Apache
The Phantom President 1932	The Country Needs a Man
	Somebody Ought to Wave a Flag
	Give Her a Kiss
	The Convention
Hallelujah, I'm a Bum 1933	You Are too Beautiful
	I'll Do it Again
	I've Gotta Get Back to New York
	What Do You Want with Money?
Dancing Lady 1933	That's the Rhythm of the Day
Hollywood Party 1934	Hello
	Hollywood Party
	Reincarnation
Ever Green 1934, England	Dear, Dear
	If I Give in to You
	Dancing on the Ceiling

Nana 1934	That's Love
Manhattan Melodrama 1934	The Bad in Every Man
Mississippi 1935	Soon
	It's Easy to Remember
	Down by the River
Dancing Pirate 1936	Are You My Love?
	When You're Dancing the Waltz
Fools for Scandal 1938	Fools for Scandal
	How Can You Forget?
	There's a Boy in Harlem
Babes in Arms 1939	Stage score
On Your Toes 1939	Stage score
The Boys from Syracuse 1940	Stage score
	Who are You?
Too Many Girls 1940	Stage score
	You're Nearer
They Met in Argentina 1941	Amarillo
	Simpatica
	You've Got the Best of Me
I Married an Angel 1942	Stage score
Higher and Higher 1943	Some of the stage score
Stage Door Canteen 1943	The Girl I Love to Leave Behind
Words and Music 1948	Rodgers and Hart story with their songs
Pal Joey 1957	Stage score plus other Rodgers and Hart songs
Jumbo 1962	Some of the stage score

Oscar Hammerstein II

Born 12 July 1895, New York.
Died 23 August 1960, Doylestown, Pa.

Shows

Always You 1920 66p
    Always You (music: Herbert Stothart)
Tickle Me 1920 207p
    Tickle Me
    Music: Herbert Stothart
    Until You Say Goodbye
    Lyrics: O.H. and Otto Harbach
    If a Wish Could Make it So
Jimmie 1920 71p
    Jimmie
    Music: Herbert Stothart
    Baby Dreams
    Lyrics: O.H. and Otto Harbach
    Cute Little Two by Four
Daffy Dill 1922 71p
    Daffy Dill
    Music: Herbert Stothart
    I'll Build a Bungalow
    Two Little Ruby Rings
    A Coachman's Heart

Queen o' Hearts 1922 39p
    Queen o' Hearts
    Music: Lewis Gensler and Dudley
    You Need Someone, Someone Needs
    Wilkinson
    You
    Lyrics: O.H. and Sidney Mitchell
Wildflower 1923 477p
    Wildflower
    London 1926 115p
    La Bambalina
    Music: Vincent Youmans
    April Blossoms
    Lyrics: O.H. and Otto Harbach
    'Course I Will
Mary Jane McKane 1924 151p
    Mary Jane McKane
    Music: Vincent Youmans and
    The Rumble of the Subway
    Herbert Stothart
    You're Never Too Old to Learn
    Lyrics: O.H. and William Cary
    Just Look Around
    Duncan
Rose Marie 1924 557p
    Hard Boiled Herman
    London 1925 851p
    Rose Marie
    Music: Rudolf Friml and Herbert
    Song of the Mounties
    Stothart
    Indian Love Call
    Lyrics: O.H. and Otto Harbach
    Totem Tom-Tom
    Only a Kiss

Sunny 1925 517p
    Sunny
    London 1926 363p
    Who?
    Music: Jerome Kern
    Dream a Dream

Song of the Flame 1925 194p
    Song of the Flame
    Music: George Gershwin and
    Cossack Love Song
    Herbert Stothart
    Lyrics: O.H. and Otto Harbach
The Desert Song 1926 471p
    The Riff Song
    London 1927 432p
    Romance
    Music: Sigmund Romberg
    'It'
    Lyrics: O.H. and Otto Harbach
    One Flower Grows Alone in Your
    Garden
    One Alone
    Farewell
The Wild Rose 1926 61p
    The Wild Rose
    Music: Rudolf Friml
    Brown Eyes
    Lyrics: O.H. and Otto Harbach
    One Golden Hour
    We'll Have a Kingdom

Golden Dawn 1927 184p
  Music: Emmerich Kalman and
  Herbert Stothart
  Lyrics: O.H. and Otto Harbach

Show Boat 1927 572p
  London 1928 350p
  Music: Jerome Kern

The New Moon 1928 509p
  London 1929 148p
  Music: Sigmund Romberg

Rainbow 1928 29p
  Music: Vincent Youmans

Sweet Adeline 1929 234p
  Music: Jerome Kern

Ballyhoo 1930 68p
  Music: Louis Alter

East Wind 1931 23p
  Music: Sigmund Romberg

Free for All 1931 15p
  Music: Richard A. Whiting

Music in the Air 1932 342p
  London 1933 275p
  Music: Jerome Kern
Ball at the Savoy London 1933 40p
  Music: Paul Abraham

The Three Sisters London 1934 48p
  Music: Jerome Kern

May Wine 1935 213p
  Music: Sigmund Romberg

Very Warm for May 1939 59p
  Music: Jerome Kern

American Jubilee 1940 World Fair
  Show
Music: Arthur Schwartz
Sunny River 1941 36p
  Music: Sigmund Romberg

We Two
When I Crack My Whip
Africa
Jungle Shadows
Here in the Dark
Make Believe
Ol' Man River
Can't Help Lovin' Dat Man
Life upon the Wicked Stage
Why Do I Love You?
Bill (lyric with P. G. Wodehouse)
Softly, as in a Morning Sunrise
Stouthearted Men
One Kiss
Lover, Come Back to Me
The One Girl
I Want a Man
I Like You as You Are
Why Was I Born?
Don't Ever Leave Me
Here am I
'Twas Not so Long Ago
I'm One of God's Children who
    Hasn't Got Wings (lyric with
    Harry Ruskin)
No Wonder I'm Blue
East Wind
Are You Love?
I'd Be a Fool
You are My Woman
Not That I Care
Living in Sin
Tonight
I've Told every Little Star
The Song is You
When the Spring is in the Air
A Girl Like Nina
I Live for Love
I'll Show You Off
Now that I Have Springtime
Somebody Wants to go to Sleep
Roll On, Rolling Road
Hand in Hand
I Built a Dream One Day
Just Once Around the Clock
Dance, My Darling
All the Things You are
All in Fun
That Lucky Fellow
Heaven in My Arms
How Can I Ever be Alone?
Tennessee Fish Fry

Sunny River
Along the Winding Road

Carmen Jones 1943 502p
  Music: Georges Bizet

Oklahoma! 1943 2212p
  London 1947 1543p
  Music: Richard Rodgers

Carousel 1945 890p
  London 1950 566p
  Music: Richard Rodgers

Happy Birthday 1946 564p

Allegro 1947 315p
  Music: Richard Rodgers

South Pacific 1949 1925p
  London 1951 792p
  Music: Richard Rodgers

The King and I 1951 1246p
  London 1953 946p
  Music: Richard Rodgers

Me and Juliet 1953 358p
  Music: Richard Rodgers

Pipe Dream 1955 246p
  Music: Richard Rodgers

Cinderella 1957 Television
  Music: Richard Rodgers

Flower Drum Song 1958 600p
  London 464p
  Music: Richard Rodgers

Call It a Dream
My Girl and I
Dat's Love
Beat Out Dat Rhythm on a Drum
Stan' Up and Fight
Oh, What a Beautiful Mornin'
The Surrey with the Fringe on Top
Many a New Day
People Will Say We're in Love
Out of My Dreams
The Farmer and The Cowman
When I Marry Mr Snow
If I Loved You
June is Bustin' Out all Over
When the Children are Asleep
You'll Never Walk Alone
A Play with one song: I Haven't a
  Worry in the World (music:
  Richard Rodgers)
A Fellow Needs a Girl
The Gentleman is a Dope
You Are Never Away
A Cockeyed Optimist
Some Enchanted Evening
There is Nothin' Like a Dame
Bali Ha'i
I'm Gonna Wash That Man Right out
  of My Hair
Younger than Springtime
Happy Talk
Honey Bun
Carefully Taught
I Whistle a Happy Tune
Hello, Young Lovers
Getting to Know You
We Kiss in the Shadow
Something Wonderful
I Have Dreamed
Shall We Dance?
A Very Special Day
Marriage Type Love
No Other Love
Will You Marry Me?
Thinkin'
How Long?
Do I Love You because You're
  Beautiful?
A Lovely Night
In My Own Little Corner
You Are Beautiful
A Hundred Million Miracles
I Enjoy Being a Girl
Grant Avenue
Love, Look Away
Sunday

Cinderella London 1958 168p	Based on the television production, plus
London revival 1960 104p	No Other Love
Music: Richard Rodgers	Maria
The Sound of Music 1959 1443p	My Favourite Things
London 1961 2386p	Do-Re-Mi
Music: Richard Rodgers	Climb Ev'ry Mountain
	Edelweiss
Cinderella 1965 Television	The same score as the 1958 production plus
	Loneliness of Evening

Films

The Desert Song 1929	Stage score
Golden Dawn 1930	Stage score
Song of the Flame 1930	Stage score
Song of the West 1930	Film version of *Rainbow*
Viennese Nights 1930	I Bring a Love Song
Music: Sigmund Romberg	You Will Remember Vienna
	Here We Are
	I'm Lonely
	Ja Ja Ja
	Regimental March
Sunny 1930	Stage score
	I Was Alone
New Moon 1931	Stage score
Reckless 1935	Title song
Music: Jerome Kern	
The Night is Young 1935	When I Grow Too Old to Dream
Music: Sigmund Romberg	The Night is Young
Sweet Adeline 1935	Stage score
Music in the Air 1935	Stage score
Give Us This Night 1936	Give Us This Night
Music: Erich Wolfgang Korngold	
Rose Marie 1936	Stage score
Show Boat 1936	Stage score
High, Wide and Handsome 1937	High, Wide and Handsome
Music: Jerome Kern	The Folks Who Live on the Hill
	Can I Forget You?
	The Things I Want
	Allegheny Al
	Will You Marry Me Tomorrow, Maria?
I'll Take Romance 1937	Title song
Music: Ben Oakland	
The Great Waltz 1938	One Day when We Were Young
Music: Dimitri Tiomkin	
The Lady Objects 1938	When You're in the Room
Music: Ben Oakland	That Week in Paris
	A Mist is Over the Moon
New Moon 1940	Stage score
Lady Be Good 1941	The Last Time I saw Paris (music: Jerome Kern)
Sunny 1941	Stage score
The Desert Song 1944	Stage score, only part used

State Fair 1945 Music: Richard Rodgers	It Might as Well be Spring That's for Me It's a Grand Night for Singing Isn't Kinda Fun? Our State Fair
Centennial Summer 1946	All Through the Day (music: Jerome Kern)
The Strip 1951	A Kiss to Build a Dream On (music: Harry Ruby, lyric: O.H. and Bert Kalmar)
Main Street to Broadway 1953	There's Music in You (music: Richard Rodgers)
The Desert Song 1953	Stage score
Rose Marie 1954	Stage score
Carmen Jones 1954	Stage score
Oklahoma! 1955	Stage score
Carousel 1956	Stage score
The King and I 1956	Stage score
South Pacific 1958	Stage score My Girl Back Home
Flower Drum Song 1961	Stage score
The Sound of Music 1965	Stage score plus two songs with lyrics by Richard Rodgers

Dorothy Fields

Born 15 July 1904, Allenhurst, N.J.
Died 28 March 1974, New York.

Shows

Cotton Club Revue 1927,
  Night Club Revue
  Music: Jimmy McHugh

Delmar's Revels 1927   I Can't Give You Anything but Love
  Music: Jimmy McHugh   (song used for one performance
                            only)

Blackbirds of 1928 1928 518p   I Can't Give You Anything but Love
  Music: Jimmy McHugh   Diga Diga Doo
                         I Must Have that Man
                         Porgy
                         Doin' the New Low Down
                         Baby

Hello Daddy 1928 198p   In a Great Big Way
  Music: Jimmy McHugh   Let's Sit and Talk About It
                         Out Where the Blues Begin
                         Futuristic Rhythm

The International Revue 1930 95p   On the Sunny Side of the Street
  Music: Jimmy McHugh   Exactly Like You

The Vanderbilt Revue 1930 13p   Blue Again
  Music: Jimmy McHugh   Button up Your Heart

Rhapsody in Black 1931 80p   I'm Feelin' Blue (Music: Jimmy
                         McHugh)

Shoot the Works 1931 87p   How's Your Uncle (Music: Jimmy
                         McHugh)

Singin' the Blues 1931 45p   A Play with two songs:
  Music: Jimmy McHugh   Singin' the Blues
                         It's the Darndest Thing

Clowns in Clover 1932 Chicago   Don't Blame Me

Stars in Your Eyes 1939 127p   It's All Yours
  Music: Arthur Schwartz   This Is It
                         Okay for Sound
                         A Lady Needs a Change
                         Never a Dull Moment
                         I'll Pay the Check

Up in Central Park 1945 504p   Close as Pages in a Book
  Music: Sigmund Romberg   It Doesn't Cost You Anything to
                         Dream
                         When You Walk in the Room
                         April Snow
                         The Big Back Yard

Arms and the Girl 1950 134p   A Cow and a Plough and a Frau
  Music: Morton Gould   Nothin' for Nothin'
                         There Must be Somethin' Better than
                         Love

A Tree Grows in Brooklyn 1951 270p   He Had Refinement
  Music: Arthur Schwartz   Make the Man Love Me
                         Love is the Reason
                         Look Who's Dancing

By the Beautiful Sea 1954 270p Music: Arthur Schwartz	Happy Habit Old Enough to Love Alone too Long I'd Rather Wake Up by Myself
Redhead 1959 452p Music: Albert Hague	The Right Finger on My Left Hand Merely Marvelous The Uncle Sam Rag Behave Yourself Erbie Fitch's Twitch
Sweet Charity 1966 608p London 1967 476p Music: Cy Coleman	Big Spender If My Friends Could See Me Now There's Gotta be Something Better than This Where Am I Going I'm a Brass Band I Love to Cry at Weddings Baby, Dream Your Dream
See-Saw 1973 296p Music: Cy Coleman	Nobody Does It Like Me It's Not Where You Start Welcome to Holiday Inn Spanglish

Television

Junior Miss 1957 Music: Burton Lane	The Happy Heart I'll Buy It Let's Make it Christmas All Year 'Round

Films

Love in the Rough 1930 Music: Jimmy McHugh	Go Home
Cuban Love Song 1931 Music: Jimmy McHugh	Cuban Love Song
Dancing Lady 1933 Music: Jimmy McHugh	My Dancing Lady
The Nitwits 1935 Music: Jimmy McHugh	Music in My Heart

Roberta 1935
Music: Jerome Kern
	Stage score plus
	I Won't Dance (Lyric with Oscar
	    Hammerstein II, Otto Harbach and
	    Jimmy McHugh)
	Lovely to Look At (Lyric with
	    Jimmy McHugh)

Every Night at Eight 1935 Music: Jimmy McHugh	I'm in the Mood for Love I Feel a Song Comin' On Speaking Confidentially Take it Easy
Hooray for Love 1935 Music: Jimmy McHugh	Hooray for Love Livin' in a Great Big Way I'm in Love all over Again You're an Angel
In Person 1935 Music: Oscar Levant	Don't Mention Love to Me Out of Sight, Out of Mind

	I've Got a New Lease on Life
I Dream Too Much 1935	I Dream Too Much
Music: Jerome Kern	I Got Love
	I'm the Echo, You're the Song
	The Jockey on the Carousel
Alice Adams 1935	I Can't Waltz Alone
Music: Max Steiner	
Swing Time 1936	The Way You Look Tonight
Music: Jerome Kern	A Fine Romance
	Pick Yourself Up
	Bojangles of Harlem
	Never Gonna Dance
	Waltz in Swing Time
The King Steps Out 1936	Stars in My Eyes
Music: Fritz Kreisler	Madly in Love
When You're In Love 1937	Our Song
Music: Jerome Kern	Whistling Boy
Joy of Living 1938	What's Good About Goodnight?
Music: Jerome Kern	You Couldn't Be Cuter
	Just Let Me Look at You
	A Heavenly Party
One Night in the Tropics 1940	Remind Me
Music: Jerome Kern	You and Your Kiss
	Ferendola
	Simple Philosophy
Up in Central Park 1948	Stage score
Excuse My Dust 1951	Spring has Sprung
Music: Arthur Schwartz	
Texas Carnival 1951	Young Folks Should Get Married
Music: Harry Warren	Whoa, Emma
Mr Imperium 1951	Let Me Look at You
Music: Harold Arlen	Andiamo
	My Love an' My Mule
Lovely to Look at 1952	Remake of *Roberta*
Music: Jerome Kern	
The Farmer Takes a Wife 1953	Today I Love Ev'rybody
Music: Harold Arlen	
Sweet Charity 1970	Stage score plus
	My Personal Property
	It's a Nice Face

Howard Dietz

Born 8 September 1896, New York.
Died 30 July 1983, New York.

Shows

Poppy 1922 328p — Alibi Baby (music: Arthur Samuels)

Dear Sir 1924 15p — Grab a Girl
  Music: Jerome Kern
- What's the Use
- A Mormon Life
- Dancing Time
- All Lanes Must Reach a Turning
- My Houseboat on the Harlem

Oh, Kay! 1924 256p — Heaven on Earth (lyric: H.D. and Ira
  London 1927 214p   Gershwin)
  Music: George Gershwin
- Oh, Kay! (as above)
- Clap Yo' Hands (verse)

Merry-Go-Round 1927 135p — Hogan's Alley
  Music: Henry Souvaine and
  Jay Gorney
  Lyrics: H.D. and Morrie Ryskind
- Gabriel is Blowing his Horn
- What D'Ya Say?
- Tampa

The Little Show 1929 321p — I Guess I'll Have to Change My Plan
  Music: Arthur Schwartz
- I've Made a Habit of You
- Man about Town
- Get Up on a New Routine
- Little Old New York
- Caught in the Rain (music: Henry Sullivan)
- Moanin' Low (music: Ralph Rainger)

Grand Street Follies 1929 85p — I Need You so (music: Arthur Schwartz, lyric: H.D. and David Goldberg)

Three's a Crowd 1930 272p — The Moment I Saw You
  Music: Arthur Schwartz
- Right at the Start of It
- Something to Remember You By
- Night after Night
- Je t'Aime
- All the King's Horses (music and lyric: H.D., Alec Wilder and Eddie Brandt)

The Second Little Show 1930 63p — Lucky Seven
  Music: Arthur Schwartz
- Sunrise
- What a Case I've Got on You
- I Like Your Face

The Band Wagon 1931 260p — Dancing in the Dark
  Music: Arthur Schwartz
- High and Low
- I Love Louisa
- New Sun in the Sky
- Where Can He Be?
- Miserable With You

Flying Colors 1932 188p — Louisiana Hayride
  Music: Arthur Schwartz
- A Shine on Your Shoes
- Alone Together
- Smokin' Reefers

Revenge with Music 1934 158p Music: Arthur Schwartz	You and the Night and the Music When You Love Only One If There is Someone Lovelier Than You
At Home Abroad 1935 198p Music: Arthur Schwartz	Got a Bran' New Suit Farewell, My Lovely Thief in the Night Love is a Dancing Thing Get Yourself a Geisha Girl
Between the Devil 1937 93p Music: Arthur Schwartz	I See Your Face Before Me By Myself You Have Everything Triplets
Keep Off the Grass 1940 44p	A Fugitive from Esquire (music: Jimmy McHugh) Two in a Taxi (as above) The Old Park Bench (as above)
Sadie Thompson 1944 60p Music: Vernon Duke	The Love I Long For Poor as a Church Mouse Garden in the Sky Born all over again
Jackpot 1944 69p Music: Vernon Duke	The Last Long Mile I Kissed My Girl Goodbye Sugarfoot What Happened? He's Good for Nothing but Me What's Mine is Yours
Inside USA 1948 337p Music: Arthur Schwartz	Inside USA Blue Grass At the Mardi Gras My Gal is Mine Once More Haunted Heart Rhode Island is Famous for You An Element of Doubt (music: Sammy Fain)
Ziegfeld Follies 1957 123p	
The Gay Life 1961 113p Music: Arthur Schwartz	What a Charming Couple This Kind of Girl You Will Never be Lonely For the First Time
Jennie 1963 82p Music: Arthur Schwartz	Waitin' for the Evening Train I Still Look at You That Way For Better or Worse Before I Kiss the World Goodbye High is Better than Low

New Versions of Operas
Die Fledermaus 1950
La Bohème 1952

Films

Hollywood Party 1934 — Feelin' High (music: Walter Donaldson)

Under Your Spell 1937 — Title song (music: Arthur Schwartz)

Three Darling Daughters 1948 — The Dickey-Bird Song (music: Sammy Fain)

Dancing in the Dark 1950 — Title song and other old songs

The Band Wagon 1953 — Stage score; That's Entertainment (music: Arthur Schwartz)

E. Y. Harburg

Born 8 April 1898, New York.
Died 5 March 1981, Los Angeles.

* Music: Jay Gorney
** Music: Jay Gorney and Phil Cohan
*** Music: Lewis E. Gensler

Shows

Earl Carroll's Sketchbook 1929 400p	Crashing the Golden Gate**
	Legs, Legs, Legs*
	Kinda Cute*
	Like Me Less, Love Me More*
	Papa Likes a Hot Papoose*
Earl Carroll's Vanities 1930 215p	Knee Deep in Daisies*
	Love Boats*
	Going Up*
	I Came to Life*
Garrick Gaieties 1930 158p	Too, Too Divine (music: Vernon Duke)
	I'm Only Human after all (music: Vernon Duke; lyric: E.Y.H. and Ira Gershwin)
The Vanderbilt Revue 1930 13p	Ex Gigolo (music: Mario Braggiotti)
Shoot the Works 1931 87p	Muchacha (music: Vernon Duke and J. Gurney)
	Hot Moonlight*
	My Heart's a Banjo*
Ballyhoo of 1932 1932 94p	Thrill Me***
	Falling Off the Wagon***
	Riddle Me This***
	Old-fashioned Wedding***
	Nuts and Noddles***
	How Do You Do it?***
	Man about Yonkers***
	Ballyhujah***
	What Have You Got to Have***
Americana 1932 76p	Brother Can You Spare a Dime*
	Whistling for a Kiss (music: Richard Myers; lyric: E.Y.H. and Johnny Mercer)
	Satan's Little Lamb (music: Harold Arlen; lyric: E.Y.H. and J. Mercer)
	Let Me Match my Private Life with Yours (music: Vernon Duke)
	Five Minutes of Spring*
	You're Not Pretty but You're Mine (music: Burton Lane)
	Get That Sun into You (music: Richard Myers)
Walk a Little Faster 1932 119p	April in Paris (music: Vernon Duke)
	Where Have We Met Before? (as above)
	Time and Tide (as above)
	That's Life (as above)

The Great Magoo 1932 11p

A Play with one song:
It's Only a Paper Moon (music: H. Arlen; lyric: Billy Rose and E.Y.H.)

Ziegfeld Follies of 1934 1934 182p

I Like the Likes of You (music: Vernon Duke)
Smart to be Smart (as above)
Water Under the Bridge (as above)
What is There to Say? (as above)

Life Begins at 8.40 1934 237p
    Music: Harold Arlen
    Lyrics: E.Y.H. and Ira Gershwin

What Can You Say in a Love Song
You're a Builder Upper
Fun to be Fooled
Shoein' the Mare
Let's Take a Walk Around the Block
Things
Quartet Erotica

New Faces of 1934 1934 148p

'Cause You Won't Play House (music: Morgan Lewis)

The Show is On 1936 237p

Long as You've Got Your Health (music: Will Irwin; lyric: E.Y.H. and Norman Zeno)
Song of the Woodman (music: H. Arlen)
Josephine Waters (as above)

Hooray for What? 1937 200p
    Music: Harold Arlen

Moanin' in the Mornin'
Down With Love
I've Gone Romantic on You
God's Country
In the Shade of the New Apple Tree

Hold on to Your Hats 1940 158p
    Music: Burton Lane

The World is in My Arms
Don't Let It Get You Down
There's a Great Day Coming Manana
Life Was Pie for the Pioneer
She Came, She Saw, She Can-Canned

Bloomer Girl 1944 654p
    Music: Harold Arlen

The Eagle and Me
When the Boys Come Home
I Never Was Born
It Was Good Enough for Grandma

Finian's Rainbow 1947 725p
    London 1947 54p
    Music: Burton Lane

How Are Things in Glocca Morra?
If This Isn't Love
Look to the Rainbow
Old Devil Moon
The Begat
When the Idle Poor Become the Idle Rich
When I'm Not Near the Girl I Love
That Great Come-and-Get-It Day

Flahooley 1951 40p
    Music: Sammy Fain

The World is Your Balloon
Happy Hunting
The Springtime Cometh

Jamaica 1957 558p
    Music: Harold Arlen

Push de Button
Yankee Dollar
Ain't It the Truth
Leave the Atom Alone

For Every Fish
Monkey in the Mango Tree

The Happiest Girl in the World
1961 97p
Music: Jacques Offenbach

Never Trust a Virgin
Shall We Say Farewell?
Never Be-Devil the Devil

Darling of the Day 1968 32p
Music: Jule Styne

A Gentleman's Gentleman
I've Got a Rainbow Working for Me

Films

Applause 1929
Rio Rita 1929

What Wouldn't I Do for That Man*
Stage score
Long Before You Came Along
(music: H. Arlen)

Glorifying the American Girl 1930
Moonlight and Pretzels 1933

What Wouldn't I Do for That Man*
Moonlight and Pretzels*
Ah, But Is It Love?*

Take a Chance 1933

It's Only a Paper Moon from *The Great Magoo*

The Count of Monte Cristo 1934

The World is Mine (music: Johnny Green)

The Singing Kid 1935
Music: Harold Arlen

You're the Cure for What Ails Me
I Love to Sing-a
Keep That Hi-De-Ho in Your Soul
Save Me, Sister

Stage Struck 1936
Music: Harold Arlen

Fancy Meeting You
In Your Own Quiet Way
You're Kinda Grandish

Gold Diggers of 1937 1936
Music: Harold Arlen
The Wizard of Oz 1938
Music: Harold Arlen

Speaking of the Weather
Let's Put Our Heads Together
Over the Rainbow
Ding-Dong the Witch is Dead
We're Off to See the Wizard
If I Only Had a Brain
The Jitterbug
Follow the Yellow Brick Road

The Marx Brothers at the Circus 1939
Music: Harold Arlen
Andy Hardy Meets Débutante 1940

Lydia, the Tattooed Lady
Two Blind Loves
Buds Won't Bud (music: Harold Arlen)

Babes on Broadway 1941

Chin Up, Cheerio, Carry On (music: Harold Arlen)

Ship Ahoy 1942
Music: Burton Lane

Poor You
Last Call for Love
I'll Take Tallulah
Tampico
Moonlight Bay

Cabin in the Sky 1943

Stage score
Happiness is Just a Thing Called Joe (music: Harold Arlen)

Thousands Cheer 1943

Let There be Music (music: Earl Brent)

Can't Help Singing 1944
  Music: Jerome Kern

Can't Help Singing
More and More
Any Moment Now
Califor-niay

Hollywood Canteen 1944

You Can Always Tell a Yank (music: Burton Lane)

Song of Russia 1944

And Russia is Her Name (music: Jerome Kern)

Kismet 1944
  Music: Harold Arlen

Stage score
Willow in the Wind
Tell Me, Tell Me, Evening Star

Centennial Summer 1946

California Sue (music: Jerome Kern)

California 1946
  Music: Earl Robinson

California
Said I to My Heart Said I
California or Bust
I Shoulda Stood in Pennsylvania
Lily-I-Lay-De-O

Gay Purr-ee 1962
  Music: Harold Arlen

Little Drops of Rain
Paris is a Lonely Town
Roses Red – Violets Blue
Mewsette
Take My Hand Paree

I Could Go on Singing 1963

I Could Go on Singing (music: H. Arlen)

Finian's Rainbow 1968

Stage score

Noël Coward

Born 16 December 1899, Teddington, Middlesex.
Died 26 March 1973, Jamaica.

Shows

London Calling! 1923 London 316p	Tamarisk Town
	Other Girls
	When My Ship Comes Home
	Carrie**
	There's Life in the Old Girl Yet*
	Russian Blues**
	Prenez Garde, Lisette
	Sentiment*
	Parisian Pierrot*
	What Love Means to Girls Like Me
	When We Were Girls Together
	Spanish Grandee
The Co-optimists 1923 London	Songs were used in the 7th and 8th editions of this long running revue:
	There May be Days (with Melville Gideon)
	Down With the Whole Damn Lot!
	Back to Nature
André Charlot Revue of 1924 1924 Broadway 285p	Used the songs marked * from *London Calling!*
On With the Dance 1925 London 229p	Cosmopolitan Lady
	I'm So in Love
	Poor Little Rich Girl**
	First Love
	Couldn't We Keep on Dancing
	Raspberry Time in Runcorn
	Spinsters' Song
	The Vicarage Dance
	Choir Boys' Song
	Even Clergymen Are Naughty Now and Then
	Church Parade
	Come a Little Closer
André Charlot Revue of 1925 1925 Broadway 138p	Used the songs marked ** from *London Calling!* and *On With the Dance* plus
	The Roses Have Made Me Remember
	The Girls I Am Leaving in England Today
This Year of Grace 1928 London 316p 1928 Broadway 157p	Dance Little Lady
	Waiting in a Queue
	Mary Make-Believe
	I'm Mad About You
	Lorelei
	A Room With a View
	It Doesn't Matter How Old You Are
	Teach Me to Dance Like Grandma
	Little Women

The Lido
English Lido
Mother's Complaint
Britannia Rules the Waves
Chauve-Souris
Try to Learn to Love
Caballero
Finale London Production
Love, Life and Laughter (New
    York)
World Weary (New York)
Lilac Time (New York)
I Can't Think (New York)
The Sun, The Moon and You (New
    York)
Playing the Game (New York)

Bitter Sweet
    1929 London 697p
    1929 New York 159p

I'll See You Again
Ladies of the Town
Dear Little Café
Tokay
Zigeuner
If Love Were All
Green Carnations
A Play with the song:
Someday I'll Find You

Private Lives
    1930 London 101p
    1931 Broadway 256p
Cochran's 1931 Revue
    1931 London 27p

Any Little Fish
Half-Caste Woman
City
Bright Young People
Twentieth Century Blues
Mad Dogs and Englishmen

Cavalcade 1931 London 405p
The Third Little Show
    1931 Broadway 136p
Ziegfeld Follies of 1931
    1931 Broadway 165p
Words and Music 1932 London 164p

Half-caste Woman

Maggie
Débutantes
Let's Live Dangerously
Children of the Ritz
Mad Dogs and Englishmen
Planters' Wives
Let's Say Goodbye
The Hall of Fame
Mad About the Boy
Journey's End
Housemaids' Knees
Three White Feathers
Description Ballets
Something to do with Spring
The Wife of an Acrobat
The Younger Generation
Midnight Matinée
The Party's Over Now

Conversation Piece
1934 London 177p
1934 Broadway 55p
	I'll Follow My Secret Heart
	Regency Rakes
	Charming, Charming
	Dear Little Soldiers
	There's Always Something Fishy
	    About the French
	English Lesson
	There Was Once a Little Village by
	    the Sea
	Nevermore

Tonight at 8.30 1936 London 157p 1936 Broadway 118p	We Were Dancing Then Play, Orchestra, Play! You Were There Has Anybody Seen Our Ship? Men About Town Here's a Toast Princes and Princesses Let's Play a Tune on the Music Box Hearts and Flowers
Operette 1938 London 133p	Pom-Pom Countess Mitzi Dearest Love Foolish Virgins The Stately Homes of England Where Are the Songs We Sung? The Island of Bollamazoo Sing for Joy My Dear Miss Dale Operette
Set to Music 1939 Broadway 129p	Songs from the English shows plus I'm So Weary of It All I've Been to a Marvellous Party Rug of Persia
Sigh No More 1945 London 213p	Sigh No More The Parting of the Ways Mother and Daughter I Wonder What Happened to Him Never Again (also used in *Set To Music*) That is the End of the News Loch Lomond Willy Wait a Bit, Joe Nina The Merry Wives of Windsor Matelot The Burchells of Battersea Rise Japanese Spies
Pacific 1860 1946 London 129p	Family Grace If I Were a Man Bright Was the Day Invitation to the Waltz His Excellency Regrets This is a Night for Lovers I Never Knew

Ace of Clubs 1950 London 211p

Pretty Little Bridesmaids
Uncle Harry
This is a Changing World
My Kind of Man
This Could Be True
Nothing Can Last Forever
Something About a Sailor
I'd Never Know
Three Juvenile Delinquents
Sail Away
Josephine
I Like America
Chase Me, Charlie

The Lyric Revue 1951 London 454p
The Globe Revue 1952
   London 234p
After the Ball 1954 London 188p

Don't Make Fun of the Fair
Give Me the Kingston
   By-Pass
Sweet Day
Crème de la Crème
Light is the Heart
May I Have the Pleasure
London at Night
Farewell Song
Faraway Land

Together with Music
   American Television Show 1955

London Morning 1959
Sail Away
   1961 Broadway 167p
   1962 London 252p

Together with Music
Ninety Minutes is a Long, Long
   Time
Ballet Music
Come to Me
Sail Away
Where Shall I Find Him?
Beatnik Love Affair
Later than Spring
The Passenger's Always Right
Useless Useful Phrases
Go Slow, Johnny
You're a Long Long Way from
   America
Something Very Strange
Why Do the Wrong People Travel?

The Girl Who Came to Supper 1963
   Broadway 112p

I've Been Invited to a Party
London
The Coconut Girl
This Time It's True Love
I'll Remember Her

Miscellaneous songs
Marvellous Party
Alice Is at it Again
Why Must the Show Go On?
Spinning Song
Could You Please Oblige Us with a
   Bren-Gun

Louisa
Mrs Worthington
Let's Do It (lyrics to Porter's song)
London Pride
Don't Let's Be Beastly to the Germans
A Bar on the Piccola Marina

Johnny Mercer

Born 18 November 1909, Savannah, Ga.
Died 25 June 1976, Los Angeles.

Shows

The Garrick Gaieties Third edition 1930 155p	Out of Breath (music: Everett Miller)
Americana 1932 76p	Whistling for a Kiss (music: Richard Myers; lyric: J.M. and E. Y. Harburg)
	Satan's Little Lamb (music: Harold Arlen; lyric: J.M. and E. Y. Harburg)
	Would'ja for a Big Red Apple (music: Henry Souvaine; lyric: J.M. and Everett Miller)
Tattle Tales 1933 28p	Another Case of the Blues (music: Richard Myers)
Walk with Music 1940 55p Music: Hoagy Carmichael	I Walk with Music
	What'll They Think of Next?
	Ooh, What You Said
	'Way Back in 1939 AD
	The Rhumba Jumps
	How Nice for Me
	Even If I Say it Myself
St Louis Woman 1946 113p Music: Harold Arlen	Any Place I Hang my Hat is Home
	Legalise my Name
	Come Rain or Come Shine
	A Woman's Prerogative
	Ridin' on the Moon
Texas, Li'l Darlin' 1949 293p Music: Robert Emmett Dolan	They Talk a Different Language
	A Month of Sundays
	The Big Movie Show in the Sky
	It's Great to be Alive
Top Banana 1951 350p	The Man of the Year This Week
	You're So Beautiful That . . .
	Top Banana
	Only if You're in Love
Li'l Abner 1956 693p Music: Gene de Paul	It's a Typical Day
	Jubilation T. Cornpone
	Namely You
	The Country's in the Very Best of Hands
	Past My Prime
Saratoga 1959 80p Music: Harold Arlen	I'll be Respectable
	One Step – Two Step
	Gettin' a Man (music and lyric)
	Why Fight This? (music and lyric)
	Countin' our Chickens
	You or No One
	The Man in my Life
Foxy 1964 72p Music: Robert Emmett Dolan	Many Ways to Skin a Cat
	My Weight in Gold
	Money Isn't Everything

The Good Companions
London 1974 235p
Music: André Previn

Talk to Me, Baby
It's Easy When You Know How
Bon Vivant
Camaraderie
Footloose
Pleasure of Your Company
Stage Struck
Dance of Life
Slippin' Around the Corner
Darkest Before the Dawn

Seven Brides for Seven Brothers
1982 5p
Music: Gene de Paul

A musical based on the film using
some of the original score

Films

Transatlantic Merry-Go-Round 1934

If I Had a Million Dollars (music:
Matty Malneck)

To Beat the Band 1935
Music: Matty Malneck

If You Were Mine
Eeny Meeny Miney Mo
Santa Claus Came in the Spring
Meet Miss America
I Saw Her at Eight O'clock

Old Man Rhythm 1935

I Never Saw a Better Night (music:
Lewis Gensler)

Rhythm on the Range 1936
Ready, Willing and Able 1937
Music: Richard Whiting

I'm an Old Cowhand
Too Marvellous for Words
Just a Quiet Evening
Sentimental and Melancholy
Handy With Your Feet

The Singing Marine 1937

Night Over Shanghai (music: Harry
Warren)

Varsity Show 1937
Music: Richard Whiting

Have You Got any Castles, Baby?
You've Got Something There
Old King Cole
We're Working our Way through
College
On with the Dance
Moonlight on the Campus
Love Is on the Air Tonight

Hollywood Hotel 1938
Music: Richard Whiting

Hooray for Hollywood
I've Hitched My Wagon to a Star
Silhouetted in the Moonlight
Can't Teach My Old Heart New
Tricks
I'm Like a Fish out of Water

Cowboy from Brooklyn 1938
Music: Richard Whiting

Cowboy from Brooklyn
I'll Dream Tonight
Ride, Tenderfoot, Ride
I've Got a Heart Full of Music

Going Places 1938
Music: Harry Warren

Jeepers Creepers
Say It with a Kiss
Mutiny in the Nursery (music and
lyric)

Garden of the Moon 1938
  Music: Harry Warren
  Lyrics: J.M. and Al Dubin

Garden of the Moon
Love is Where You Find It
Girl Friend of the Whirling
  Dervish
Confidentially
The Lady on the Two-Cent Stamp

Gold Diggers in Paris 1938

Day Dreaming (music: Harry
  Warren)

Jezebel 1938
Naughty but Nice 1939
  Music: Harry Warren

Title song (music: Harry Warren)
In a Moment of Weakness
Hooray for Spinach
I'm Happy about the Whole Thing
Corn Pickin'

You'll Find Out 1940
  Music: Jimmy McHugh

You've Got Me This Way
I'd Know You Anywhere
The Bad Humor Man
I've Got a One-Track Mind
Don't Think It Ain't Been Charming

Second Chorus 1941
Birth of the Blues 1941

Love of my Life (music: Arti Shaw)
The Waiter and The Porter and the
  Upstairs Maid

Navy Blues 1941
  Music: Arthur Schwartz

You're a Natural
In Waikiki
When Are We Going to Land
  Abroad?

Blues in the Night 1941
  Music: Harold Arlen

Blues in the Night
This Time the Dreams on Me
Says Who? Says You, Says I!

You're the One 1941
  Music: Jimmy McHugh

You're the One
Strawberry Lane
I Could Kiss You for That
Gee, I Wish I'd Listened to my
  Mother

The Fleet's In 1942
  Music: Victor Schertzinger

Tangerine
I Remember You
Not Mine
Arthur Murray Taught me Dancing
If You Build a Better Mousetrap
When You Hear the Time Signal
The Fleet's In

You Were Never Lovelier 1942
  Music: Jerome Kern

You Were Never Lovelier
Dearly Beloved
I'm Old-Fashioned
Wedding in the Spring
The Shorty George
On the Beam

Star Spangled Rhythm 1942
  Music: Harold Arlen

That Old Black Magic
Hit the Road to Dreamland
Old Glory
I'm Doing It for Defense
A Sweater, A Sarong and A
  Peekaboo Bang
Sharp as a Tack
On the Swing Shift

Captain of the Clouds 1942
The Sky's the Limit 1943
  Music: Harold Arlen

Riding High 1943

True to Life 1943
  Music: Hoagy Carmichael

Here Come the Waves 1944
  Music: Harold Arlen

To Have or Not to Have 1944

Out of This World 1945
  Music: Harold Arlen

Laura 1945
The Harvey Girls 1946
  Music: Harry Warren

Forever Amber 1947
The Pretty Girl 1950
Here Comes the Groom 1951

The Belle of New York 1952
  Music: Harry Warren

Dangerous When Wet 1953
  Music: Arthur Schwartz

Top Banana 1954
Seven Brides for Seven Brothers
  Music: Gene de Paul

He Loved Me Till the All-Clear
  Came
Title song (music: Harold Arlen)
My Shining Hour
One for my Baby
I've Got a Lot in Common With You
He Loved Me Till the All-Clear Came
  (music: Harold Arlen)
The Old Music Master
There She Was
Miss Pollyana
Accent-tchu-ate the Positive
I Promise You
Let's Take the Long Way Home
There's a Fellow Waiting in
  Ploughkeepsie
My Mama Thinks I'm a Star
Here Come the Waves
How Little We Know (music:
  Hoagy Carmichael)
Out of This World
I'd Rather Be Me
June Comes around Every Year
Title song (music: David Raksin)
On the Atchison, Topeka and the
  Santa Fe
Wait and See
The Wild Wild West
It's a Great Big World
Swing Your Partner Round and
  Round
In the Valley Where the Evening Sun
  Goes Down
Title song (music: David Raksin)
Fancy Free (music: Harold Arlen)
In the Cool, Cool, Cool of the
  Evening (music: Hoagy
  Carmichael)
The Belle of New York
Baby Doll
I Want to be a Dancin' Man
Naughty but Nice
Batchelor Dinner Song
Oops
Seeing's Believing
I Got Out of Bed on the
  Right Side
Ain't Nature Grand

Stage score
Spring, Spring, Spring
Bless Your Beautiful Hide
Sobbin' Women
June Bride
When You're in Love

	Lament
	Goin' Co'tin'
Daddy Long-Legs 1955	Something's Gotta Give
	Sluefoot
	History of the Beat
	Welcome Egghead
	C-A-T Spells Cat
	Dream
Bernadine 1957	Title song
Merry Andrew 1958	The Pipes of Pan
Music: Saul Chaplin	Chin Up, Stout Fella
	Everything is Tickety Boo
	Salud
	The Square of the Hypotenuse
	You Can't Always Have What You Want
Li'l Abner 1959	Stage score
Breakfast at Tiffany's 1961	Moon River (music: Henry Mancini)
The Days of Wine and Roses 1962	Title song (music: Henry Mancini)
Hatari! 1962	Just for Tonight (music: Henry Mancini)
Charade 1963	Title song (music: Henry Mancini)
How the West Was Won 1963	Raise a Ruckus Tonight
Music: Robert Emmett Dolan	Wait for the Hoedown
	What Was Your Name in the States?
The Great Race 1965	The Sweetheart Tree (music: Henry Mancini)
Darling Lili 1970	Whistling away the Dark
Music: Henry Mancini	The Little Birds
	The Girl in No Man's Land
	I'll Give You Three Guesses
	Skal
	Your Good-Will Ambassador

Other songs not originally written for either stage or film scores

Satin Doll (music: Duke Ellington)
Lazy Bones (music: Hoagy Carmichael)
Sky Lark (music: Hoagy Carmichael)
In the Cool, Cool, Cool of the Evening (music: Hoagy Carmichael)
The Dixieland Band (music: Bernie Hanighen)
And the Angels Sing (music: Ziggy Elman)
The Yogi Who Lost His Willpower

Frank Loesser

Born 29 June 1910, New York.
Died 26 July 1969, New York.

Shows

The Illustrators' Show 1936 5p	Bang, the Bell Rang! (music: Irving Actman)
	I'm You (as above)
	Give Me the Wild Trumpets (as above)
Where's Charley? 1948 792p	My Darling, My Darling
1958 London 380p	Make a Miracle
	Lovelier than Ever
	Once in Love with Amy
	The New Ashmolean Marching Society and Students' Conservatory Band
Guys and Dolls 1950 1200p	A Bushel and a Peck
1953 London 555p	Adelaide's Lament
	Guys and Dolls
	If I Were a Bell
	I've Never Been in Love Before
	Take Back Your Mink
	More I Cannot Wish You
	Luck Be a Lady
	Sit Down, You're Rockin' the Boat
	The Oldest Established
	I'll Know
The Most Happy Fella 1956 676p	Standing on the Corner
1960 London 288p	Happy to Make Your Acquaintance
	Big "D"
	I Like Everybody
	Joey, Joey, Joey
	Abbondanza
Greenwillow 1960 95p	Summertime Love
	Never Will I Marry
How to Succeed in Business Without Really Trying 1961 1416p	Happy to Keep his Dinner Warm
1963 London 520p	Coffee Break
	The Company Way
	A Secretary is Not a Toy
	Been a Long Day
	Paris Original
	Rosemary
	I Believe in You
	Brotherhood of Man
Pleasures and Palaces 1965, opened and closed on its pre-Broadway tour in Detroit	

Films

Vogues of 1938 1937	Lovely One (music: Manning Sherwin)
Cocoanut Grove 1938	Says My Heart (music: Burton Lane)
College Swing 1938	Moments Like This (music: Burton Lane)

How'dja Like to Love Me? (as above)
You're a Natural (music: Manning
Sherwin)
I Fall in Love With You Every Day
(as above)

Sing You Sinners 1938

Small Fry (music: Hoagy
Carmichael)

Thanks for the Memory 1938

Two Sleepy People (music: Hoagy
Carmichael)

Spawn of the North 1938

Wish I Was the Willow (music:
Burton Lane)

St Louis Blues 1938
   Music: Burton Lane

I Go for That

The Hurricane 1938

Blue Nightfall
Moon of Manakoora (music: Alfred
Newman)

Hawaiian Nights 1939

Hey, Good Looking (music: Matty
Malneck)

Man about Town 1939
   Music: Fred Hollander

Strange Enchantment
That Sentimental Sandwich
Man about Town
Fidgety Feet

Some Like it Hot 1939
   Music: Burton Lane

Some Like it Hot
The Lady's in Love With You

Destry Rides Again 1939
   Music: Frederick Hollander

See What the Boys in the Back Room
Will Have
You've Got that Look that Leaves Me
Weak

Typhoon 1940

Palms of Paradise (music: Fred
Hollander)

Arizona Sketches 1940

Prairieland Lullaby (music: Victor
Young)

Buck Benny Rides Again 1940
   Music: Jimmy McHugh

My! My!
Say It
My Kind of Country

A Night at Earl Carroll's 1940

Li'l Boy Love (music: Fred
Hollander)
I Hear Music

Dancing on a Dime 1940
   Music: Burton Lane

Dancing on a Dime

Northwest Mounted Police 1940

Does the Moon Shine Through the
Tall Pine? (music: Victor Young)
I've Been in Love Before (music:
Frank Hollander)

Seven Sinners 1940

Las Vegas Nights 1941
   Music: Louis Alter

Dolores
I Gotta Ride
Mary, Mary, Quite Contrary

Kiss the Boys Goodbye 1941
   Music: Victor Schertzinger

Kiss the Boys Goodbye
Sand in my Shoes
I'll Never Let a Day Pass By

Sis Hopkins 1941
   Music: Jule Styne

Well! Well!
I Said Yes, She Said No
This isn't Hay, It's the USA

Caught in the Draft 1941

Love Me as I Am (music: Louis Alter)

Sweater Girl 1942
   Music: Jule Styne

I Don't Want to Walk Without You
The Liberty Magazine Song

	I Said No
Priorities on Parade 1942	You're in Love With Someone Else (music: Jule Styne)
Forest Rangers 1942	Jingle Jangle Jingle (music: Joseph Lilley)
Happy Go Lucky 1943 Music: Jimmy McHugh	Happy Go Lucky
	Let's Get Lost
	Sing a Tropical Song
	'Murder' He Says
	The Fuddy Duddy Watchmaker
Seven Days' Leave 1943 Music: Jimmy McHugh	Can't Get You Out of this Mood
	A Touch of Texas
	Soft-Hearted
	I Get the Neck of the Chicken
	Please, Won't You Leave My Girl Alone?
	Baby
	Puerto Rico
	You Speak My Language
Thank Your Lucky Stars 1943 Music: Arthur Schwartz	Thank Your Lucky Stars
	They're Either Too Young or Too Old
	How Sweet You are
	I'm Ridin' for a Fall
	The Dreamer
	Good Night, Neighbor
	Love Isn't Born
	Ice Cold Katy
Christmas Holiday 1944	Spring Will be a Little Late This Year
Duffy's Tavern 1945	Leave Us Face It (music: Abe Burroughs)
The Perils of Pauline 1947	I Wish I Didn't Love You So
	The Sewing Machine
	Poppa, Don't Preach to Me
Variety Girl 1947	Tallahassee
	He Can Waltz
	Your Heart Calling Mine
	I Must Have Been Madly in Love
	I Want my Money Back
	Impossible Things
	The French
Neptune's Daughter 1949	Baby's It's Cold Outside
	My Heart Beats Faster
	I Love Those Men
Red, Hot and Blue 1949	Now That I Need You
	I Wake Up in the Morning Feeling Fine
	Hamlet
	That's Loyalty
Let's Dance 1950	Why Fight the Feeling?
	Oh Them Dudes
	Can't Stop Talking
	Tunnel of Love
	The Hyacinth
Where's Charley? 1952	Stage score

Hans Christian Andersen 1952
  Made into a stage musical
  London 1974 383p

Wonderful Copenhagen
No Two People
Thumbelina
Anywhere I Wander
Inchworm
I'm Hans Christian Andersen
The Ugly Duckling

Guys and Dolls 1955

Stage score plus:
A Woman in Love
Adelaide
Pet Me, Poppa

*How to Succeed in Business Without
  Really Trying* 1967

Stage score

Miscellaneous songs
Snug as a Bug in a Rug (music: Matt
  Malneck)
Praise the Lord and Pass the
  Ammunition

What Do You Do in the infantry?
The Road to Victory
Rodger Young

Alan Jay Lerner

Born 31 August 1918, New York.

Shows

What's Up? 1943 63p
  Music: Frederick Loewe

From the Chimney to the Cellar
You've Got a Hold on Me
A Girl is Like a Book
Joshua
Three Girls in a Boat
My Last Love

The Day Before Spring 1945 165p
  Music: Frederick Loewe

The Day Before Spring
God's Green World
I Love You This Morning
A Jug of Wine
Where's my Wife?

Brigadoon 1947 581p
  London 1949 685p
  Music: Frederick Loewe

I'll Home with Bonnie Jean
The Heather on the Hill
The Love of my Life
Come to Me, Bend to Me
Almost Like Being in Love
There But for You Go I
From This Day On

Love Life 1948 252p
  Music: Kurt Weill

Here I'll Stay
I Remember It Well
Economics
My Kind of Night
Taking No Chances

Paint Your Wagon 1951 289p
  London 1953 477p
  Music: Frederick Loewe

I'm on my Way
I Talk to the Trees
They Call the Wind Maria
I Still See Elisa
There's a Coach Comin' In
Hand Me Down That Can o' Beans
Wand'rin' Star

My Fair Lady 1956 2717p
  London 1958 2281p
  Music: Frederick Loewe

Why Can't the English
Wouldn't It Be Loverly?
With a Little Bit of Luck
I'm an Ordinary Man
Just You Wait
The Rain in Spain
I Could Have Danced All Night
Ascot Gavotte
On the Street Where You Live
Embassy Waltz
You Did It
Show Me
Get Me to the Church on Time
A Hymn to Him
Without You
I've Grown Accustomed to her Face

Camelot 1960 873p
  London 1964 518p
  Music: Frederick Loewe

I Wonder What the King is Doing Tonight?
The Simple Joys of Maidenhood

Camelot

C'est Moi
The Lusty Month of May
How to Handle a Woman
If Ever I Would Leave You
The Seven Deadly Virtues
What Do Simple Folk Do?
I Loved You Once in Silence
Come Back to Me

On a Clear Day You Can See Forever
1965 280p
Music: Burton Lane

On a Clear Day You Can See
  Forever
On the SS Bernard Cohn
She Wasn't You
Hurry! It's Lovely up Here
What Did I Have That I Don't Have

Coco 1969 332p
Music: André Previn

The World Belongs to the Young
The Money Rings out Like Freedom
A Brand New Dress
A Woman is How She Loves
How Far is it to the Next Town?

Lolita, My Love 1971 Boston
Music: John Barry

Gigi 1973 103p
  Music: Frederick Loewe

Stage version of the film with the
  following numbers added:
The Earth and Other Minor Things
Paris is Paris Again
The Contract
In This Wide, Wide World
Rehearse!

1600 Pennsylvania Avenue 1976 7p
Music: Leonard Bernstein

If I Was a Dove
Take Care of This House
I Love my Wife
The Mark of a Man
We Must Have a Ball
Pity the Poor

Carmelina 1979 17p
Music: Burton Lane

It's Time for a Love Song
Someone in April
Love Before Breakfast
I'm a Woman
Why Him?

Dance a Little Closer 1983 1p
Music: Charles Strouse

Dance a Little Closer
I Got a New Girl
It Never Would've Worked
No Man is Worth It
A Woman who Thinks I'm
  Wonderful

Films

Royal Wedding 1951
  Music: Burton Lane

Too Late Now
I Left My Hat in Haiti
Open Your Eyes
Happiest Day of My Life
You're All the World to Me
Every Night at Seven
How Could You Believe Me

Sunday Jumps
What a Lovely Day for a Wedding

Brigadoon 1954   Stage score
Gigi 1958   Gigi
 Music: Frederick Loewe I Remember It well
      Thank Heaven for Little Girls
      I'm Glad I'm not Young Anymore
      The Night They Invented
       Champagne
      She's Not Thinking of Me

My Fair Lady 1964 Stage score
Camelot 1967   Stage score
On a Clear Day You Can See Forever Stage score plus:
 1969   Go to Sleep
      Love With all the Trimmings
Paint Your Wagon 1969 Stage score plus the following
       written with André Previn:
      Best Things in Life are Dirty
      The First Thing You Know
      Gold Fever
      The Gospel of No Name City
      A Million Miles away Behind the
       Door

The Little Prince 1974 Little Prince
 Music: Frederick Loewe I Need Air
      Be Happy
      I'm on Your Side
      I Never Met a Rose
      A Snake in the Grass
      Why is the Desert?
      Closer and Closer and Closer
      You're a Child

Sheldon Harnick

Born 30 April 1924, Chicago Ill.

Shows

New Faces of 1952 1952 365p	Boston Beguine
Two's Company 1952 91p	A Man's Home
John Murray Anderson's Almanac 1953 227p	Merry Little Minuet
Shoestring Revue 1955 off-Broadway 100p	Someone is Sending Me Flowers (music: David Baker)
	The Sea is All Around Us (as above)
	Garbage
	Medea in Disneyland (music: Lloyd Norlin)
The Littlest Revue 1956 off-Broadway 32p	The Shape of Things
Shangri-la 1956 21p	Uncredited interpolations
Shoestring Revue 1957 off-Broadway 110p	Best Loved Girls (music: David Baker)
The Body Beautiful 1958 60p Music: Jerry Bock	Where Are They?
	Leave Well Enough Alone
	All of These and More
	The Honeymoon is Over
	Just my Luck
	Summer Is
Fiorello 1959 795p London 1962 56p Music: Jerry Bock	On the Side of the Angels
	Politics and Poker
	I Love a Cop
	Till Tomorrow
	Little Tin Box
	The Very Next Man
	The Name's La Guardia
	Gentleman Jimmy
Vintage '60 1960 off-Broadway 8p	All American (music: David Baker)
	Forget Me (as above)
Tenderloin 1960 216p Music: Jerry Bock	Little Old New York
	Artificial Flowers
	A Picture of Happiness
	How the Money Changes Hands
	Good Clean Fun
	My Gentle Young Johnny
Smiling the Boy Fell Dead 1961 off-Broadway 22p Music: David Baker	The ABC's of Success
	If I Felt any Younger Today
	More than Ever Now
	I've Got a Wonderful Future
	Daydreams
	Two by Two
Never Too Late 1962 1007p	A play with one song:
	Never Too Late Cha-Cha (music: Jerry Bock)
She Loves Me 1963 301p London 1964 189p Music: Jerry Bock	Good Morning, Good Day
	Days Gone By
	Tonight at Eight
	Will He Like Me?

Dear Friend
Ice Cream
She Loves Me

Man in the Moon 1963 7p
  A Marionette Show
  Music: Jerry Bock

Look Where I Am
Itch to be Rich
Worlds Apart
You Treacherous Men
Ain't You Never Been Afraid?

Fiddler on the Roof 1964 3242p
  London 1967 2030p
  Music: Jerry Bock

Tradition
Matchmaker, Matchmaker
If I Were a Rich Man
To Life
Miracle of Miracles
Sunrise, Sunset
Do You Love Me?
Anatevka

Wet Paint 1965 off-Broadway 16p
The Apple Tree 1966 463p
  Music: Jerry Bock

Concert Encore
Here in Eden
The Apple Tree
What Makes Me Love Him?
Make Way
Forbidden Love (in Gaul)
Tiger, Tiger
Oh, To Be a Movie Star
Gorgeous

The Rothschilds 1970 505p
  Music: Jerry Bock

One Room
He Tossed a Coin
Sons
Everything
Rothschild and Sons
In My Own Lifetime

Pinocchio 1973 134p
  A Marionette Show
  Music: Mary Rodgers

Rex 1976 49p
  Music: Richard Rodgers

Away from You
As Once I Loved You
Christmas at Hampton Court
In Time

The Umbrellas of Cherbourg
  1979 off-Broadway 78p
  London 1980 12p
  Music: Michel Legrand

The English translation from the
original by Jacques Demy with
additional lyrics

Opera
Captain Jinks of the Horse Marines
  Kansas City 1975
  Music: Jack Beeson

Other translations including *The Merry Widow*

Stephen Sondheim

Born 22 March 1930, New York.

Shows

Girls of Summer 1956 56p

A play with the musical theme: Girls of Summer

West Side Story 1957 732p
249 on return engagement
London 1958 1040p
Music: Leonard Bernstein

Jet Song
Something's Coming
Maria
Tonight
America
One Hand, One Heart
I Feel Pretty
Somewhere
Gee, Officer Krupke
A Boy Like That

Gypsy 1959 702p
London 1970 300p
Music: Jule Styne

Let Me Entertain You
Some People
Small World
Little Lamb
You'll Never Get Away from Me
Broadway
If Momma was Married
Everything's Coming up Roses
You Gotta Get a Gimmick

A Funny Thing Happened on the Way to the Forum 1962 964p
London 1963 762p

A Comedy Tonight
Free
The House of Marcus Lycus
Lovely
Pretty Little Picture
Everybody Ought to Have a Maid
Impossible

Anyone Can Whistle 1964 9p

Me and My Town
Simple
Come Play Wiz Me
Anyone Can Whistle
A Parade in Town
I've Got You to Lean on
With so Little to be Sure of

Do I Hear a Waltz? 1965 220p
Music: Richard Rodgers

What Do We Do? We Fly!
Here We Are Again
No Understand
Take the Moment
Moon in my Window
We're Gonna be All Right
Do I Hear a Waltz?

The Mad Show 1966 off-Broadway
871p
Evening Primrose 1966 Television

The Boy From (under the name Esteban Ria Nido)
I'm Here
I Remember
When?
Take Me to the World

Company 1970 690p
1972 London 344p

Company

The Little Things We Do Together
You Could Drive a Person Crazy
Another Hundred People
Not Getting Married Today
Side by Side by Side
Barcelona
The Ladies Who Lunch
Being Alive

Follies 1971 522p

Beautiful Girls
Waiting for the Girls Upstairs
Broadway Baby
In Buddy's Eyes
Who's That Woman?
I'm Still Here
Too Many Mornings
Could I Leave You?
You're Gonna Love Tomorrow
Love Will See Us Through
Losing My Mind

Twigs 1971 289p

A play with one song:
Hollywood and Vine

*A Funny Thing Happened on
the Way to the Forum*
1972 Revival 156p
A Little Night Music 1973 601p
1975 London 406p

The original score plus:
Farewell
Echo Song
The Glamorous Life
You Must Meet My Wife
Liaisons
Every Day a Little Death
A Weekend in the Country
Send in the Clowns
The Miller's Son

The Frogs 1974
Yale Swimming Pool 8p

Invocation to the Gods and
    Instructions to the Audience
The Frogs
Dionysos
It's Only a Play
Evoe for the Dead
The Sound of Poets

Candide 1974 740p
A revival of the Leonard
Bernstein/Richard Wilbur/John
Latouche 1956 show, with
additional lyrics by Sondheim.

Life is Happiness Indeed
Auto Da Fe (What a Day)
This World
Sheep's Song

Pacific Overtues 1976 193p

There is no Other Way
Chrysanthemum Tea
Poems
Welcome to Kanagawa
Someone in a Tree
Pretty Lady
Next

Side by Side by Sondheim
1976 London 558p
1977 390p

A revue of Sondheim songs

Sweeney Todd 1979 558p
1980 London 157p

The Ballad of Sweeney Todd
The Worst Pies in London

Johanna
Pretty Women
A Little Priest
By the Sea
Not While I'm Around

Marry Me a Little
   1981 off-Broadway 96p

A musical entertainment using only
   the songs of Sondheim to tell the
   story.

Merrily We Roll Along 1981 16p

Rich and Happy
Merrily We Roll Along
Old Friends
Like It Was
Not a Day Goes By
Good Thing Going

Sunday in the Park with George
   1983 Played at the Playwright
   Horizons as 'a new musical work-in-
   progress': 23 April 1984 planned
   opening on Broadway.

Films

West Side Story 1961
Gypsy 1963
*A Funny Thing Happened on the Way to
   the Forum* 1966
The Last of Sheila 1973

Stage score
Stage score
Stage score

Screenplay by Sondheim and
   Anthony Perkins

Stavisky 1974
A Little Night Music 1978
The 7% Solution 1976

Musical score
Stage score with minor alterations
I Never Do Anything Twice

BIBLIOGRAPHY

General

Gerald Bordman, *The American Musical Theatre*, Oxford University Press, New York, 1979.

Hoagy Carmichael with Stephen Longstreet, *Sometimes I Wonder*, Alvin Redman, London, 1966.

Vernon Duke, *Passport to Paris*, Little, Brown & Co., Boston, 1955.

Lehman Engel, *Their Words are Music*, Crown, New York, 1975.

Lehman Engel, *Words with Music*, Macmillan, New York, 1972.

Stanley Green, *The World of Musical Comedy* (2nd ed.), Barnes, New Jersey, 1974.

Stanley Green, *Encyclopaedia of the Musical*, Cassell, London, 1976.

Joshua Logan, *Josh*, Delacorte, New York, 1976.

Richard Rodgers, *Musical Stages*, Random House, New York, 1975.

Alec Wilder, *American Popular Song*, Oxford University Press, New York, 1972.

Max Wilk, *They're Playing Our Song*, Atheneum, New York, 1973.

Irving Berlin

David Ewen, *The Story of Irving Berlin*, Holt Rinehart Winston, New York, 1950.

Michael Freedland, *Irving Berlin*, W. H. Allen, London, 1974.

Lloyd Morris, *Incredible New York*, Random House, New York, 1953.

Alexander Woollcott, *The Story of Irving Berlin*, Putnam, New York, 1925.

Cole Porter

Robert Kimball and Brendan Gill, *Cole*, Michael Joseph, London, 1971.

The Cole Porter Songbook (Foreword Moss Hart), Simon & Schuster, New York, 1959.

George Eels, *The Life that Late He Led: Cole Porter*, W. H. Allen, London, 1967.

Ira Gershwin

David Ewen, *The Story of George Gershwin*, Holt Rinehart Winston, New York, 1943.

Ira Gershwin, *Lyrics on Several Occasions*, Knopf, New York, 1959.

Robert Kimball and Alfred Simon, *The Gershwins*, Atheneum, New York, 1973.

Edward Jablonski and Lawrence Stewart, *The Gershwin Years*, Doubleday, New York, 1958.

Robert Rushmore, *The Life of George Gershwin*, Crowell, Collier, Macmillan, New York, 1966.

Charles Schwartz, *Gershwin, His Life and Music*, Bobbs-Merrill, Indiana, 1973.

P. G. Wodehouse and Guy Bolton, *Bring on the Girls!*, Simon & Schuster, New York, 1953.

Lorenz Hart

Dorothy Hart, *Thou Swell Thou Witty*, Harper & Row, New York, 1976.

Samuel Marx and Jan Clayton, *Rodgers and Hart*, Putnam, New York, 1976.

The Rodgers and Hart Songbook (Preface by Oscar Hammerstein II and further Preface by Richard Rodgers), Simon & Schuster, New York, 1951.

Oscar Hammerstein II

Hugh Fordin, *Getting to Know Him*, Random House, New York, 1977.

Vincent Sheean, *The Amazing Oscar Hammerstein* (Preface by Oscar Hammerstein II), Weidenfeld & Nicholson, London, 1956.

Deems Taylor, *Some Enchanted Evenings*, Greenwood Press, London, 1955.

Lyrics by Oscar Hammerstein II (Preface by Oscar Hammerstein II), Simon & Schuster, New York, 1949.

The Jerome Kern Songbook (Ed. Oscar Hammerstein II), Simon & Schuster, New York, 1955.

The Rodgers and Hammerstein Songbook (Ed. Richard Rodgers and Oscar Hammerstein II), Simon & Schuster and Williamson Music, New York, 1958.

Dorothy Fields
Douglas Gilbert, *American Vaudeville: Its Life and Times*, Dover, New York, 1960.

Felix Isman, *Weber and Fields: Their Tribulations, Triumphs and Their Associates*, Boni and Liveright, New York, 1924.

Mark Sullivan, *Our Times: The United States 1900, 1904*, Scribner, New York, 1926.

Howard Dietz
Howard Dietz, *Dancing in the Dark*, Quadrangle, New York, 1974.

E. Y. Harburg
E. Y. Harburg, *Rhymes for the Irreverent*, Grossman, New York, 1965.

E. Y. Harburg, *At this Point in Rhyme*, Crown, New York, 1976.

John Lahr, *Notes on a Cowardly Lion*, Knopf, New York, 1969.

William Stott, *Documentary Expression and Thirties America*, Oxford University Press, New York, 1976.

Theodore Taylor, *Jule: The Story of Composer, Jule Styne*, Random House, New York, 1979.

Noël Coward
Noël Coward, *Present Indicative*, Heinemann, London, 1937.

Noël Coward, *Future Indefinite*, Heinemann, London, 1954.

Noël Coward, *Not Yet the Dodo*, Heinemann, London, 1967.

Noël Coward, *The Lyrics of Noël Coward*, Heinemann, London, 1965.

Cole Lesley, *The Life of Noël Coward*, Jonathan Cape, London, 1976.

Sheridan Morley, *A Talent to Amuse*, Heinemann, London, 1969.

Frank Loesser
The Frank Loesser Songbook (Ed. Cynthia Lindsay), Simon & Schuster, New York, 1972.

Alan Jay Lerner
Alan Jay Lerner, *On The Street Where I Live*, Hodder & Stoughton, London, 1978.

Lee Snider (ed.), *Kurt Weill in America* (Introduction by Miles Kreuger), Chappell, London, 1975.

Sheldon Harnick
Hal Prince, *Contradictions*, Dodd Mead, New York, 1974.

Stephen Sondheim
Craig Zadan, *Sondheim & Co.*, Macmillan, New York, 1974.

Recorded Lectures
Sheldon Harnick, *Lyrics and Lyricists* lecture, 92nd Street YMHA LL603, 1970.

Alan Jay Lerner, *Lyrics and Lyricists* lecture, 92nd Street YMHA LL601, 1971.

Johnny Mercer, *Lyrics and Lyricists* lecture, 92nd Street YMHA LL601, 1971.

(All Laureate and all produced by Maurice Levine.)

Sleeve Notes
Ben Bagley, *Frank Loesser Revisited*, P.S. 1359.

Alan Ayres, *Side by Side by Sondheim*, BL 21851, 1976.

COPYRIGHT NOTICES

DOROTHY FIELDS
T. B. Harms Co. – The Way You Look Tonight (1936), Lovely To Look At (1935), A Fine Romance (1936), Remind Me (1940), He Had Refinement (1951).

HOWARD DIETZ
Harms Inc. – Hammacher Schlemmer, I Love You (1948), I Have No Words (1930), Something To Remember You By (1930), Shine On Your Shoes (1932), Smokin' Reefers (1932).
Chappell & Co. Inc. – Hottentot Potentate (1935), That's Entertainment (1935), Get A Little Geisha Girl (1935).
T. B. Harms Co. – On Our Houseboat On The Harlem (1924).

YIP HARBURG
Harms Inc. – Brother Can You Spare A Dime (1932), It's Only A Paper Moon (1933), April In Paris (1932), Things (1934), The Quartet Erotica (1934).
Players Music Corp. – It Was Good Enough For Grandma (1944), When The Idle Poor Become The Idle Rich (1946), When I'm Not Near The Girl I Love (1946), The Begat (1947).

HAROLD ARLEN/YIP HARBURG
Push De Button (1957), Monkey In The Mango (1957).
Harwin Music Corp. – Paris Is A Lonely Town (1961).

JOHNNY MERCER
Harms Inc. – Too Marvellous For Words (1937), The Girl Friend Of The Whirling Dervish (1938), Hooray For Hollywood (1938), Blues In The Night (1941).
Burvan Music Corp. – In The Cool, Cool, Cool Of The Evening (1950).
Paramount Music Corp. – The Yogi Who Lost His Willpower (1941).
Capitol Songs Inc. – G.I. Jive (1943).
A.M. Music Corp. – Legalise My Name (1946).
T. B. Harms Co. – I'm Old Fashioned (1942).
Harwin Music Corp. – One For My Baby (1943).

JOHNNY MERCER/ANDRE PREVIN
Bon Vivant (1974).

FRANK LOESSER
Paramount Music Corp. – I Don't Want To Walk Without You, Baby (1941), 'Murder' – He Says (1943).
Famous Music Corp. – Hamlet (1949).

ALAN JAY LERNER
ALAN JAY LERNER/FREDERICK LOEWE
I'm On My Way (1951), Wandrin' Star (1951), Why Can't The English (1956), If Ever I Would Leave You (1960), Camelot (1960).
Lowal Corp. – Gigi (1958).
Chappell & Co. Inc. – On A Clear Day (1965).

ALAN JAY LERNER/JOHN BARRY
How Far Is It To The Next Town (1971).

NOEL COWARD
Chappell & Co. Ltd. – Half-Caste Woman (1931), Mad About The Boy (1932), There's Always Something Fishy About The French (1934), There Have Been Songs In England (1941), Uncle Harry (1947), Josephine (1952), I Like America (1950), After The Ball (1954), London At Night (1954), If Love Were All (1929).
Chappell & Co. Inc. – Why Do The Wrong People Travel (1961).

E. Y. HARBURG
Somewhere Over The Rainbow, The Song Of The Woodman, Lydia, The Tattooed Lady.

JOHNNY MERCER
Spring, Spring, Spring.

INDEX OF LYRIC WRITERS
AND COMPOSERS

GENERAL INDEX

(of names appearing in more than one chapter)